St

STUDENT'S SOLUTIONS MANUAL FOR

STATISTICS

FOR MANAGEMENT AND ECONOMICS

ABBREVIATED FOURTH EDITION

Gerald Keller

Wilfrid Laurier University

Brian Warrack

Wilfrid Laurier University

DUXBURY PRESS

An Imprint of Brooks/Cole Publishing Company

I(T)P® An International Thomson Publishing Company

Pacific Grove • Albany • Belmont • Bonn • Boston • Cincinnati • Detroit
Johannesburg • London • Madrid • Melbourne • Mexico City • New York
Paris • Singapore • Tokyo • Toronto • Washington

Assistant Editor: *Cindy Mazow*
Editorial Assistant: *Rita Jaramillo*
Marketing Representative: *Laura Hubrich*
Production Editor: *Mary Vezilich*

For more information, contact Duxbury Press at Brooks/Cole Publishing Company,
or electronically at **http://www.duxbury.com**

BROOKS/COLE PUBLISHING COMPANY
511 Forest Lodge Road
Pacific Grove, CA 93950
USA

International Thomson Editores
Seneca 53
Col. Polanco
11560 México, D. F., México

International Thomson Publishing Europe
Berkshire House 168-173
High Holborn
London WC1V 7AA
England

International Thomson Publishing Japan
Hirakawacho Kyowa Building, 3F
2-2-1 Hirakawacho
Chiyoda-ku, Tokyo 102
Japan

Thomas Nelson Australia
102 Dodds Street
South Melbourne, 3205
Victoria, Australia

International Thomson Publishing Asia
221 Henderson Road
#05-10 Henderson Building
Singapore 0315

Nelson Canada
1120 Birchmount Road
Scarborough, Ontario
Canada M1K 5G4

International Thomson Publishing GmbH
Königswinterer Strasse 418
53227 Bonn
Germany

Printed in Canada

5   4   3   2   1

ISBN 0-534-36184-6

Contents

Preface

This Study Guide was written to supplement *Statistics for Management and Economics,* Fourth Edition. It is designed to help students who are encountering difficulties in understanding the material and in applying the techniques covered in the book. We have written this guide to appeal to both students who apply statistical techniques manually and to students who are using the computer extensively. All of the examples and exercises are designed to be solved manually. To encourage students to approach all problems in a systematic way, we have left spaces to fill in answers. For example, following hypothesis testing exercises students are asked to specify the hypotheses, the test statistics, the rejection region, the value of the test statistic, and the conclusion. We urge you to use these spaces and then check the solutions at the back of the Study Guide. The solutions are shown in similar format.

Students using a computer software package can use the exercises to practice their technique-identification skills. That is, identify the technique to be used and set up the hypotheses.

For students who are using either Minitab or Excel, we provide a method to use the computer to illustrate important statistical concepts. In the appendixes of Chapters 8, 9, and 10 we present simulation experiments to be conducted on the computer. These experiments permit students to illustrate for themselves some of the concepts and techniques introduced in the book.

Additionally, throughout the Study Guide, we have attempted to anticipate specific problem areas by posing typical student questions (based on our experience) and providing answers.

Because of the importance of being able to identify the appropriate statistical technique, we have included two review chapters (Chapters 13 and 19), containing 28 exercises. We recommend that students proceed through the flowcharts in Chapters 13 and 19 to identify the correct method. Students applying their skills manually can complete the solution. Students using the computer only should ensure that they know how to command their software package to produce the answer (assuming the existence of raw data).

We have attempted to make this Study Guide as error-free as we can. We acknowledge, however, that there is a high probability that a few errors still exist. We would appreciate being informed about any errors. Please visit our web site at www.globalserve.net/~gkeller for corrections and other useful information. You can also contact us through the publisher. Write to

> Dr. Gerald Keller
> c/o Wadsworth Publishing Company
> 10 Davis Drive
> Belmont, CA 94002

You can e-mail the author at gkeller@mach1.wlu.ca.

Chapter 1: What Is Statistics?

1.1   Introduction

This chapter provided an introduction to the two general bodies of methods that together constitute the subject called statistics: descriptive statistics and inferential statistics. Descriptive statistics consists of methods for organizing, summarizing, and presenting data in a convenient and usable form. Inferential statistics, which occupies the larger portion of the textbook, consists of a body of methods for drawing conclusions about characteristics of a population based on information contained in a sample taken from the population.

1.2   Key Statistical Concepts

This section described the three key considerations present in the solution to any statistical problem: the population, the sample, and the statistical inference. The population refers to the collection of all measurements of interest in a statistical problem, such as the salaries of all workers in a community. A characteristic of the population, such as the average salary, is called a parameter of the population. Suppose the problem is to estimate the value of this population parameter. This estimate is called an inference, or conclusion, about the population parameter (that is, about the average salary). An estimate can be obtained by soliciting the salaries of a properly selected group of workers (called the sample) from the community and calculating the average of this sample of salaries. As always, this sample is a subset of the entire population. The average salary of the group of workers is called a sample statistic—a descriptive measure of the sample. If we use the average salary of the group of workers as an estimate of the average salary of the entire population, then we are drawing a statistical inference, or conclusion, about the population based on information provided by a sample taken from the population.

Example 1.1

An election is to be held soon to determine who will be the mayor of a certain city. Based on the results of a pollster's survey of 400 eligible voters, a newspaper has reported the proportion of eligible voters who favor Ms. Winn, one of the candidates. Identify the population and its parameter, the sample and its statistic, and the inference of interest in the situation described.

Solution

The population is the collection of all residents of the city who are eligible to vote in the election. The population parameter is the proportion of all eligible voters who favor Ms. Winn. The 400 eligible voters surveyed by the pollster constitute the sample, and the sample statistic is the proportion of these 400 eligible voters who favor Ms. Winn. The inference is the estimate (reported by the newspaper) of the proportion of all eligible voters who favor Ms. Winn.

Example 1.2

According to *U.S.A. Today* (15 October 1987), the average size of an American household had fallen from 3.14 persons in 1970 to 2.66 persons in 1987.

a) The 1987 figure of 2.66 is claimed to be the value of a population parameter. What are the population and the parameter? *P= American Home*

b) What procedure must be taken to be 100% certain that the value of the population parameter is exactly 2.66?

b) What procedure was likely used to arrive at the 1987 figure of 2.66? Use the terms *sample, sample statistic,* and *inference* in your answer.

Solution

a) One can imagine determining the number of persons living in each and every household in the United States. The set of all these (millions of) numbers is the population of interest. The average of this population of numbers is the parameter of interest, which is claimed to be 2.66.

b) You would have to collect all the numbers in the population (called taking a census) and then compute the average of all the numbers.

c) It is likely that only a relatively small subset of all American households was selected and the number of persons living in each of these households obtained. The set of numbers obtained for the selected group of households is a sample drawn from the population. The average of the sample values, called the sample statistic, was then computed to be 2.66. The statement that 2.66 is the average size of *all* American households is an inference about the population parameter; it may or may not be correct.

EXERCISES

1.1 Thousands of customers have accounts at a large department store. An accountant claims that the average unpaid balance for these accounts is $75, a figure obtained by computing the average of the unpaid balances for 50 of the accounts.

a) Identify the population and its parameter.

P= Customers with accounts (unpaid)

P = Average unpaid bal $75

b) What is the sample?

60 accounts

c) Is the figure of $75 a parameter or a (statistic?)

1.2   A psychologist has interviewed 250 school children throughout New York State and found that 80% of them spend at least 25 hours a week watching television.

a) Identify the population parameter and the sample statistic of interest here.

Pop. Par. Is the percentage of Ny school children that watch 25 hrs. of TV. Por week

Samp. stat = Is the 80% of the 250 that watched 25 hrs Por week

b) Comment on the following inference, which is based on the results of the psychologist's interviews: 80 percent of American school children spend at least 25 hours a week watching television.

should state (New york state)

3

Chapter 2: Graphical Descriptive Techniques

2.1 Introduction

This chapter discussed graphical descriptive methods used to summarize and describe sets of data. At the completion of this chapter, you are expected to know the following:

1. How to recognize whether the type of data under consideration is quantitative, qualitative, or ranked.
2. How to summarize a set of quantitative data by means of a frequency distribution, histogram, relative frequency polygon, and stem and leaf display.
3. How to summarize a set of qualitative data by means of a pie chart and bar chart.

2.2 Types of Data

This section introduced the two main types of data that are referred to throughout the text: quantitative (numerical) data and qualitative (categorical) data. The appropriate graphical method to be used in presenting data depends, in part, on the type of data under consideration. Later in the text, when statistical inference is covered, the data type will help to identify the appropriate statistical technique to be used in solving a problem. In a few situations, it will be necessary to recognize whether or not a set of nonquantitative data can be ordered. If the categories for a set of nonquantitative data can be ordered or ranked, we have a third type of data, called ranked data.

At the completion of this section, you should be able to identify whether the type of data under consideration is quantitative, qualitative, or ranked.

> *Question:* How do I identify quantitative data?
>
> *Answer:* Quantitative data are real numbers. They are not numbers arbitrarily assigned to represent qualitative data. An experiment that produces qualitative data always asks for verbal, nonnumerical responses (e.g., yes and no; defective and nondefective; Catholic, Protestant, and other).

Example 2.1

For each of the following examples of data, determine whether the data type is quantitative, qualitative, or ranked.

a) the weekly level of the prime interest rate during the past year
b) the make of car driven by each of a sample of executives
c) the number of contacts made by each of a company's salespersons during a week

d) the rating (excellent, good, fair, or poor) given to a particular television program by each of a sample of viewers

e) the number of shares traded on the New York Stock Exchange each week throughout 1987

Solution

a) Quantitative, if the interest rate level is expressed as a percentage. If the level is simply observed as being high, moderate, or low, then the data type is qualitative.

b) Qualitative

c) Quantitative

d) Ranked, because the categories can be ordered

e) Quantitative

EXERCISES

2.1 Describe the difference between quantitative data and qualitative data.

2.2 For each of the following examples of data, determine whether the data are quantitative, qualitative, or ranked.

qual a) the month of the highest sales for each firm in a sample

qual b) the department in which each of a sample of university professors teaches

quant c) the weekly closing price of gold throughout a year

Rank d) the size of soft drink (large, medium, or small) ordered by a sample of customers in a restaurant

quant e) the number of barrels of crude oil imported monthly by the United States

2.3 Identify the type of data observed for each of the following variables.

quant a) the number of students in a statistics class

Ranked b) the student evaluations of the professor (1 = poor, 5 = excellent)

qual. c) the political preferences of voters

qual d) the states in the United States of America

quant e) the size of a condominium (in square feet)

2.3   Graphical Techniques for Quantitative Data

This section introduced the basic methods of descriptive statistics used for organizing a set of numerical data in tabular form and presenting it graphically. Summarizing data in this way requires that you first group the data into classes. Judgment is required concerning the number and the size of the classes to be used. The important point to bear in mind when making this judgment is that the presentation of the grouped data should enable the user to quickly grasp the general shape of the distribution of the data.

At the completion of this section, you should be able to summarize a set of numerical data in the following ways:

1. Organize the data into a frequency distribution.
2. Construct a histogram.
3. Construct a frequency polygon.
4. Construct the relative frequency counterparts of points 1, 2, and 3.
5. Construct an ogive—the graph of a cumulative relative frequency distribution.
6. Construct a stem and leaf display.

Question: How do I choose the number of classes and the width of the classes to be used in constructing a frequency distribution?

Answer: Although this choice is arbitrary and no hard and fast rules can be given, here are a few useful guidelines:

1.   The classes must be nonoverlapping, so that each measurement falls into exactly one class. Therefore, choose the classes so that no measurement falls on a class boundary.

2.   Choose the number of classes to be used as a number between 5 and 20, with smaller numbers of classes being chosen for smaller data sets.

3.   The approximate width of each class is given by the following:

$$\text{Approximate class width} = \frac{\text{Largest value} - \text{Smallest value}}{\text{Number of classes}}$$

Choose the actual class width to be a value close to the approximate width that is convenient to work with. Avoid awkward fractional values.

Example 2.2

The weights in pounds of a group of workers are as follows.

173	165	171	175	188
183	177	160	151	169
162	179	145	171	175
168	158	186	182	162
154	180	164	166	157

a) Construct a stem and leaf display for these data.
b) Construct a frequency distribution for these data

Solution

a) The first step in constructing a stem and leaf display is to decide how to split each observation (weight) into two parts: a stem and a leaf. For this example, we will define the first two digits of an observation to be its stem and the third digit to be its leaf. Thus, the first two weights are split into a stem and a leaf as follows:

Weight	Stem	Leaf
173	17	3
183	18	3

Scanning the remaining weights, we find that there are five possible stems (14, 15, 16, 17 and 18), which we list in a column from smallest to largest, as shown below. Next, we consider each observation in turn and place its leaf in the same row as its stem, to the right of the vertical line. The resulting stem and leaf display shown below has grouped the 25 weights into five categories. The second row of the display, corresponding to the stem 15, has four leaves: 4, 8, 1 and 7. The four weights represented in the second row are therefore 154, 158, 151, and 157.

Stem	Leaf
14	5
15	4 8 1 7
16	2 8 5 0 4 6 9 2
17	3 7 9 1 5 1 5
18	3 0 6 2 8

b)   The hardest, and most important, step in constructing a frequency distribution is choosing the number and width of the classes. Constructing a stem and leaf display first is often helpful. For this example, the display in part a) suggests using five classes, each with a width of 10 pounds. The number (or frequency) of weights falling into each class is then recorded as shown in the table that follows. Care must be taken to define the classes in such a way that each measurement belongs to exactly one class. We will follow the convention that a class (such as 140 up to 150) contains all measurements from the lower limit (140) up to, but not including, the upper limit (150).

Class Limits	Frequency
140 up to 150	1
150 up to 160	4
160 up to 170	8
170 up to 180	7
180 up to 190	5
Total	25

Suppose that we hadn't first constructed a stem and leaf display, or that the stem and leaf display contained only a few, or too many, categories. (If the number of measurements is less than 50, the frequency distribution should contain between 5 and 7 classes.) We might then begin by noting that the smallest and largest measurements are 145 and 188, respectively, so that the range of the measurements is $188 - 145 = 43$. If we decide to use five classes, the approximate width of each class is $43/5 = 8.6$. In order to work with "round" numbers, we have chosen to use a class width of 10 and to set the lower limit of the first class at 140.

Example 2.3

Refer to the data in Example 2.2.

a)   Construct a relative frequency histogram for the data.
b)   Construct a relative frequency polygon for the data.
c)   Construct an ogive for the data.

Solution

a) The relative frequencies, obtained by dividing each frequency by 25, are shown below:

Class Limits	Frequency	Relative Frequency	Cumulative Relative Frequency
140 up to 150	1	.04	.04
150 up to 160	4	.16	.20
160 up to 170	8	.32	.52
170 up to 180	7	.28	.80
180 up to 190	5	.20	1.00

The relative frequency histogram is constructed by erecting over each class interval a rectangle, the height of which equals the relative frequency of that class.

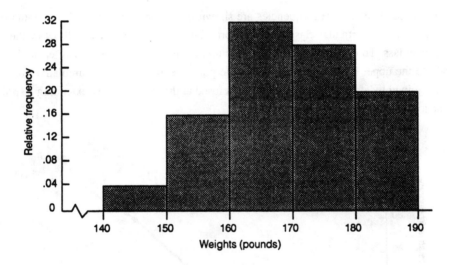

b) The relative frequency polygon is constructed by plotting the relative frequency of each class above the midpoint of that class and then joining the points with straight lines. The polygon is closed by considering one additional class (with zero frequency) at each end of the distribution and extending a straight line to the midpoint of each of these classes.

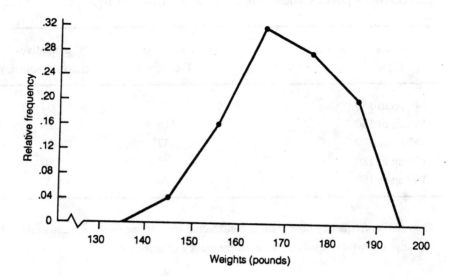

c) The cumulative relative frequencies are shown in the table in part a). The cumulative relative frequency of a particular class is the proportion of measurements that fall below the upper limit of that class. To construct the ogive, the cumulative relative frequency of each class is plotted above the upper limit of that class, and the points representing the cumulative frequencies are then joined by straight lines. The ogive is closed at the lower end by extending a straight line to the lower limit of the first class.

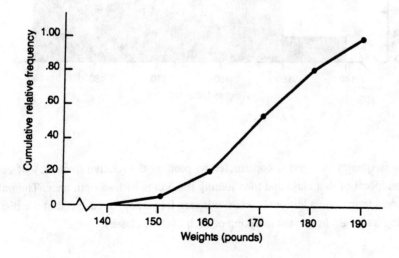

EXERCISES

2.4   The salaries (in hundreds of dollars) of a sample of 40 government employees are as follows:

208	160	175	334	228	211	179	354
265	215	191	239	298	226	220	260
173	263	226	165	252	422	284	232
225	348	290	180	300	200	245	204
256	281	230	275	158	224	315	217

a) Construct a stem and leaf display for these data. (When leaves consist of two digits, they should be separated from one another by commas.)

b) Construct a frequency distribution for these data.

150 -185
185 - 220
220 - 255
255 - 290
290 - 325
325 - 360
360 - 395
395 - 430

2.5   Refer to the data in Exercise 2.4.

a) Construct a relative frequency histogram for the data.

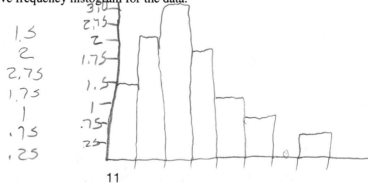

11

b) Construct a relative frequency polygon for the data.

c) Construct an ogive for the data.

2.4 Scatter Diagrams

This section introduced the notion of the relationship between two *quantitative* variables. Economists, for example, are interested in the relationship between inflation rates and unemployment rates. Business owners are interested in many variables, including the relationship between their advertising expenditures and sales levels. The graphical technique used to depict the relationship between the variables X and Y is the **scatter diagram,** which is a plot of all pairs of values (x, y) for the variables X and Y.

Example 2.4

An educational economist wants to establish the relationship between an individual's income and education. She takes a random sample of 10 individuals and asks for their income (in $1,000s) and education (in years). The results are shown below. Construct a scatter diagram for these data, and describe the relationship between the number of years of education and income level.

x (education)	y (income)
11	25
12	33
11	22
15	41
8	18
10	28
11	32
12	24
17	53
11	26

Solution

If we feel that the value of one variable (such as income) depends to some degree on the value of the other variable (such as years of education), the first variable (income) is called the **dependent variable** and is plotted on the vertical axis. The ten pairs of values for education (*x*) and income (*y*) are plotted in Figure 2.1, forming a scatter diagram.

The scatter diagram allows us to observe two characteristics about the relationship between education (x) and income (y):

1. Because these two variables move together—that is, their values tend to increase together and decrease together—there is a **positive relationship** between the two variables.
2. The relationship between income and years of education appears to be **linear,** since we can imagine drawing a straight line (as opposed to a curved line) through the scatter diagram that approximates the positive relationship between the two variables.

The pattern of a scatter diagram provides us with information about the relationship between two variables. Figure 2.1 depicts a positive linear relationship. If two variables move in opposite directions, and the scatter diagram consists of points that appear to cluster around a straight line, then the variables have a **negative linear relationship** (see Figure 2.2). It is possible to have **nonlinear relationships** (see Figures 2.3 and 2.4), as well as situations in which the two variables are **unrelated** (see Figure 2.5). In Section 4.5, we will compute numerical measures of the **strength** of the linear relationship between two variables.

Figure 2.1
Scatter Diagram for Example 2.4

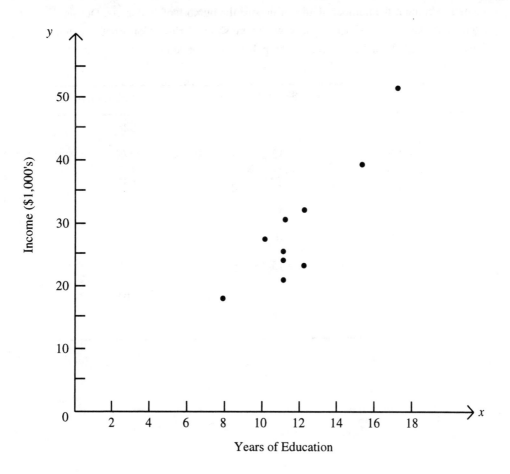

Years of Education

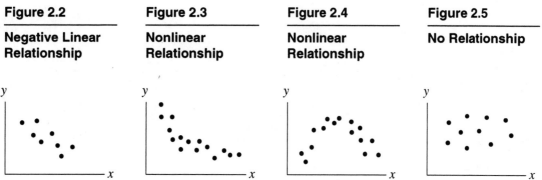

Figure 2.2

Negative Linear Relationship

Figure 2.3

Nonlinear Relationship

Figure 2.4

Nonlinear Relationship

Figure 2.5

No Relationship

EXERCISE

2.6 The manager of a large furniture store wanted to determine the effectiveness of her advertising. The furniture sotre regularly runs several ads per month in the local newspaper. The manager wanted to know if the number of ads influenced the number of customers. During the past eight months, she kept track of both figures, which are shown below. Construct a scatter diagram for these data, and describe the relationship between the number of ads and the number of customers.

Month	Number of Ads, x	Number of customers, y
1	5	528
2	12	876
3	8	653
4	6	571
5	4	556
6	15	1,058
7	10	963
8	7	719

2.5   Pie Charts, Bar Charts, and Line Charts

The methods described in the previous section are appropriate for summarizing data that are quantitative, or numerical measurements. But we must also be able to describe data that are qualitative, or categorical data. These data consist of attributes, which are the names of the categories into which the observations are sorted.

A pie chart is a useful method for displaying the percentage of observations that fall into each category of qualitative data, while a bar chart can be used to display the frequency of observations that fall into each category. If the categories consist of points in time and the objective is to focus on the trend in frequencies over time, a line chart is useful.

At the completion of this section, you should be able to do the following:

1.   Construct a pie chart.
2.   Construct a bar chart.
3.   Construct a line chart.

Example 2.5

According to the *New York Times* (27 September 1987, p. 1F), the June levels of unemployment in the United States for five years were as follows:

Year	Unemployed (millions)
1983	10.7
1984	8.5
1985	8.3
1986	8.2
1987	7.3

a) Use a bar chart to depict these data.
b) Use a line chart to depict these data.

Solution

a) The five years, or categories, are represented by intervals of equal width on the horizontal axis. The height of the vertical bar erected above any year is proportional to the frequency (number of unemployed) corresponding to that year.

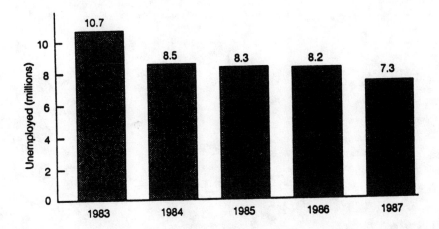

b) A line chart is obtained by plotting the frequency of a category above the point on the horizontal axis representing that category and then joining the points with straight lines.

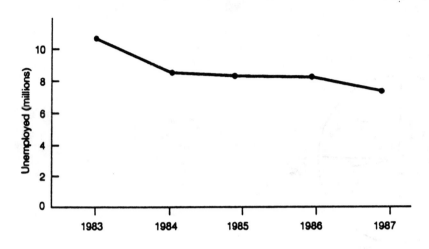

Example 2.6

The *New York Times* article alluded to in Example 2.4 reported that "6 million Americans who say they want work are not even seeking jobs." A breakdown of these 6 million Americans by race follows:

Race	Frequency
White	4,320,000
Black	1,500,000
Other	1 80,000

Use a pie chart to depict these data.

Solution

A pie chart is an effective method of showing the percentage breakdown of a whole entity into its component parts. We must first determine the percentage of the 6 million Americans belonging to each of the three racial categories: 72% white, 25% black, and 3% other. Each category is represented by a slice of the pie (a circle) that is proportional in size to the percentage (or relative frequency) correspond-ing to that category. Since the entire circle corresponds to 360°, the angle between the lines demarcating the White sector is therefore (.72)(360) = 259.2°. In a similar manner, we can determine that the angles for the Black and Other sectors are 90° and 10.8°, respectively.

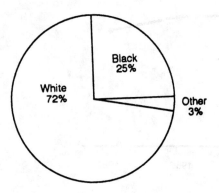

EXERCISES

2.7 Refer to Example 2.6. A breakdown by age group of the 6 million Americans not seeking jobs follows:

Age	Frequency
16 up to 20	1,560,000
20 up to 25	960,000
25 up to 60	3,000,000
60 and over	480,000

Use a pie chart to depict these data.

2.8 The number of men and women who have received an M.B.A. degree from a particular university in each of five years is shown below.

Year	Men	Women
1988	74	12
1989	85	20
1990	90	32
1991	112	48
1992	128	67

a) Use a component bar chart to depict these data.

b) Use a line chart to depict these data.

Chapter 3: Art and Science of Graphical Presentations

This chapter discussed how to make effective use of the techniques introduced in Chapter 2. We do not believe that it is necessary to elaborate on Chapter 3 in this Study Guide.

Chapter 4: Numerical Descriptive Measures

4.1   Introduction

This chapter discussed numerical descriptive measures used to summarize and describe sets of data. At the completion of this chapter, you are expected to know the following:

1.   How to calculate the basic numerical measures of central location and dispersion.
2.   How to use the Empirical Rule.
3.   How to approximate the mean and standard deviation of a set of grouped data.

4.2   Measures of Central Location

This section discussed three commonly used numerical measures of the central, or average, value of a data set: the mean, the median, and the mode. You are expected to know how to compute each of these measures for a given data set. Moreover, you are expected to know the advantages and disadvantages of each of these measures, as well as the type of data for which each is an appropriate measure.

Question: How do I determine which measure of central location should be used—the mean, the median, or the mode?

Answer: If the data are qualitative, the only appropriate measure of central location is the mode. If the data are ranked, the most appropriate measure of central location is the median.

For quantitative data, however, it is possible to compute all three measures. Which measure you should use depends on your objective. The mean is most popular because it is easy to compute and to interpret. (In particular, the mean is generally the best measure of central location for purposes of statistical inference, as you'll see in later chapters.) It has the disadvantage, however, of being unduly influenced by a few very small or very large measurements.

To avoid this influence, you might choose to use the median. This could well be the case if the data consisted, for example, of salaries or of house prices. The mode, representing the value occurring most frequently (or the midpoint of the class with the largest frequency) should be used when the objective is to indicate the value (such as shirt size or house price) that is most popular with consumers.

Example 4.1

Find the mean, mode, and median of the following sample of measurements:

8, 12, 6, 6, 10, 8, 4, 6

Solution

The mean value is

$$\bar{x} = \frac{\sum\limits_{i=1}^{n} x_i}{n} = \frac{\sum\limits_{i=1}^{8} x_i}{8}$$

$$= \frac{8 + 12 + 6 + 6 + 10 + 8 + 4 + 6}{8} = \frac{60}{8} = 7.5$$

The mode is 6, because that is the value that occurs most frequently. To find the median, we must first arrange the measurements in ascending order:

4, 6, 6, 6, 8, 8, 10, 12

Since the number of measurements is even, the median is the midpoint between the two middle values, 6 and 8. Thus, the median is 7.

Example 4.2

Consider the following sample of measurements, which is obtained from the sample in Example 4.1 by adding one extreme value, 21:

8, 12, 6, 6, 10, 8, 4, 6, 21

Which measure of central location is most affected by the addition of the single value?

Solution

The mean value is now

$$\bar{x} = \frac{8 + 12 + 6 + 6 + 10 + 8 + 4 + 6 + 21}{9} = 9$$

The mode is still 6.

We arrange the new sample of measurements in ascending order:

4, 6, 6, 6, 8, 8, 10, 12, 21

The median is now equal to 8, the middle value. Thus, the mean is the measure that is most affected by the addition of one extreme value.

Example 4.3

In Example 2.2, we considered the following weights, in pounds, of a group of workers:

173	165	171	175	188
183	177	160	151	169
162	179	145	171	175
168	158	186	182	162
154	180	164	166	157

a) Find the mean of the weights of the sample of 25 workers.
b) Find the median of the weights.
c) Find the modal class of the frequency distribution of weights that was constructed in the solution to part b) of Example 2.2.

Solution

a) The mean of the 25 weights is

$$\bar{x} = \frac{\sum_{i=1}^{25} x_i}{25} = \frac{173 + 183 + 162 + \ldots + 175 + 162 + 177}{25}$$

$$= 168.8 \text{ pounds}$$

b) The middle value of the 25 weights is most easily found by referring to the stem and leaf display constructed in the solution to part a) of Example 2.2. We find that the median, or middle value, is 169 pounds.

c) The modal class is the class with the largest frequency, which is "160 up to 170." The mode may be taken to be the midpoint of this class, which is 165 pounds.

EXERCISES

4.1   Consider the following sample of measurements:

27, 32, 30, 28, 30, 32, 35, 28, 32, 29

Compute each of the following:

a) the mean

b) the median

c)   the mode

4.2   Refer to Exercise 2.4 (page 11).

a)   Find the mean of the salaries of the sample of 40 employees.

b)   Find the median of the salaries.

c)   Find the modal class of the frequency distribution of salaries that you constructed in part b) of Exercise 2.4.

4.3   Identify the measure(s) of central location that is (are) appropriate if the data type is:

a)   quantitative

b)   qualitative

c)   ranked

4.3   Measures of Variability

This section discussed the most common numerical measures of dispersion, or variability, of a set of measurements. For either a population or a sample of measurements, you should be able to compute the range, the variance, and the standard deviation.

Example 4.4

Compute the mean, range, variance, and standard deviation for the following sample of data:

6, 10, 2, 4, 12, 8

Solution

The sample mean is

$$\bar{x} = \frac{\sum\limits_{i=1}^{n} x_i}{n} = \frac{\sum\limits_{i=1}^{6} x_i}{6}$$

$$= \frac{6 + 10 + 2 + 4 + 12 + 8}{6} = \frac{42}{6} = 7$$

The range is $(12 - 2) = 10$, which is the difference between the largest and smallest values.

The sample variance is

$$s^2 = \frac{\sum\limits_{i=1}^{n} (x_i - \bar{x})^2}{n-1} = \frac{\sum\limits_{i=1}^{6} (x_i - 7)^2}{5}$$

$$= \frac{(6-7)^2 + (10-7)^2 + (2-7)^2 + (4-7)^2 + (12-7)^2 + (8-7)^2}{5}$$

$$= \frac{(-1)^2 + (3)^2 + (-5)^2 + (-3)^2 + (5)^2 + (1)^2}{5}$$

$$= \frac{70}{5}$$

$$= 14$$

In an example such as this one, where we have already computed $\sum\limits_{i=1}^{n} x_i$ in order to find $\bar{x}$, it is easier to use the shortcut formula for computing the sample variance. This saves us from having to compute numerous squared deviations. To use the shortcut formula, we need to compute

$$\sum\limits_{i=1}^{n} x_i^2 = \sum\limits_{i=1}^{6} x_i^2$$

$$= 6^2 + 10^2 + 2^2 + 4^2 + 12^2 + 8^2 = 364$$

27

Using the shortcut formula for s^2, we obtain

$$s^2 = \frac{1}{n-1}\left[\sum_{i=1}^{n} x_i^2 - \frac{\left(\sum_{i=1}^{n} x_i\right)^2}{n}\right]$$

$$= \frac{1}{5}\left[364 - \frac{(42)^2}{6}\right]$$

$$= 14$$

Thus, the sample standard deviation is

$$s = \sqrt{s^2} = \sqrt{14} = 3.74$$

Example 4.5

Treating the data in Example 4.4 as a population, calculate the mean, variance, and standard deviation of the population of data.

Solution

If we treat the data as a population, our solution will differ from that of Example 4.4 in the notation used for the descriptive measures and in the divisor used to compute the variance (and hence the standard deviation). The population mean is

$$\mu = \frac{\sum_{i=1}^{N} x_i}{N} = \frac{\sum_{i=1}^{6} x_i}{6}$$

$$= \frac{6 + 10 + 2 + 4 + 12 + 8}{6} = \frac{42}{6} = 7$$

The population variance is

$$\sigma^2 = \frac{\sum_{i=1}^{N}(x_i - \mu)^2}{N} = \frac{\sum_{i=1}^{6}(x_i - 7)^2}{6}$$

$$= \frac{(6-7)^2 + (10-7)^2 + (2-7)^2 + (4-7)^2 + (12-7)^2 + (8-7)^2}{6}$$

$$= \frac{70}{6}$$

$$= 11.67$$

Thus, the population standard deviation is

$$\sigma = \sqrt{\sigma^2} = \sqrt{11.67} = 3.42$$

EXERCISES

4.4   Consider the following sample of data:

17, 25, 18, 14, 28, 21

Compute each of the following for this sample:

a)   the mean

b)   the range

c)   the variance

d)   the standard deviation

4.5   Treating the data in Exercise 4.4 as a population, calculate each of the following for this population:

a)   the mean

b)   the variance

c)   the standard deviation

4.4   Interpreting Standard Deviation

The standard deviation of a set of measurements, taken by itself, is difficult to interpret. This section described one way in which we can use the standard deviation to make a statement regarding the proportion of measurements that fall within various intervals of values centered at the mean value.

The Empirical Rule makes statements that apply only to samples of measurements with a mound-shaped distribution. For such a sample of measurements, the Empirical Rule states that approximately 68% of the measurements fall within one standard deviation of the mean, approximately 95% of the measurements fall within two standard deviations of the mean, and virtually all the measurements fall within three standard deviations of the mean.

A crude method of approximating the standard deviation of a sample of measurements that have a mound-shaped distribution follows from the Empirical Rule. Called the range approximation of s, because it uses the range of the sample of measurements, it states that

$$s \cong \text{Range}/4$$

Example 4.6

A professor has announced that the grades on a statistics exam have a mean value of 72 and a standard deviation of 6. If the grades have a mound-sloped distribution, what can we say about the proportion of grades that are between:

a)   66 and 78?
b)   60 and 84?
c)   54 and 90?

Solution

a)   Since the grades have a mound-shaped distribution, we can use the Empirical Rule, which states that approximately 68% of the grades fall within one standard deviation of the mean. In other words, 68% of the grades fall between 66 and 78. Notice that this implies that approximately 32% of the grades do not fall between 66 and 78. Furthermore, since a mound-shaped distribution is symmetrical, approximately 16% of the grades are lower than 66 and 16% are higher than 78.

b)   Approximately 95% of the grades fall between 60 and 84.

c)   Virtually all the grades fall between 54 and 90.

EXERCISES

4.6   Refer to Example 2.2. The mean and standard deviation of the weights of the sample of 25 workers are 168.8 pounds and 11.2 pounds, respectively. If the distribution of these weights were mound-shaped, what proportion of the weights would be:

a)   between 157.6 and 1800 pounds?

b)   below 146.4 pounds?

4.7   Refer to Example 2.2. Estimate the standard deviation of the sample of 25 weights using the range approximation of s. Why is your answer not closer to the true value of $s = 11.2$ pounds?

4.5 Measures of Relative Standing and Box Plots

Sections 4.2 and 4.3 dealt with measures of central location and variability of a data set. Additional information concerning a data set can be obtained by computing percentiles, which describe the relative location of observations within a data set.

A box plot is a graphical summary of quantitative data. A box plot indicates what the two extreme values of a data set are, where the data are centered, and how spread out the data are. It does this by plotting the values of five descriptive statistics of the data: the smallest value, lower quartile, median, upper quartile, and largest value.

At the completion of this section, you should be able to do the following:

1. Compute the percentiles for a set of quantitative data.
2. Construct a box plot for a set of quantitative data.
3. Detect any outliers in the data set.
4. Comment on the skewness of the distribution of the data.

Example 4.7

Refer to Example 2.2 (page 7).

a) Find the 25th percentile of the weights of the 25 workers.

b) Find the 50th percentile of the weights.

c) Find the 75th percentile of the weights.

Solution

a) The 25th percentile, or lower quartile, is the value for which at most $.25 \times 25 = 6.25$ of the weights are smaller and at most $.75 \times 25 = 18.75$ of the weights are larger. In other words, it is the value for which at most 6 of the weights are smaller and at most 18 of the weights are larger. Thus, the 25th percentile must be the 7th smallest weight. This can be found either by arranging the 25 weights in ascending order or, more easily, by reading from the stem and leaf display constructed in the solution to part a) of Example 2.2. Using either method, the 25th percentile is found to be 162 pounds.

b) The 50th percentile of the weights is simply the median, which was found in part b) of Example 4.3 to be 169 pounds.

c) The 75th percentile, or upper quartile, is the value for which at most $.75 \times 25 = 18.75$ of the weights are smaller and at most $.25 \times 25 = 6.25$ of the weights are larger. In other words, the 75th percentile must be the 7th largest (or 19th smallest) weight. Reading once again from the stem and leaf display in the solution to part a) of Example 2.2, we find the 75th percentile to be 177 pounds.

Example 4.8

In Example 2.2, we considered the following weights, in pounds, of a group of workers:

173	165	171	175	188
183	177	160	151	169
162	179	145	171	175
168	158	186	182	162
154	180	164	166	157

a) Construct a box plot for these weights.

b) Compute the interquartile range and identify any outliers.

c) Compare the information conveyed by your box plot with that of the corresponding histogram constructed in Example 2.3.

Solution

a) The first step in constructing a box plot is to rank the data, in order to determine the numerical values of the five descriptive statistics to be plotted. We suggest that you rank the data from smallest to largest, determine the rank of each of the five descriptive statistics, and then determine the numerical value of each descriptive statistic. In this example, the smallest weight has rank 1 and the largest weight has rank 25 (since there are a total of 25 weights).

Descriptive Statistic		Rank	Numerical Value
Smallest	(S)	1	145
Lower Quartile	(Q_1)	7	162
Median	(Q_2)	13	169
Upper Quartile	(Q_3)	19	177
Largest	(L)	25	188

The median, being the middle value, has a rank of $13 \left(= \dfrac{1 + 25}{2} \right)$. The lower quartile ($Q_1$) has a rank that is (*approximately*) midway between the ranks of the smallest and median values; in this case, a rank of $7 \left(= \dfrac{1 + 13}{2} \right)$. (This rank would only be *approximate* if it were not an integer value. If that were the case, you would have to choose the integer either just below or just above the fractional rank, depending on which integer would satisfy the requirements for the lower quartile). However you find it, the rank of the lower quartile (Q_1) must be such that at most 25% of the ranks are less than the rank of Q_1 and at most 75% of the ranks are greater than the rank of Q_1.

Similarly, the upper quartile (Q_3) has a rank that is (approximately) midway between the ranks of the median and the largest values; in this case, a rank of $19 \left(= \dfrac{13 + 25}{2} \right)$.

Having determined the five ranks of interest, we can now identify the five numerical values to be plotted. We could do this either by arranging the 25 weights in ascending order or, more easily, by reading from the stem and leaf display constructed in the solution to part a) of Example 2.2. Either way, we obtain the five numerical values shown in the table. (Notice that the quartiles were also found in Example 3.6.)

We can now begin to construct the box plot by plotting the five values, as shown in the accompanying figure. Construct a box with endpoints Q_1 and Q_3 (i.e., 162 and 177). This box contains about 50% of the weights. Draw a vertical line inside the box to indicate the location of the median (169). Before completing the box plot by drawing the lines, or whiskers, emanating from each end of the box, we must compute the interquartile range and check for any unusually small or large values, known as outliers.

The interquartile range (IQR) is equal to

$$\text{IQR} = Q_3 - Q_1$$

$$= 177 - 162 = 15 \text{ pounds}$$

An outlier is defined to be any value that is more than 1.5 interquartile ranges away from the box containing 50% of the data. That is, an outlier is any weight that is at least 1.5(IQR) pounds less than Q_1 or at least 1.5(IQR) pounds greater than Q_3. Since 1.5(IQR) = 1.5(15) = 22.5 pounds, an outlier is any value lying outside the interval

$$(162 - 22.5, 177 + 22.5) = (139.5, 199.5)$$

There are no outliers in this data set, since none of the 25 weights lies outside this interval.

Because the whiskers in a box plot extend from each end of the box to the most extreme value that is *not* an outlier, in this example the whiskers extend all the way to the two extreme values, since these values are not outliers.

Box Plot for 25 Weights

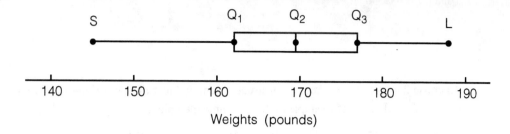

Weights (pounds)

Notice that if the data set contained a weight exceeding 200 pounds, that weight would be an outlier and the right whisker would still extend only to the value 188.

b) From part a), the interquartile range is 15 pounds, and there are no outliers.

c) From the box plot, the weights range from 145 to 188, with about a quarter below 162 and a quarter above 177. The distribution is skewed to the left, because the left whisker is longer than the right whisker. The histogram also reveals this skewness, but not the information concerning quartiles.

EXERCISES

4.8 Refer to Exercise 2.4 (page 11).

a) Find the 25th percentile of the salaries of the 40 employees.

b) Find the 50th percentile.

c) Find the 75th percentile.

d) Find the 90th percentile.

4.9   In Exercise 2.4, you were asked to construct a stem and leaf display for the following salaries (in hundreds of dollars) of a sample of 40 government employees:

208	160	175	334	228	211	179	354
265	215	191	239	298	226	220	260
173	263	226	165	252	422	284	232
225	348	290	180	300	200	245	204
256	281	230	275	158	224	315	217

a) Construct a box plot for these data.

b) Compute the interquartile range and identify any outliers.

c) Comment on the skewness of the data.

4.6   Measures of Association

In Chapter 2 (Section 2.4), we learned how a scatter diagram can be used to assess whether or not there is a relationship between two variables, and to determine if the relationship is linear, nonlinear, positive, or negative. This section introduced numerical measures of the linear relationship between two variables X and Y: the **covariance** and the **coefficient of correlation.**

If we had access to the entire population of values for X and Y, we could compute the population covariance:

Population covariance $= \text{COV}(X, Y) = \dfrac{\sum(x_i - \mu_x)(y_i - \mu_y)}{N}$

where μ_x is the population mean of the first variable, X; μ_y is the population mean of the second variable, Y; and N is the size of the population.

Usually, we will be working with only a sample of observations for X and Y. The sample covariance is defined in a similar manner, where n is the number of pairs of observations in the sample.

Sample covariance $= \text{cov}(X, Y) = \dfrac{\sum(x_i - \bar{x})(y_i - \bar{y})}{n - 1}$

For convenience, we label the population covariance $\text{COV}(X, Y)$ and the sample covariance $\text{cov}(X, Y)$.

Recall, from the discussion of scatter diagrams (Section 2.4), that there is a **positive relationship** between two variables if their values tend to increase together and decrease together. Moreover, the relationship is **linear** if a straight line can be drawn through the scatter diagram that approximates the positive relationship between the two variables.

In general, if two variables have a positive linear relationship, the covariance between the two variables will be a positive number (Figure 4.1(a)).

On the other hand, if two variables have a negative linear relationship, the covariance between the two variables will be a negative number (Figure 4.1(b)). Finally, if two variables are unrelated the covariance will be close to zero (Figure 4.1(c)).

Figure 4.1
Covariance and Correlation for Various Scatter Diagrams

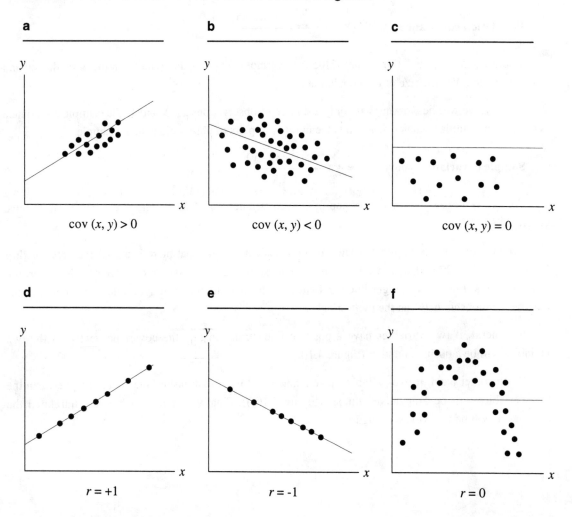

It is difficult to ascertain the **strength** of the relationship between X and Y from their covariance. A better measure for this purpose is the coefficient of correlation, obtained by dividing the covariance by the standard deviations of X and Y. The **population** coefficient of **correlation** is labeled ρ (Greek letter rho) and is defined as

$$\rho = \frac{\text{COV}(X, Y)}{\sigma_x \sigma_y}$$

where σ_x and σ_y are the standard deviations of X and Y, respectively.

As mentioned previously, you will usually be working with only a sample of observations for X and Y. The **sample** coefficient of **correlation,** r, is defined as

$$r = \frac{\text{cov}(X, Y)}{s_x s_y}$$

where s_x and s_y are the sample standard deviations of X and Y, respectively.

The coefficient of correlation will always lie between -1 and +1. Its sign will be the same as the sign of the covariance and is interpreted in the same way. The closer the correlation is to +1, the stronger is the **positive** relationship between X and Y. Figure 4.1(d) depicts two variables whose correlation coefficient is +1. On the other hand, the closer the correlation is to −1, the stronger is the **negative** relationship between X and Y. Figure 4.1(e) depicts two variables that are perfectly negatively correlated. Finally, a correlation close to zero indicates that **no linear relationship** exists, as in Figure 4.1(f).

Example 4.9

In Example 2.4, we used a scatter diagram to determine that there is a positive linear relationship between years of education and income level (in $1,000s), based on the sample of data shown below. Using the same data, measure how these two variables are related by computing their covariance and coefficient of correlation.

x (years of education)	y (income in $1,000s)
11	25
12	33
11	22
15	41
8	18
10	28
11	32
12	24
17	53
11	26

Solution

We begin by calculating the sample means and standard deviations:

$\bar{x} = 11.8$

$s_x = 2.53$

$\bar{y} = 30.2$

$s_y = 10.28$

We then compute the deviations from the mean for both x and y, and compute their products. The following table summarizes these calculations.

x	y	$(x - \bar{x})$	$(y - \bar{y})$	$(x - \bar{x})(y - \bar{y})$
11	25	−0.8	−5.2	4.16
12	33	0.2	2.8	0.56
11	22	−0.8	−8.2	6.56
15	41	3.2	10.8	34.56
8	18	−3.8	−12.2	46.36
10	28	−1.8	−2.2	3.96
11	32	−0.8	1.8	−1.44
12	24	0.2	−6.2	−1.24
17	53	5.2	22.8	118.56
11	26	−0.8	−4.2	3.36

Total = 215.4

Thus,

$$\text{cov}(X, Y) = \frac{\sum(x_i - \bar{x})(y_i - \bar{y})}{n-1} = \frac{215.4}{9} = 23.9333$$

The coefficient of correlation is

$$r = \frac{\text{cov}(X, Y)}{s_x s_y} = \frac{23.9333}{(2.53)(10.28)} = 0.92$$

There is a reasonably strong linear relationship between X and Y.

EXERCISE

4.10 In Exercise 2.4, you were asked to construct a scatter diagram and use it to assess the relationship between the number of ads placed by a store and the number of customers, based on the sample of data shown below. Using the same data, measure how these two variables are related by computing their covariance and coefficient of correlation.

Month	Number of Ads (x)	Number of Customers (y)
1	5	528
2	12	876
3	8	653
4	6	571
5	4	556
6	15	1,058
7	10	963
8	7	719

Chapter 5: Data Collection and Sampling

In this chapter we presented methods by which statisticians gather data. This material is quite straight-forward requiring no additional help from this study guide.

Chapter 6: Probability and Discrete Probability Distributions

6.1 Introduction

This chapter introduced the basic concepts of probability. It outlined rules and techniques for assigning probabilities to events. At the completion of this chapter, you are expected to know the following:

1. The meaning of the many new terms introduced.
2. The three general approaches for assigning probabilities.
3. How to define a sample space for a random experiment.
4. The meaning of conditional probability and independent events.
5. How to employ the three rules of probability.
6. How to construct and use a probability tree.
7. The concept of a random variable and its probability distribution.
8. How to compute the mean and standard deviation of a discrete probability distribution.
9. How to recognize when it is appropriate to use a binomial distribution, and how to use the table of binomial probabilities.
10. How to recognize when it is appropriate to use a Poisson distribution, and how to use the table of Poisson probabilities.

6.2 Assigning Probabilities to Events

This section introduced the notion of a random experiment and described the outcomes, or events, that may result from such an experiment. When attempting to solve any problem involving probabilities, you should begin by defining the random experiment and the sample space. You are expected to know the meaning of the many new terms introduced in this section, such as simple event, mutually exclusive, exhaustive, union, intersection, and complement.

This section also described procedures for assigning probabilities to events and outlined the basic requirements that must be satisfied by probabilities assigned to simple events. Probabilities can be assigned to the simple events (or, for that matter, to any events) using the classical approach, the relative frequency approach, or the subjective approach.

Whatever method is used to assign probabilities to the simple events that form a sample space, two basic requirements must be satisfied:

1. Each simple event probability must lie between 0 and 1, inclusive.
2. The probabilities assigned to the simple events in a sample space must sum to 1.

The probability of any event A is then obtained by summing the probabilities assigned to the simple events contained in A.

Question: How do I know whether I should combine two events A and B using "and" or "or"?

Answer: The key here is to fully understand the meaning of the combined statement.

$$P(A \text{ and } B) = P(A \text{ and } B \text{ both occur})$$
$$P(A \text{ or } B) = P(A \text{ or } B \text{ or both occur})$$

Sometimes it will be necessary to reword the statement of a given event so that it conforms with one of the two expressions given above. For example, suppose your friend Karen is about to write two exams and you define the events as follows:

    A: Karen will pass the statistics exam.
    B: Karen will pass the accounting exam.

The event "Karen will pass at least one of the two exams" can be reworded as "Karen will either pass the statistics exam *or* she'll pass the accounting exam, *or* she'll pass both exams." This new event can therefore be denoted $(A \text{ or } B)$.

On the other hand, the event "Karen will not fail either exam" is the same as "Karen will pass both her statistics exam *and* her accounting exam." This event can therefore be denoted $(A \text{ and } B)$.

Example 6.1

An investor has asked his stockbroker to rate three stocks (A, B, and C) and list them in the order in which she would recommend them. Consider the following events:

    L: Stock A doesn't receive the lowest rating.
    M: Stock B doesn't receive the lowest rating.
    N: Stock C receives the highest rating.

a) Define the random experiment and list the simple events in the sample space.
b) List the simple events in each of the events L, M, and N.
c) List the simple events belonging to each of the following events: $(L \text{ or } N)$, $(L \text{ and } M)$, and $\overline{M}$.
d) Is there a pair of mutually exclusive events among L, M, and N?
e) Is there a pair of exhaustive events among L, M, and N?

Solution

a) The random experiment consists of observing the order in which the stockbroker recommends the three stocks. The sample space consists of the set of all possible orderings:

$$S = \{ABC, ACB, BAC, BCA, CAB, CBA\}$$

b) $L = \{ABC, ACB, BAC, CAB\}$

$M = \{ABC, BAC, BCA, CBA\}$

$N = \{CAB, CBA\}$

c) The event (L or N) consists of all simple events in L or N or both:

$$(L \text{ or } N) = \{ABC, ACB, BAC, CAB, CBA\}$$

The event (L and M) consists of all simple events in both L and M:

$$(L \text{ and } M) = \{ABC, BAC\}$$

The complement of M consists of all simple events that do not belong to M:

$$\overline{M} = \{ACB, CAB\}$$

d) No, there is not a pair of mutually exclusive events among L, M, and N, since each pair of events has at least one simple event in common.

$$(L \text{ and } M) = \{ABC, BAC\}$$

$$(L \text{ and } N) = \{CAB\}$$

$$(M \text{ and } N) = \{CBA\}$$

e) Yes, L and M are an exhaustive pair of events, since every simple event in the sample space is contained either in L or M, or both. That is, (L or M) = S.

Example 6.2

The five top-selling cars in Canada in the 1986 model year are shown below, together with assumed sales levels. One registration form is selected at random from a file of the registration forms for the 200,000 cars, and the type of car appearing on the form is observed.

Car	Sales Level
Ford Tempo	50,000
Hyundai Pony	44,000
Pontiac 6000	40,000
Chevrolet Cavalier	34,000
Chevrolet Celebrity	32,000
	200,000

a) List the simple events in the sample space for this random experiment.

b) Assign a probability to each simple event.

c) Find the probability that each of the following events will occur:

  L: The form selected is for a car made by Ford.
  M: The form selected is for a North American car.
  N: The form selected is not for a car made by General Motors.

Solution

a) There are five possible simple events that could be observed, distinguished from one another by the five different types of cars that could appear on the registration form selected. Let "Tempo" represent the simple event that the registration form selected is for a Ford Tempo, and define the other four simple events in a similar manner. Then the sample space is

$$S = \{\text{Tempo, Pony, 6000, Cavalier, Celebrity}\}$$

b) Since each of the 200,000 registration forms has the same chance of being selected and there are 50,000 forms for a Tempo,

$$P(\text{Tempo}) = \frac{50,000}{200,000} = .25$$

Similarly, $P(\text{Pony}) = \dfrac{44,000}{200,000} = .22$

$$P(6000) = \frac{40,000}{200,000} = .20$$

$$P(\text{Cavalier}) = \frac{34,000}{200,000} = .17$$

$$P(\text{Celebrity}) = \frac{32,000}{200,000} = .16$$

46

c) Recall that the probability of an event is obtained by summing the probabilities assigned to the simple events contained in that event.

$$P(L) = P(\text{Tempo}) = .25$$

$$P(M) = P\,\{\text{Tempo, 6000, Cavalier, Celebrity}\}$$
$$= P(\text{Tempo}) + P(6000) + P(\text{Cavalier}) + P(\text{Celebrity})$$
$$= .25 + .20 + .17 + .16 = .78$$

$$P(N) = P\,\{\text{Tempo, Pony}\}$$
$$= P(\text{Tempo}) + P(\text{Pony})$$
$$= .25 + .22 = .47$$

Example 6.3

A manufacturing plant conducted a survey to determine its employees' reactions toward a proposed change in working hours. A breakdown of the responses is shown in the following table:

WORK AREA	REACTION	
	Agree	Disagree
Production	17	23
Office	8	2

Suppose an employee is chosen at random, with the relevant events being defined as follows:

A: The employee works in production.
B: The employee agrees with the proposed change.

Express each of the following events in words:

a) $\bar{A}$ b) $(A \text{ or } B)$ c) $(A \text{ and } B)$ d) $(A \text{ or } \bar{B})$

Solution

a) $\bar{A}$:   The employee works in the office.

b) $(A \text{ or } B)$:   The employee either works in production or agrees with the proposed change, or both.

c) $(A \text{ and } B)$:   The employee works in production and agrees with the proposed change.

d) $(A \text{ or } \bar{B})$: The employee either works in production or disagrees with the proposed change, or both.

Example 6.4

Refer to Example 6.3, and find the following probabilities:

a) $P(\bar{A})$ b) $P(A \text{ or } B)$ c) $P(A \text{ and } B)$ d) $P(A \text{ or } \bar{B})$

Solution

a) $P(\bar{A}) = \dfrac{8}{50} + \dfrac{2}{50} = \dfrac{10}{50} = .20$

b) $P(A \text{ or } B) = \dfrac{17}{50} + \dfrac{23}{50} + \dfrac{8}{50} = \dfrac{48}{50} = .96$

c) $P(A \text{ and } B) = \dfrac{17}{50} = .34$

d) $P(A \text{ or } \bar{B}) = \dfrac{17}{50} + \dfrac{23}{50} + \dfrac{2}{50} = \dfrac{42}{50} = .84$

Conditional Probability

This subsection introduced the notion of conditional probability. The (marginal) probability that an event A will occur is denoted by $P(A)$. You should understand the distinction between $P(A)$ and $P(A|B)$, which is the conditional probability that A will occur given that the event B has occurred. You should also be able to compute this conditional probability, which is obtained by dividing the probability that both A and B will occur by the probability that B will occur:

$$P(A|B) = \frac{P(A \text{ and } B)}{P(B)}$$

Whenever you are given joint probabilities and are asked to find a conditional probability, it is often useful to display the given information using a two-way cross-classification table.

The second important concept introduced in this section was that of independent events. Two events A and B are said to be independent if the knowledge that B has occurred does not affect the probability that A will occur. In other words, A and B are independent events if

$$P(A|B) = P(A)$$

Equivalently, A and B are independent events if $P(B|A) = P(B)$.

Example 6.5

A company's employees have been classified according to age and salary, as shown in the following table:

AGE	SALARY			TOTAL
	Under $25,000	$25,000–$45,000	Over $45,000	
Under 30	32	3	0	35
30–45	10	18	21	49
Over 45	1	10	5	16
TOTAL	43	31	26	100

One employee is selected at random, and two events are defined as follows:

A: The employee is under 30.
B: The employee's salary is under $25,000.

Express each of the following probabilities in words, and find its numerical value:

a) $P(A \vert B)$ b) $P(B \vert A)$ c) $P(A \vert \overline{B})$ d) $P(\overline{A} \vert B)$

Solution

a) Given that the employee's salary is under $25,000, the probability that the employee is under 30 is

$$P(A|B) = \frac{P(A \text{ and } B)}{P(B)} = \frac{32/100}{(32+10+1)/100} = \frac{32}{43} \cong .74$$

Alternatively, rather than using the formula directly, we can find $P(A|B)$ in the following manner. Given that the selected employee's salary is under $25,000, the sample space of possible outcomes is reduced to the 43 employees classified in the first column of the table. Of these employees, 32 are under the age of 30. Therefore,

$$P(A|B) = \frac{32}{43} = .74$$

While this procedure may likewise be used to find the remaining conditional probabilities, we have chosen to use the formula.

b) Given that the employee is under 30, the probability that the employee's salary is under $25,000 is

$$P(B|A) = \frac{P(B \text{ and } A)}{P(A)} = \frac{32/100}{(32+3+1)/100} = \frac{32}{35} \cong .91$$

c) Given that the employee's salary is at least $25,000, the probability that the employee is under 30 is

$$P(A|\bar{B}) = \frac{P(A \text{ and } \bar{B})}{P(\bar{B})} = \frac{(3+0)/100}{(31+26)/100} = \frac{3}{57} \cong .05$$

d) Given that the employee's salary is under $25,000, the probability that the employee is at least 30 is

$$P(\bar{A}|B) = \frac{P(\bar{A} \text{ and } B)}{P(B)} = \frac{(10+1)/100}{43/100} = \frac{11}{43} \cong .26$$

Example 6.6

Refer to Example 6.5.

a) Find the probability that the employee's salary is at least $25,000, given that the employee is at least 30 years of age.

b) Are A and B independent events?

Solution

a) Using the notation established in Example 6.5, we must find $P(\overline{B}|\overline{A})$.

$$P(\overline{B}|\overline{A}) = \frac{P(\overline{B} \text{ and } \overline{A})}{P(\overline{A})} = \frac{(18+21+10+5)/100}{(49+16)/100} = \frac{54}{65} \cong .83$$

b) For A and B to be independent events, we must have $P(A|B) = P(A)$. But $P(A) = .35$ and $P(A|B) \cong .74$, from part a) of Example 6.5. Therefore, A and B are not independent events. Alternatively, we can conclude that A and B are not independent events by observing that $P(B|A) \ne P(B)$. This inequality holds because $P(B|A) \cong .91$, from part b) of Example 6.5, and $P(B) = .43$.

EXERCISES

6.1   The number of spots turning up when a six-sided die is tossed is observed. Consider the following events:

  A: An even number is observed.
  B: A number greater than 2 is observed.
  C: A number less than 5 is observed.
  D: A 6 is observed.

a) List the simple events in the sample space.

$S = \{1,2,3,4,5,6\}$

b) List the simple events in each of the events A, B, C, and D.

$A\ S = \{2,4,6\} \quad B, S = \{3,4,5,6\}$

$C\ S = \{1,2,3,4\} \quad D\ S = \{6\}$

c) List the simple events belonging to each of the following events:
    (A or B), (A and C), and $\overline{D}$.

$S = \{2,3,4,5,6\} \quad S = \{2,4\} \quad , \quad S\ \{1,2,3,4,5\}$

d) Is there a pair of mutually exclusive events among *A, B, C,* and *D*? Explain.

   $C + D$

e) Is there a pair of exhaustive events among *A, B, C,* and *D*? Explain.

   $B + C$

6.2 Refer to Example 6.1

   a) Assuming that each possible ordering of the three stocks is equally likely, assign a probability to each of the simple events.

   b) Express each of the following events in words, and find its probability:
      $(L$ or $N)$, $(L$ and $M)$, and $\overline{M}$.

6.3 Two hundred employees of a company have been classified according to their sex and their length of employment with the company, as shown in the following table:

	Male	Female	
Less than two years	28	26	54
Two years or more	82	64	146
	110	90	200

One employee is selected at random, and two events are defined as follows:

$A = 100$

$B = 146$

   A: The employee is male.
   B: The employee has worked for the company for two years or more.

$\frac{146}{}$

$\frac{82}{100}$

Express each of the following events in words:

a) $\bar{B}$ b) $(A \text{ or } B)$ c) $(A \text{ and } B)$ d) $(\bar{A} \text{ or } \bar{B})$

female

work Less than 2 years

6.4   Refer to Exercise 6.3, and find the following probabilities:

a) $P(\bar{B})$ b) $P(A \text{ or } B)$ c) $P(A \text{ and } B)$ d) $P(\bar{A} \text{ or } \bar{B})$

$A=.55$

$B=.73$

a) $.27$ $\dfrac{54}{200}$ b) $.87$ $\dfrac{174}{200}$ c) $.41$ $\dfrac{82}{200}$ d) $.59$ $\dfrac{\begin{array}{r}54\\+64\\\hline118\end{array}}{200}$

6.5   An accounting firm has advertised the availability of its report describing recent changes to the federal income tax act. The first 200 callers requesting a copy of the report are classified in the following table according to the medium by which the caller became aware of the report and the caller's primary interest.

PRIMARY INTEREST	MEDIUM		
	Radio	Newspaper	Word of Mouth
Personal Tax	34	20	26
Corporate Tax	36	70	14

One caller is selected at random, and two events are defined as follows:

A: The caller is primarily interested in corporate tax.
B: The caller became aware of the report through the newspaper.

Express each of the following probabilities in words, and find its numerical value:

a) $P(A|B)$

Both

b) $P(B|A)$

c) $P(\overline{A}|B)$

d) $P(\overline{A}|\overline{B})$

6.6   Refer to Exercise 6.5.

a)   Find the probability that the caller became aware of the report either by radio or by newspaper, given that the caller is primarily interested in corporate tax.

b)   Are A and B independent events?

6.3   Probability Rules and Trees

This section outlined three rules of probability that allow you to calculate the probabilities of three special events [$\overline{A}$, $(A$ or $B)$, and $(A$ and $B)$] from known probabilities of various related events. The three rules are as follows:

1.   *Complement Rule:*

$P(\overline{A}) = 1 - P(A)$

2.   *Addition Rule:*

$P(A$ or $B) = P(A) + P(B) - P(A$ and $B)$

3.   *Multiplication Rule:*

$P(A$ and $B) = P(A) \cdot P(B|A)$

or

$$P(A \text{ and } B) = P(B) \cdot P(A|B)$$

We note that the addition rule and the multiplication rule can be expressed more simply under certain conditions. If A and B are *mutually exclusive* events, then $P(A \cap B) = 0$, so the addition rule becomes

$$P(A \text{ or } B) = P(A) + P(B) \quad \text{if } A \text{ and } B \text{ are mutually exclusive}$$

If A and B are independent events, then $P(B|A) = P(B)$, so the multiplication rule becomes

$$P(A \text{ and } B) = P(A) \cdot P(B) \quad \text{if } A \text{ and } B \text{ are independent}$$

Remember, though, that these two simple formulas hold only when A and B satisfy the conditions specified.

Probability Trees

This section expanded upon the use of probability trees. A probability tree is a useful device both for identifying all of the simple events in a sample space and for finding the probability that any simple event will occur. Whenever the outcome to be observed in a random experiment can be broken down into a series of observations of simpler, component outcomes (observing one component outcome at each stage), it will be useful to depict the situation with a probability tree, if only to clarify the problem to be addressed.

A probability tree will usually be helpful if you are asked to find the probability of a joint event, such as $P(A \text{ and } B)$. On the other hand, if you are given some joint probabilities and are asked to find a conditional probability, it will usually be helpful to use a two-way cross-classification table.

Example 6.7

A chemical company has two divisions: household and industrial. A financial analyst estimates that the industrial division has a 70% chance of showing a profit this year. He maintains that the household division has only a 50% chance of showing a profit, but if it does so, he feels 90% certain that the industrial division will also be profitable.

a) Find the probability that both divisions will be profitable.
b) Find the probability that at least one division will be profitable.

Solution

a) Define the events:

A: The industrial division will be profitable.

B: The household division will be profitable.

Summarize the given information:

$P(A)\quad = .7$
$P(B)\quad = .5$
$P(A|B)\ = .9$

We must find $P(A$ and $B)$. According to the multiplication rule,

$$P(A \text{ and } B)\ = P(A) \cdot P(B|A)$$

$$= P(B) \cdot P(A|B)$$

The given information is such that only the second form of the multiplication rule is useful here. Therefore,

$$P(A \text{ and } B) = P(B) \cdot P(A|B) = (.5)(.9) = .45$$

b) The probability that at least one division will be profitable can be expressed notationally as $P(A$ or $B)$. Using the addition rule,

$$P(A \text{ or } B)\ = P(A) + P(B) - P(A \text{ and } B)$$

$$= .7 + .5 - .45 = .75$$

Example 6.8

Refer to Example 6.7.

a) Are A and B independent events?

b) Are A and B mutually exclusive events?

Solution

a) A and B are not independent events, since $P(A) \neq P(A|B)$; that is, $.7 \neq .9$.

b) A and B are not mutually exclusive, since $P(A$ and $B) = .45 \neq 0$.

Example 6.9

Solve Example 6.7 using a probability tree.

Solution

Summarizing Example 6.7, we were given

$P(A) = .7, P(B) = .5, P(A|B) = .9$

and asked to find a) $P(A \text{ and } B)$ and b) $P(A \text{ or } B)$. Because the conditional probability that is given is for event A, event A should appear at the second stage of the probability tree, as shown in the figure below. The probabilities shown on the tree are either given or deduced from the fact that the sum of the probabilities on branches emanating from a common node must equal 1.

The one probability that is given but cannot be assigned to a branch is $P(A) = .7$, which is the sum of the two joint probabilities $P(B \text{ and } A)$ and $P(\overline{B} \text{ and } A)$.

a) Recall that the probability of a simple event, such as $(A \text{ and } B)$, is the product of the probabilities attached to the branches leading to that event. Therefore,

$$P(A \text{ and } B) = P(B \text{ and } A) = P(B) \cdot P(A|B) = (.5)(.9) = .45$$

b) Looking at the four simple events listed at the right of the tree, we observe that the event $(A \text{ or } B)$ occurs if any one of the first three simple events occurs:

$$
\begin{aligned}
P(A \text{ or } B) &= (B \text{ and } A) &+ P(B \text{ and } \overline{A}) &+ P(\overline{B} \text{ and } A) \\
&= (.5)(.9) &+ (.5)(.1) &+ P(\overline{B} \text{ and } A)
\end{aligned}
$$

Because $P(A) = P(B \text{ and } A) + P(\overline{B} \text{ and } A)$, we obtain

$$P(\overline{B} \text{ and } A) = P(A) - P(B \text{ and } A) = .7 - .45 = .25$$

Thus, $P(A \text{ or } B) = (.5)(.9) + (.5)(.1) + .25 = .75$.

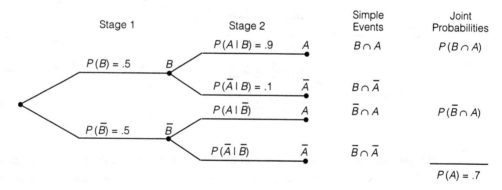

Example 6.10

A company's records show that 80% of the male employees have a college education, while only 50% of the female employees have a college education. Sixty percent of the company's employees are female. One employee is selected at random.

a) Find the probability that the employee selected is a male who does not have a college education.

b) Find the probability that the employee selected has a college education.

Solution

a) The first step is to define the events of interest:

M: The employee is male.

C: The employee selected has a college education.

The second step is to summarize the given information, recognizing that $\overline{M}$ denotes the selection of a female employee:

$$P(\overline{M}) = .6, \quad P(C|M) = .8, \quad P(C|\overline{M}) = .5$$

To ensure that a conditional probability is expressed correctly in notational form, it is helpful to reword the statement of the conditional event using the words "given that." For example, the statement that 80% of the male employees have a college education can be reworded as "Given that an employee is male, the probability that he has a college education is .8." It then becomes easy to express this statement in notational form as $P(C|M) = .8$, recalling that the symbol "|" is read "given that."

Recognizing that we can observe in two stages whether or not the events M and C occur, we can depict the situation using the following probability tree:

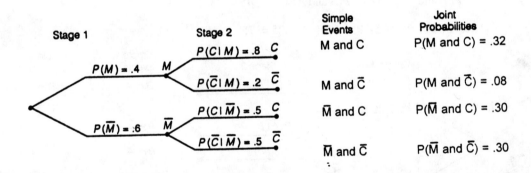

When you are assigning probabilities to the branches, recall that the probabilities assigned to a set of branches, all of which emanate from a common node, must sum to 1. You should next write down the simple event corresponding to each possible path through the tree, together with its associated (joint) probability. Finally, you should check that the joint probabilities sum to 1. Once you have proceeded this far, it will be relatively easy to answer any question asked of you.

Reading from the probability tree, the probability that the employee selected is a male who does not have a college education is

$$P(M \text{ or } \overline{C}) = .08$$

b) The probability we want to find is $P(C)$. The event C occurs only if one of two simple events, $(M$ and $C)$ or $(\overline{M}$ and $C)$, occurs. Since these two simple events are mutually exclusive,

$$P(C) = P(M \text{ and } C) + P(\overline{M} \text{ and } C)$$

$$= .32 + .30 = .62$$

Example 6.11 (Optional: high level of difficulty)

A textile firm employs three knitting machines to produce bedspreads. Forty percent of the firm's daily bedspread production comes from machine A, while the remainder of the production is split equally between machines B and C. One percent of the bedspreads produced on machine A are flawed, while the flaw rates for machines B and C are 2% and 3%, respectively. If one bedspread is selected at random from a day's production and is found to contain a flaw, what is the probability that it was produced on machine B?

Solution

The events of interest are as follows:

   A: The bedspread selected was produced on machine A.

   B: The bedspread selected was produced on machine B.

   C: The bedspread selected was produced on machine C.

   F: The bedspread selected contains a flaw.

Summarizing the given information, we have

$$P(A) = .4, \qquad P(B) = .3, \qquad P(C) = .3$$

$$P(F|A) = .02 \qquad P(F|B) = .02, \qquad P(F|C) = .03$$

We can now depict the situation with a probability tree.

Prior Probabilities	Conditional Probabilities	Simple Events	Joint Probabilities
$P(A) = .4$ — A	$P(F|A) = .01$ F	A and F	$P(A \text{ and } F) = .004$
	$P(\overline{F}|A) = .99$ $\overline{F}$	A and $\overline{F}$	$P(A \text{ and } \overline{F}) = .396$
$P(B) = .3$ — B	$P(F|B) = .02$ F	B and F	$P(B \text{ and } F) = .006$
	$P(\overline{F}|B) = .98$ $\overline{F}$	B and $\overline{F}$	$P(B \text{ and } \overline{F}) = .294$
$P(C) = .3$ — C	$P(F|C) = .03$ F	C and F	$P(C \text{ and } F) = .009$
	$P(\overline{F}|C) = .97$ $\overline{F}$	C and $\overline{F}$	$P(C \text{ and } \overline{F}) = .291$

59

The probability that we are required to find is

$$P(B|F) = \frac{P(B \text{ and } F)}{P(F)}$$

The value of the numerator is obtained easily from the probability tree:

$$P(B \cap F) = P(B) \cdot P(F|B) = (.3)(.02) = .006$$

To find $P(F)$, note that event F occurs only if one of three simple events occurs: (A and F), (B and F), or (C and F). Since these three simple events are mutually exclusive,

$$P(F) = P(A \text{ and } F) + P(B \text{ and } F) + P(C \text{ and } F)$$

$$= .004 + .006 + .009 = .019$$

We therefore have

$$P(B|F) = \frac{P(B \text{ and } F)}{P(F)} = \frac{.006}{.019} = .316$$

EXERCISES

6.7   A firm's employees were surveyed to determine their feelings toward a new dental plan and a new life insurance plan. The results showed that 81% favored the insurance plan, while only 35% favored the dental plan. Of those who favored the insurance plan, 30% also favored the dental plan.

a)   What percentage of the employees favored both plans?

$A = .81$
$B = .35$
$(A|B) = .30$
$A + B) =$

$.81 \cdot .30 = .243$

$= 24.3\%$

24.3

b)   What percentage of the employees favored at least one of the plans?

$, .81 + .35 - .243 = .917$

$= 91.7\%$

91.7

6.8   Consider two events, A and B, for which $P(A) = .2$, $P(B) = .6$, and $P(A \text{ or } B) = .68$.

a)   Find $P(A \text{ and } B)$.

$.12$

b)   Are A and B independent events?   Yes

c)   Are A and B mutually exclusive events?
                                     NO

6.9   An electrical contractor has observed that 90% of his accounts are paid within 30 days. Of those that are not paid within 30 days, 40% remain unpaid after 60 days. If one account is selected at random, what is the probability that it is paid within 60 days?

A. = .90   .36   .96   (.94)
B = .40
$(A+B) = .56$
$A|B = 1.4$

6.10   A mechanic has removed six spark plugs from an engine and finds two to be defective. If two spark plugs are selected at random from among these six, what is the probability that exactly one of them is defective?

A 6   16/30

B 2

6.11   (Optional: High level of difficulty)

Lona has reached the finals of her tennis club's annual tournament but must await the outcome of a match between Cayleigh and Marnie before knowing who her opponent will be. Observers feel that Lona has a 70% chance of winning if she plays Cayleigh and a 40% chance of winning if she plays Marnie. They also believe that the probability that Marnie will reach the finals is .9. After the final match is played, you are told that Lona won. What is the probability that she played Marnie?

6.12 (Optional: High level of difficulty)

Marvin employs two able legal assistants, Shirley and Pat. The assistant who is the last to leave the office each day is supposed to set the telephone answering machine to receive messages while the office is closed. Shirley leaves the office after Pat 60% of the time and forgets to set the machine on 5% of these occasions. Pat forgets to set the machine 10% of the time when she is the last to leave. (Since the two assistants don't get along with one another, they never leave the office together.) Upon arriving at the office one morning, Marvin discovers that the answering machine hasn't been set to receive messages. What is the probability that Shirley is at fault?

6.4 Random Variables and Probability Distributions

This section introduced the concept of a random variable, which assigns a numerical value to each simple event in a sample space, thereby enabling us to work with numerical-valued outcomes. A random variable is discrete if the number of possible values that it can assume is finite or countably infinite; otherwise, the random variable is continuous. The second important concept introduced was that of a discrete probability distribution, which lists all possible values that a discrete random variable can take on, together with the probability that each value will be assumed. When constructing a discrete probability distribution, bear in mind that the probabilities must sum to 1.

Example 6.12

The local taxation office claims that 10% of the income tax forms processed this year contain errors. Suppose that two of these forms are selected at random. Find the probability distribution of the random variable X, defined as the number of forms selected that contain an error.

Solution

A sample space for this random experiment is

$$S = \left\{ F_1 F_2, F_1 \overline{F}_2, \overline{F}_1 F_2, \overline{F}_1 \overline{F}_2 \right\}$$

where, for example, $F_1 \overline{F}_2$ indicates that the first form selected contains an error and the second form does not. The random variable X assigns a value of 0, 1, or 2 to each of these simple events. To find the probability that each of these values will be assumed, we must determine the simple events that result in each of these values being assumed and the probabilities that the simple events will occur. For example, $X = 2$ if and only if the event $F_1 F_2$ occurs. Since the occurrence of an error on one form is independent of the occurrence of an error on the other form,

$$P(X = 2) = p(2) = P(F_1 F_2) = P(F_1)P(F_2) = (.1)(.1) = .01$$

Similarly,

$$P(X = 1) = p(1) = P(F_1 \overline{F}_2) + P(\overline{F}_1 F_2)$$
$$= P(F_1)P(\overline{F}_2) + P(\overline{F}_1)P(F_2)$$
$$= (.1)(.9) + (.9)(.1) = .18$$
$$P(X = 0) = p(0) = P(\overline{F}_1 \overline{F}_2) = P(\overline{F}_1)P(\overline{F}_2) = (.9)(.9) = .81$$

Summarizing the probability distribution of X in tabular form, we obtain

x	$p(x)$
0	.81
1	.18
1	.01

Note that we could have used a probability tree to identify the simple events and their associated probabilities.

EXERCISES

6.13 For each of the following random variables, indicate whether the variable is discrete or continuous and specify the possible values that it can assume.

a) X = the number of customers served by a restaurant on a given day

b) X = the time in minutes required to complete a particular assembly

c) X = the number of accidents at a particular intersection in a given week

d) X = the number of questions answered correctly by a randomly selected student who wrote a quiz consisting of 15 multiple choice questions

e) X = the weight in ounces of a newborn baby chosen at random

6.14 The following table gives the probability distribution of X, the number of telephones in a randomly selected home in a certain community.

x	$p(x)$
0	.021
1	.412
2	.283
3	.188
4	.096

If one home is selected at random, find the probability that it will have:

a) no telephone;

b) fewer than two telephones;

c)   at least three telephones;

d)   between one and three telephones (inclusive).

6.15   The security force on a particular campus estimates that 80% of the cars that are parked illegally on campus are detected and issued a $10 parking ticket. Suppose your car will be parked illegally on two occasions during the coming year. Determine the probability distribution of the random variable $X =$ the total dollar amount of parking tickets that you will receive.

6.5   Expected Value and Variance

This section dealt with the two main descriptive measures of a discrete random variable: its expected value and its variance. As well as being able to calculate the numerical values of these measures, you are expected to have a general understanding of their meanings and to be familiar with the laws of expected value and of variance.

The expected value (or mean value) of a discrete random variable X is a weighted average of the values that X can assume:

$$E(X) = \mu = \sum_{i=1}^{n} x_i p(x_i)$$

The variance of a discrete random variable X is a weighted average of the squared deviations of the values of X from their mean μ:

$$V(X) = \sigma^2 = \sum_{i=1}^{n} (x_i - \mu)^2 p(x_i)$$

When computing the variance of X by hand, it is usually easier to use the shortcut formula:

$$\sigma^2 = E(X^2) - \mu^2$$

A related measure of the dispersion of the values of X about their mean value μ is the standard deviation of X, defined to be the positive square root of the variance of X. The standard deviation of X, denoted σ, has the advantage of being expressed in the same units as both the values of X and their mean value μ.

Example 6.13

Let X be a random variable with the following probability distribution:

x	$p(x)$
-2	.1
4	.3
6	.4
8	.2

a) Find the mean and standard deviation of X.
b) Find the mean and standard deviation of $Y = 2X + 4$.

Solution

a) From the definitions of $E(X)$ and $V(X)$:

$$E(X) = \mu = \sum_{i=1}^{4} x_i p(x_i)$$
$$= -2(.1) + 4(.3) + 6(.4) + 8(.2)$$
$$= -.2 + 1.2 + 2.4 + 1.6 = 5.0$$

$$V(X) = \sigma^2 = \sum_{i=1}^{4} (x_i - \mu)^2 p(x_i)$$
$$= (-2 - 5)^2(.1) + (4 - 5)^2(.3) + (6 - 5)^2(.4) + (8 - 5)^2(.2)$$
$$= (-7)^2(.1) + (-1)^2(.3) + (1)^2(.4) + (3)^2(.2)$$
$$= (49)(.1) + (1)(.3) + (1)(.4) + (9)(.2)$$
$$= 7.4$$

Therefore, the mean value of X is $\mu = 5$, and the standard deviation of X is $\sigma = \sqrt{7.4} = 2.72$.

A convenient alternative for computing the expected value and variance of X is to record the necessary computations in a table. In the accompanying table, we have recorded the computations involved in the calculation of $E(X)$ and $E(X^2)$. Recall that $E(X^2)$ is needed in the shortcut formula for computing the variance of X.

x	$p(x)$	$x\,p(x)$	x^2	$x^2 p(x)$
-2	.1	-.2	4	.4
4	.3	1.2	16	4.8
6	.4	2.4	36	14.4
8	.2	1.6	64	12.8
		$5.0 = E(X)$		$32.4 = E(X^2)$

As before, we obtain

$$E(X) = \mu = 5.0$$
$$V(X) = E(X^2) - \mu^2 = 32.4 - (5)^2 = 7.4$$
$$\sigma_x = \sqrt{7.4} = 2.72$$

b) Using the laws of expected value and variance:

$$\begin{aligned} E(Y) &= E(2X + 4) = E(2X) + E(4) \\ &= 2(5) + 4 = 14 \\ V(Y) &= V(2X + 4) = V(2X) \\ &= (2)^2 V(X) = 4(7.4) = 29.6 \\ \sigma_y &= \sqrt{29.6} = 5.44 \end{aligned}$$

In the next to last line above, a common error is to forget to square the 2 before multiplying by $V(X)$.

Example 6.14

A firm believes it has a 50–50 chance of winning an $80,000 contract if it spends $5,000 on the proposal. If the firm spends twice this amount on the proposal, it feels its chances of winning the contract will improve to 60%. If the firm bases its decision solely on expected value, how much should it spend on the proposal?

Solution

Let X be the net revenue received from the contract (net of the proposal cost) if $5,000 is spent on the proposal, and let Y be the net revenue received if $10,000 is spent. The probability distributions of X and Y are as follows:

x	$p(x)$		y	$p(y)$
−5,000	.5		−10,000	.4
75,000	.5		70,000	.6

If $5,000 is spent on the proposal, the expected net revenue is

$$E(X) = (-5,000)(.5) + (75,000)(.5) = \$35,000$$

If $10,000 is spent on the proposal, the expected net revenue is

$$E(Y) = (-10,000)(.4) + (70,000)(.6) = \$38,000$$

The firm should spend $10,000 on the proposal, since that results in the higher expected net revenue.

EXERCISES

6.16 According to the *Statistics Canada Yearbook* (1985), the distribution of the number of dependent children involved in divorces in 1981 is the following:

Number of dependent children	0	1	2	3	4	5
Percentage of divorces	48.1	22.8	20.7	6.3	1.6	0.5

a) If one divorce case is selected at random, find the probability that the number of dependent children involved is at least 2.

b) Find the expected value and the variance of the number of dependent children involved in 1981 divorces.

c) What is the probability that the number of dependent children involved in a divorce falls within two standard deviations of the mean value?

6.17   Suppose you make a $1,000 investment in a risky venture. There is a 40% chance that the pay-off from the investment will be $2,000, a 50% chance that you will just get your money back, and a 10% chance that you will receive nothing at all from your investment. Find the expected value and standard deviation of the payoff from your investment of $1,000.

6.18   Refer to Exercise 6.17.

   a)   If X is the payoff from the investment, then the net profit from the investment is $Y = X - 1,000$. Find the expected value and standard deviation of the net profit.

   b)   If you invest $3,000 in the risky venture instead of $1,000 and the possible payoffs triple accordingly, what is the expected value and standard deviation of the net profit from the $3,000 investment?

6.6   Bivariate Distributions (Optional)

This section introduced the notion of a bivariate (or joint) probability distribution of two quantitative variables, from which we can examine the relationship between the two variables.

A common measure of the strength of the **linear** relationship between two variables X and Y is the **covariance**, given by

$$COV(X, Y) = \sum_{all(x,y)} (x - \mu_x)(y - \mu_y) \bullet P(X = x \text{ and } Y = y)$$
$$= E(XY) - \mu_x \mu_y$$

A covariance can take on any numerical value between $-\infty$ and $+\infty$. To obtain a measure more amenable to interpretation, we divide COV(X, Y) by the product $\sigma_X \bullet \sigma_Y$, to obtain the **coefficient of correlation**

$$\rho = \frac{COV(X,Y)}{\sigma_x \bullet \sigma_y}$$

A correlation ρ can only assume values between -1 and +1, inclusive.

If $\rho = +1$, there is a perfect positive linear relationship between X and Y. If $\rho = -1$, there is a perfect negative linear relationship between X and Y. If $\rho = 0$, there is no linear relationship between X and Y; in this case, X and Y are said to be **independent**.

Example 6.15

Consider the following bivariate distribution of X and Y.

	x	
y	10	20
1	.4	.2
2	.1	.3

a.   Find the marginal probabilities.

b.   Determine the mean, variance, and standard deviation for *X* and for *Y*.

c.   Compute the covariance between *X* and *Y*, and determine if *X* and *Y* are independent.

d.   Compute the coefficient of correlation.

Solution

a.   The four probabilities in the interior of the table are the joint probabilities $p(x, y)$. In particular,

$p(10, 1) = .4$

$p(10, 2) = .1$

Summing these two probabilities, we obtain the marginal probability

$P(X = 10) = .5$

Proceeding similarly to find the other marginal probabilities, we obtain the marginal probability distributions of X and Y:

x	*p(x)*	*y*	*p(y)*
10	.5	1	.6
20	.5	2	.4

b. $\mu_x = \Sigma x_i p(x_i) = 10(.5) + 20(.5) = 15$

$\mu_y = \Sigma y_i p(y_i) = 1(.6) + 2(.4) = 1.4$

$V(X) = \Sigma(x_i - \mu x)^2 p(x_i)$

$\qquad = (10 - 15)^2(.5) + (20 - 15)^2(.5) = 25$

$\sigma_x = \sqrt{25} = 5$

$V(Y) = \Sigma(y_i - \mu_y)^2 p(y_i)$

$\qquad = (1 - 1.4)^2(.6) + (2-1.4)^2(.4) = .24$

$\sigma y = \sqrt{24} = .49$

c. $COV(X,Y) = \sum_{all(x,y)} (x - \mu_x)(y - \mu_y) \bullet P(X = x \text{ and } Y = y)$

$= (10 - 15)(1 - 1.4)(.4) + (10 - 15)(2 - 1.4)(.1) + (20 - 15)(1 - 1.4)(.2) + (20-15)(2 - 1.4)(.3)$

$= (-5)(-.4)(.4) + (-5)(.6)(.1) + (5)(-.4)(.2) + (5)(.6)(.3)$

$= .8 - .3 - .4 + .9$

$= 1.0$

X and Y are not independent, because COV(X, Y) $\neq 0$

d. The coefficient of correlation is

$$\rho = \frac{COV(X,Y)}{\sigma_x \sigma_y}$$

$$= \frac{1.0}{\sqrt{25}\sqrt{.24}}$$

$= .408$

Exercise

6.19   The table below lists the joint probabilities of X and Y.

X

y	2	4
4	.4	.3
8	.2	.1

a. Find the marginal probabilities

b. Determine the mean, variance, and standard deviation for X and for Y.

c. Compute the covariance and the coefficient of correlation.

d. Are X and Y independent? Explain.

6.7   Binomial Distribution

The most important discrete probability distribution is the binomial distribution. You should be able to do the following:

1. Recognize situations in which a binomial distribution is applicable.
2. Define the binomial random variable that is appropriate in a given situation.
3. Compute binomial probabilities using the formula and using Table 1 in Appendix B.

The primary characteristic of a binomial experiment is that each trial of the experiment must result in one of only two possible outcomes. More precisely, a binomial experiment possesses the following properties:

1. The experiment consists of a fixed number, n, of trials.
2. The result of each trial can be classified into one of two categories: success or failure.
3. The probability, p, of a success remains constant from trial to trial.
4. Each trial of the experiment is independent of the other trials.

The binomial random variable, X, counts the number of successes in the n trials of a binomial experiment. The probability of observing x successes in the n trials of a binomial experiment is

$$P(X = x) = \frac{n!}{x!\,(n-x)!}\, p^x (1-p)^{n-x}, \text{ for } x = 0, 1, \ldots, n$$

This probability can also be found using Table 1 in Appendix B, for selected values of n and p.

Example 6.16

The owner of a boat used for deep-sea fishing charters advertises that his clients catch at least one large salmon (over 15 pounds) on 60% of the charters. Suppose you book four charters for the coming year. Find the probability distribution of X, the number of charters on which you catch at least one large salmon.

Solution

Assuming the result of each charter is independent of the results of other charters, we are dealing with a binomial experiment. A good habit to develop when dealing with any binomial experiment is to begin by clearly identifying the following four characteristics of the experiment:

n = 4
success = a charter on which at least one large salmon is caught
p = .6
X = the number of charters on which at least one large salmon is caught

The binomial random variable X can take any one of the values 0, 1, 2, 3, and 4. The probabilities with which these values are assumed can be computed from the formulas for binomial probabilities:

$$p(0) = \frac{4!}{0!\,4!}(.6)^0(.4)^4 = \frac{4\cdot3\cdot2\cdot1}{1\cdot4\cdot3\cdot2\cdot1}(1)(.0256) = .0256$$

$$p(1) = \frac{4!}{1!\,3!}(.6)^1(.4)^3 = \frac{4\cdot3\cdot2\cdot1}{1\cdot3\cdot2\cdot1}(.6)(.0640) = .1536$$

$$p(2) = \frac{4!}{2!\,2!}(.6)^2(.4)^2 = \frac{4\cdot3\cdot2\cdot1}{2\cdot1\cdot2\cdot1}(.36)(.16) = .3456$$

$$p(3) = \frac{4!}{3!\,1!}(.6)^3(.4)^1 = \frac{4\cdot3\cdot2\cdot1}{3\cdot2\cdot1\cdot1}(.216)(.4) = .3456$$

$$p(4) = \frac{4!}{4!\,0!}(.6)^4(.4)^0 = \frac{4\cdot3\cdot2\cdot1}{4\cdot3\cdot2\cdot1\cdot1}(.1296)(1) = .1296$$

Hence, the probability distribution of X is as follows:

x	$p(x)$
0	.0256
1	.1536
2	.3456
3	.3456
4	.1296

Example 6.17

Let X be a binomial random variable with $n = 20$ and $p = .4$. Find the following probabilities using Table 1 in Appendix B:

a) $P(X \geq 10)$
b) $P(X = 2)$
c) $P(3 \leq X \leq 5)$

Solution

a) Because the cumulative binomial probabilities tabulated in Table 1 are of the form $P(X \leq k)$, any probability that we want to find must be expressed in terms of probabilities of this form. Notice that the event $(X \leq 9)$ is the complement of the event $(X \geq 10)$. Therefore, applying the complement rule, we obtain

$$P(X \geq 10) = 1 - P(X \leq 9)$$
$$= 1 - .755 = .245$$

b) Expressing $P(X = 2)$ in terms of probabilities of the form $P(X \leq k)$, we obtain

$$P(X = 2) = P(X = 0, 1, \text{ or } 2) - P(X = 0 \text{ or } 1)$$
$$= P(X \leq 2) - P(X \leq 1)$$
$$= .004 - .001 = .003$$

c) It is often helpful to begin by enumerating the x-values of interest before expressing the required probability in terms of probabilities of the form $P(X \leq k)$:

$$P(3 \leq X \leq 5) = P(X = 3, 4, \text{ or } 5)$$
$$= P(X = 0, 1, 2, 3, 4, \text{ or } 5) - P(X = 0, 1, \text{ or } 2)$$
$$= P(X \leq 5) - P(X \leq 2)$$
$$= .126 - .004 = .122$$

Example 6.18

The Globe and Mail (3 September 1987) has reported that 80% of Wall Street firms that speculate on corporate takeovers before they become public also help to underwrite such deals. A random sample of 10 firms that speculate on corporate takeovers is selected.

a) Find the probability that at least half the firms selected underwrite takeovers.
b) Find the probability that at most three of the firms selected do not underwrite takeovers.
c) Find the expected value and variance of the number of firms selected that underwrite takeovers.

Solution

a) Summarizing the characteristics of the binomial experiment:

$$n = 10$$
success = a selected firm underwrites takeovers
$$p = .8$$
$$X = \text{the number of firms selected that underwrite takeovers}$$

The required probability is

$$P(X \geq 5) = 1 - P(X \leq 4)$$
$$= 1 - .006 = .994$$

b) If we redefine a "success" to be a selected firm that does not underwrite takeovers, then we still have $n = 10$, and the probability of a success is now $p = .2$. If Y is the number of firms selected that do not underwrite takeovers, then the required probability is

$$P(Y \leq 3) = .879$$

c) Using the same notation and definition of success as in part a), the expected value of X is

$$E(X) = \mu = np = (10)(.8) = 8$$

The variance of X is

$$V(X) = \sigma^2 = npq = (10)(.8)(.2) = 1.6$$

EXERCISES

6.20 According to *Forbes Magazine*, 27% of Americans would like to fly in the Space Shuttle. Three Americans are selected at random and asked if they would like to fly in the Space Shuttle. Find the probability distribution of X, the number of persons selected who respond positively.

6.21 Consider a binomial random variable, X, with $n = 25$ and $p = .7$. Use Table 1 in Appendix B to find the following probabilities:

a) $P(X \geq 15)$

b) $P(X \leq 8)$

c) $P(X = 24)$

d) $P(18 \leq X \leq 23)$

6.22 Sixty percent of the new cars sold in the United States in 1984 were made by General Motors. A random sample of 15 purchases of new 1984 cars is selected.

a) Find the mean and standard deviation of the number of persons selected who purchased a G.M. car.

b) Find the probability that at least 10 of those selected purchased a G.M. car.

c) Find the probability that at least five of those selected did not purchase a G.M. car.

6.8   Poisson Distribution

The Poisson distribution is a second important discrete distribution. You should be able to do the following:

1. Recognize situations in which a Poisson distribution is applicable.
2. Define the Poisson random variable that is appropriate in a given situation.
3. Compute Poisson probabilities using the formula and using Table 2 in Appendix B.
4. Approximate binomial probabilities using the appropriate Poisson distribution.

The Poisson distribution is applicable when the events of interest (such as incoming telephone calls) occur randomly, independently of one another, and rarely. By "rarely" we mean that there is only a very small probability that the event of interest will occur within a very small specified time interval or region.

The Poisson random variable, X, counts the number of occurrences of an event (i.e., number of successes) in a given time interval or region.

A Poisson random variable can therefore take any one of infinitely many possible integer values. In contrast, a binomial random variable (which is also discrete) has only finitely many possible values. The probability of observing exactly x successes is given by

$$P(X = x) = \frac{e^{-\mu}\mu^x}{x!}, \text{ for } x = 0, 1, 2, \dots$$

where μ is the average number of successes in the given time interval or region. This probability can also be found using Table 2 in Appendix B, for selected values of μ.

It is important to ensure that the intervals specified in the definitions of X and μ are the same. For example, suppose X is the number of successes in a specified 2-hour period and you know that, on average, there are three successes per hour. Then μ must be defined as the average number of successes in the 2-hour period, and you set $\mu = 6$. You should not obtain a common time period by defining both X and μ in terms of a 1-hour period, since your interest lies in the number of successes in the 2-hour period specified.

A binomial distribution having n trials and a probability p of a success on each trial can be approximated by a Poisson distribution if p is very small ($p < .05$ at least). The appropriate approximating Poisson distribution is the one with $\mu = np$, the mean of the binomial distribution.

Example 6.19

Records show that there is an average of three accidents each day in a certain city between 2 and 3 P.M.

a) Use the Poisson probability formula to find the probability that there will be exactly one accident between 2 and 3 P.M. on a particular day.

b) Use the table of Poisson probabilities to check your answer to part a).

c) Find the probability that there will be at least three accidents between 2 and 3 P.M. on a particular day.

d) Find the probability that there will be at least three accidents between 2 and 2:30 P.M. on a particular day.

Solution

a) Let X be the number of accidents between 2 and 3 P.M. Then X satisfies the requirements for a Poisson random variable, since the accidents of interest occur randomly, independently, and rarely within a specified time period. Knowing that the average number of accidents within the specified time period is $\mu = 3$, we obtain

$$P(X = 1) = \frac{e^{-\mu}\mu^x}{x!} = \frac{e^{-3}3^1}{1!} = \frac{e^{-3}(3)}{(1)} = .149$$

b) Before using Table 2 in Appendix B, we must express the required probability in terms of the types of cumulative probabilities tabulated in Table 2:

$$P(X = 1) = P(X \leq 1) - P(X = 0)$$
$$= .199 - .050 = .149$$

c)
$$P(X \geq 3) = 1 - P(X \leq 2)$$
$$= 1 - .423 = .577$$

d) We must first redefine X and μ in terms of the new time period of interest. Let X be the number of accidents between 2 and 2:30 P.M. The average number of accidents in this time period is $\mu = 3/2 = 1.5$. Using Table 2, we obtain

$$P(X \geq 3) = 1 - P(X \leq 2)$$
$$= 1 - .809 = .191$$

Example 6.20

Consider a binomial random variable X with $n = 200$ and $p = .005$. Approximate the values of the following probabilities:

a) $P(X = 2)$
b) $P(X \geq 4)$

Solution

Binomial distributions with $p = .005$ are not tabulated in Table 1 in Appendix B. The required binomial probabilities can be approximated, however, using the Poisson distribution with $\mu = np = (200)(.005) = 1$.

a) $P(X = 2) = P(X \leq 2) - P(X \leq 1)$
$$\cong .920 - .736 = .184 \qquad \text{(from Table 2)}$$

b) $P(X \geq 4) = 1 - P(X \leq 3)$
$$\cong 1 - .981 = .019 \qquad \text{(from Table 2)}$$

EXERCISES

6.23 A harried executive claims that his productivity suffers from having to deal with an average of 12 random interruptions each morning between 9 A.M. and 12 noon.

    a) Use the Poisson probability formula to find the probability that he will be interrupted eight times during a particular morning.

    b) Use the table of Poisson probabilities to check your answer to part a).

    c) Find the probability that he will be interrupted at least six times between 9 and 10 A.M. on a particular morning.

6.24 The authors of a textbook claim that only 1% of the pages in the book contain an error. Suppose 20 pages from the book are selected at random.

    a) Use the binomial probability tables to find the probability that at least one of the pages selected contains an error.

    b) Use the Poisson probability tables to approximate the binomial probability found in part a).

Chapter 7: Continuous Probability Distributions

7.1   Introduction

This chapter continued our discussion of probability distributions. It began by describing continuous probability distributions in general, and then took a detailed look at the normal distribution, which is the most important specific continuous distribution. At the completion of this chapter, you are expected to understand the following:

1. The basic differences between discrete and continuous random variables.
2. How to convert a normal random variable into the standard normal random variable, and how to use the table of standard normal probabilities.
3. How to approximate binomial probabilities using either a Poisson distribution or a normal distribution.
4. How to recognize when it is appropriate to use an exponential distribution, and how to compute exponential probabilities.

7.2   Continuous Probability Distributions

This section introduced the notion of a continuous random variable, which differs from a discrete random variable both in the type of numerical events of interest and the type of function used to find probabilities. A continuous random variable X can assume any value in some interval, such as $5 < x < 20$. Since a continuous random variable can assume an uncountably infinite number of values, the probability that any particular value will be assumed is zero. Hence, for a continuous random variable X, it is only meaningful to talk about the probability that X will assume a value within a particular interval. Such a probability is found using the probability density function, $f(x)$, associated with X. The probability that X will take a value in the interval $a < x < b$ is given by the area under the graph of $f(x)$ between the values a and b. For most of the specific continuous distributions that you will encounter (such as the normal distribution), you can easily compute probabilities such as this by using probability tables appearing in the appendices. Notice that because

$$P(X = a) = P(X = b) = 0$$

the following equality holds for any continuous random variable X:

$$P(a < X < b) = P(a \leq X \leq b)$$

A specific continuous distribution that is especially simple to work with is the **uniform distribution.** A random variable X defined over an interval $a \leq x \leq b$ is uniformly distributed if its probability density function is given by

$$f(x) = \frac{1}{b - a}, \qquad a \leq x \leq b$$

Because the graph of the density function is a horizontal line, the area under the graph is a rectangle, giving rise to an alternative name for the uniform distribution—the rectangular distribution. Notice that the values of a uniform random variable X are distributed evenly, or uniformly, across the domain of X.

Example 7.1

A continuous random variable X has the following probability density function:

$$f(x) = \begin{cases} .01x + .1 & \text{for } -10 \le x \le 0 \\ -.01x + .1 & \text{for } 0 \le x \le 10 \end{cases}$$

a) Graph the density function $f(x)$.
b) Verify that $f(x)$ satisfies the requirements of a probability density function.
c) Find $P(X \ge 5)$.

Solution

a)

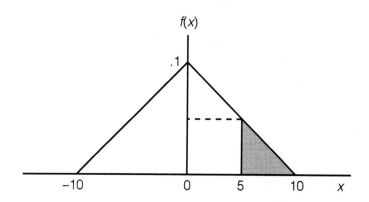

b) To verify that $f(x)$ is indeed a probability density function, we observe that:

1. $f(x) \ge 0$ for all values of x.

2. The total area under the graph of $f(x)$ is 1. To see this, recall that the area of a triangle is $bh/2$, where b is the base and h is the height of the triangle. Therefore, the area under $f(x)$ to the right of $x = 0$ is $(10)(.1)/2 = .5$. Due to symmetry, the area under $f(x)$ to the left of $x = 0$ is also .5, so the total area under $f(x)$ is $.5 + .5 = 1$.

c) To find $P(X \ge 5)$, we must find the area under the graph of $f(x)$ to the right of $x = 5$. This area is the shaded triangle shown on the graph in part a). The base of this triangle is $(10 - 5) = 5$, and the height is $f(5) = -.01(5) + .1 = .05$. Hence,

$$P(X \ge 5) = (5)(.05)/2 = .125$$

EXERCISES

7.1   Consider a uniform random variable X with the following probability density function:

$$f(x) = \frac{1}{50}, \quad 20 \le x \le 70$$

a)   Graph the density function $f(x)$.

b)   Verify that $f(x)$ satisfies the requirements of a probability density function.

c)   Find $P(X \ge 40)$.

d)   Find $P(X \le 39)$.

7.2   A continuous random variable X has the following probability density function:

$$f(x) = -.08x + .4, \quad 0 \le x \le 5$$

a)   Graph the density function $f(x)$.

b) Verify that $f(x)$ satisfies the requirements of a probability density function.

c) Find $P(X \geq 3)$.

d) Find $P(X \leq 2)$.

e) Find $P(X = 2)$.

7.3   Normal Distribution

The normal distribution is the most important specific continuous distribution. Given a problem involving a normal distribution, you should begin by clearly defining the relevant normal variable X. You should next sketch a graph of the normal distribution and label it with the given information concerning the mean, standard deviation, and probabilities. Table 3 in Appendix B tabulates probabilities for the standard normal random variable Z. Hence, before using this table, you must convert values of the normal random variable X into values of Z using the transformation.

$$Z = \frac{X - \mu_x}{\sigma_x}$$

As well as being able to deal with situations that can be modeled using a normal distribution, you should be able to approximate binomial probabilities using the appropriate normal distribution.

Example 7.2

Use Table 3 in Appendix B to find the following probabilities, where Z is the standard normal random variable:

a) $P(Z \geq 1.25)$
b) $P(-.82 \leq Z \leq 1.36)$
c) $P(.47 \leq Z \leq 2.12)$

Solution

a) We begin by sketching a graph of the normal curve and shading the area under the curve to the right of $Z = 1.25$, which corresponds to the required probability. Recall that the areas tabulated in Table 3 in Appendix B are of the form $P(0 \leq Z \leq z_0)$ for selected values of z_0, so required areas must be expressed in terms of areas of this form before Table 3 can be used. Since the total area under the curve to the right of $z = 0$ is .5,

$$P(Z \geq 1.25) = .5 - P(0 \leq Z \leq 1.25)$$
$$= .5 - .3944 = .1056$$

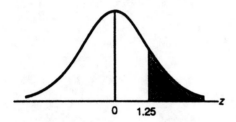

b) $\quad P(-.82 \leq Z \leq 1.36) = P(-.82 \leq Z \leq 0) + P(0 \leq Z \leq 1.36)$

Because the normal distribution is symmetrical, the area between $-.82$ and 0 is equal to the area between 0 and .82. Hence, $P(-.82 \leq Z \leq 0)$ is equal to the area between 0 and .82. Therefore,

$$P(-.82 \leq Z \leq 1.36) = P(0 \leq Z \leq .82) + P(0 \leq Z \leq 1.36)$$
$$= .2939 + .4131 = .7070$$

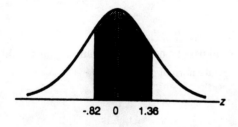

c) Expressing the required area in terms of the types of areas that are tabulated in Table 3, we obtain

$$P(.47 \leq Z \leq 2.12) = P(0 \leq Z \leq 2.12) - P(0 \leq Z \leq .47)$$
$$= .4830 - .1808$$
$$= .3022$$

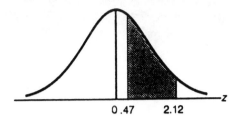

0.47   2.12

Example 7.3

If Z is the standard normal variable, find the value z_0 for which:

a) $P(-z_0 \leq Z \leq z_0) = .95$

b) $P(Z \geq z_0) = .0025$

Solution

a) Since the normal distribution is symmetrical, we know that

$$P(-z_0 \leq Z \leq 0) = P(0 \leq Z \leq z_0) = .95/2 = .4750$$

Locating .4750 in the body of Table 3, we find that the corresponding z-value is $z_0 = 1.96$.

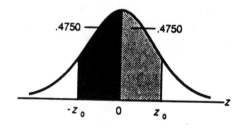

.4750   .4750

$-z_0$ 0 z_0

b) Since the area to the right of z_0 is .0025, which is less than .5, z_0 must lie to the right of 0. The area between 0 and z_0 is $(.5 - .0025) = .4975$, so

$$P(0 \leq Z \leq z_0) = .4975$$

Locating .4975 in the body of Table 3, we find that $z_0 = 2.81$.

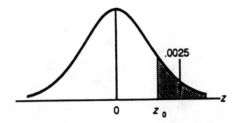

.0025

Example 7.4

A muffler company advertises that you will receive a rebate if it takes longer than 30 minutes to replace your muffler. Experience has shown that the time taken to replace a muffler is approximately normally distributed with a mean of 25 minutes and a standard deviation of 2.5 minutes.

- a) What proportion of customers receive a rebate?
- b) What proportion of mufflers take between 22 and 26 minutes to replace?
- c) What should the rebate-determining time of 30 minutes be changed to if the company wishes to provide only 1% of customers with a rebate?

Solution

- a) Let X be the number of minutes taken to replace a muffler. The proportion of customers who receive a rebate is the area under the normal curve to the right of $x = 30$. Using the transformation $Z = (X - \mu)/\sigma$, we see that this is the same as the area under the standard normal curve to the right of $Z = (30 - 25)/2.5 = 2.0$. Hence, the required proportion is

$$P(X \geq 30) = P(Z \geq 2.0)$$

$$= .5 - P(0 \leq Z \leq 2.0)$$

$$= .5 - .4772 = .0228$$

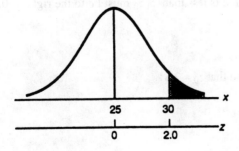

86

b) The proportion of mufflers that take between 22 and 26 minutes to replace is:

$$P(22 \leq X \leq 26) = P\left(\frac{22 - 25}{2.5} \leq Z \leq \frac{26 - 25}{2.5}\right)$$

$$= P(-1.2 \leq Z \leq .4)$$

$$= P(-1.2 \leq Z \leq 0) + P(0 \leq Z \leq .4)$$

$$= P(0 \leq Z \leq 1.2) + P(0 \leq Z \leq .4)$$

$$= .3849 + .1554$$

$$= .5403$$

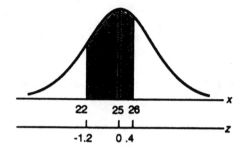

c) We must find the value, x_0, of X for which $P(X \geq x_0) = .01$. If z_0 is the value of Z corresponding to x_0,

$$z_0 = \frac{x_0 - \mu}{\sigma} = \frac{x_0 - 25}{2.5}$$

Moreover, $P(Z \geq z_0) = .01$, so $P(0 \leq Z \leq z_0) = .5 - .01 = .49$. Locating .49 in the body of Table 3, we find that $z_0 \cong 2.33$. Hence,

$$2.33 = \frac{x_0 - 25}{2.5}, \text{ or}$$

$$x_0 = 25 + (2.33)(2.5) = 30.83$$

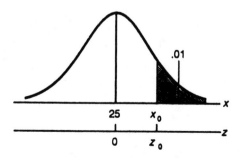

Example 7.5

Let X be a binomial random variable with $n = 400$ and $p = .2$. Approximate the following probabilities using the normal distribution:

a) $P(X = 85)$
b) $P(X \geq 90)$

Solution

a) The binomial random variable X has mean

$$\mu = np = (400)(.2) = 80$$

and standard deviation

$$\sigma = \sqrt{npq} = \sqrt{(400)(.2)(.8)} = \sqrt{64} = 8$$

Thus, we choose the normal distribution with $\mu = 80$ and $\sigma = 8$ for the approximation. If Y is the approximating normal random variable, then

$$P(X = 85) \cong P(84.5 \leq Y \leq 85.5)$$

$$= P\left(\frac{84.5 - 8}{8} \leq Z \leq \frac{85.5 - 80}{8}\right)$$

$$= P(.56 \leq Z \leq .69)$$

$$= P(0 \leq Z \leq .69) - P(0 \leq Z \leq .56)$$

$$= .2549 - .2123$$

$$= .0426$$

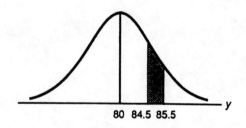

80 84.5 85.5

b) We want to approximate the probability that X will assume a value equal to 90 or more. Since $P(X = 90)$ is approximated by the area under the normal curve between 89.5 and 90.5,

$$P(X \geq 90) \cong P(Y \geq 89.5)$$

$$= P\left(Z \geq \frac{89.5 - 80}{8}\right)$$

$$= P(Z \geq 1.19)$$

$$= .5 - P(0 \leq Z \leq 1.19)$$

$$= .5 - .3830$$

$$= .1170$$

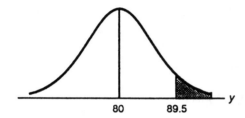

Notice that, if we had wanted to approximate $P(X > 90)$, we would have approximated the probability that X will assume a value equal to 91 or more. In that case, we would begin by writing

$$P(X > 90) = P(X \geq 91) \cong P(Y \geq 90.5)$$

EXERCISES

7.3   Use Table 3 in Appendix B to find the following probabilities, where Z is the standard normal random variable:

a) $P(Z \geq 1.85)$

b) $P(Z \geq -1.85)$

89

c) $P(-1.24 \leq Z \leq .95)$

d) $P(1.24 \leq Z \leq 2.48)$

7.4   If Z is the standard normal variable, find the value z_0 for which:

a) $P(-z_0 \leq Z \leq z_0) = .90$

b) $P(Z \geq z_0) = .01$

7.5   Records show that the playing time of major league baseball games is approximately normally distributed with a mean of 156 minutes and a standard deviation of 34 minutes. If one game is selected at random, find the probability that it will last:

a) more than 3 hours.

b) between 2 and 3 hours.

c) less than 1.5 hours.

7.6 The amount of rainfall during August at a popular resort is approximately normally distributed with a mean of 40 mm and a standard deviation of 12 mm.

a) What is the probability that the resort will have less than 5 mm of rain next August?

b) What is the probability that the resort will have more than 25 mm of rain next August?

c) What amount of rainfall is exceeded only 10% of the time in August?

7.7 A fair coin is tossed 200 times. Approximate the probability that the number of heads observed is between 95 and 105 (inclusive).

7.4 Exponential Distribution

The exponential distribution is a useful continuous distribution that is closely related to the Poisson distribution. You should be able to do the following:

1. Recognize situations in which an exponential distribution is applicable.
2. Define the exponential random variable that is appropriate in a given situation.
3. Compute exponential probabilities using the formulas.
4. Understand the relationship between the exponential and Poisson distributions.

An exponential random variable can be used to measure the time that elapses before the first occurrence of an event (or the time between occurrences of an event), where occurrences of the event (such as incoming telephone calls) follow a Poisson distribution. The exponential distribution may also be used to model the length of life of various electronic components.

A random variable X is exponentially distributed if its probability density function is given by

$$f(x) = \lambda e^{-\lambda x}, \qquad x \geq 0$$

where $e = 2.71828 \ldots$ and λ is a parameter of the distribution ($\lambda > 0$). It can be shown that $E(X) = \mu = 1/\lambda$.

Given two numbers a and b, probabilities involving X may be found as follows:

$$P(X \leq a) = 1 - e^{-\lambda a}$$

$$P(a \leq X \leq b) = e^{-\lambda a} - e^{-\lambda b}$$

The following example illustrates the relationship between the exponential and Poisson distributions.

Example 7.6

Records show that there is an average of three accidents each day in a certain city between 2 and 3 P.M., with the accidents occurring according to a Poisson distribution.

a) Use the exponential distribution to find the probability that no accident will occur between 2 and 2:30 P.M. today.

b) Use the Poisson distribution to find the probability required in part a).

Solution

a) Let X denote the time *in minutes* that will elapse after 2 P.M. before an accident occurs. It is important that X and λ be defined in terms of the same units. Thus, λ is the average number of accidents per minute: $\lambda = 3/60 = .05$. According to the formula for exponential probabilities, the probability that at least 30 minutes will elapse after 2 P.M. before an accident occurs is

$$P(X \geq 30) = e^{-.05(30)}$$

$$= e^{-1.5} = .223$$

b) Let Y denote the number of accidents that will occur between 2 and 2:30 P.M. today. Then Y is a Poisson random variable, with $\mu = 1.5$ accidents per half hour. We want to find the probability that no accidents will occur within a 30-minute period. Using the formula for a Poisson probability,

$$P(Y = 0 \mid \mu = 1.5) = \frac{(e^{-1.5})(1.5^0)}{0!}$$

$$= e^{-1.5} = .223$$

EXERCISES

7.8 A manager receives an average of 24 telephone calls between 1:00 and 3:00 P.M., with the calls arriving according to a Poisson distribution.

a) Find the probability that 10 minutes will elapse without any calls being received by the manager.

b) Find the probability that the manager will receive at most one call during a 10-minute period.

7.9 The length of life of a certain brand of light bulb is exponentially distributed with a mean of 5,000 hours.

a) Find the probability that a bulb will burn out within the first 1,000 hours.

b) Find the probability that a bulb will last more than 7,000 hours.

c) Find the probability that the lifetime of a bulb will be between 2,000 and 8,000 hours.

Chapter 8: Sampling Distributions

8.1   Introduction

This chapter connects the material in Chapters 4 through 7 (numerical descriptive statistics, sampling, and probability distributions, in particular) with statistical inference, which is introduced in Chapter 9.

You are expected to know how the sampling distribution of the mean is created and the shape and parameters of the distribution. You are also expected to be capable of calculating probabilities using the sampling distribution of the mean.

8.2   Sampling Distribution of the Mean

The most important thing to learn from this section is that if we repeatedly draw samples from any population, the values of $\bar{x}$ calculated in each sample will vary. This new random variable created by sampling will have three important characteristics:

1. $\bar{x}$ is approximately normally.
2.   The mean of $\bar{x}$ will equal the mean of the original random variable. That is, $\mu_{\bar{x}} = \mu_x$.
3.   The variance of $\bar{x}$ will equal the variance of the original random variable divided by n. That is, $\sigma_{\bar{x}}^2 = \sigma_x^2 / n$.

The sampling distribution of $\bar{x}$ allows us to make probability statements about $\bar{x}$ based on knowing the values of the sample size n and the population parameters μ and σ^2.

Example 8.1

A random variable possesses the following probability distribution:

x	$p(x)$
1	.2
2	.5
3	.3

a)   Find all possible samples of size 2 that can be drawn from this population.
b)   Using the results in part a), find the sampling distribution of $\bar{x}$.
c)   Confirm that $\mu_{\bar{x}} = \mu_x$ and $\sigma_{\bar{x}}^2 = \sigma_x^2 / n$.

Solution

a) There are nine possible samples of size 2. They are (1,1), (1,2), (1,3), (2,1), (2,2), (2,3), (3,1), (3,2), and (3,3).

b) The samples, the values of $\bar{x}$, and the probability of each sample outcome are shown below:

Sample	$\bar{x}$	Probability
(1,1)	1.0	(.2)(.2) = .04
(1,2)	1.5	(.2)(.5) = .10
(1,3)	2.0	(.2)(.3) = .06
(2,1)	1.5	(.5)(.2) = .10
(2,2)	2.0	(.5)(.5) = .25
(2,3)	2.5	(.5)(.3) = .15
(3,1)	2.0	(.3)(.2) = .06
(3,2)	2.5	(.3)(.5) = .15
(3,3)	3.0	(.3)(.3) = .09

The sampling distribution of $\bar{x}$ follows:

$\bar{x}$	$p(\bar{x})$
1.0	.04
1.5	.20
2.0	.37
2.5	.30
3.0	.09

c) Using our definitions of expected value and variance, we find the mean and variance of the random variable x:

$$\mu_x = E(x) = \sum x p(x) = 1(.2) + 2(.5) + 3(.3) = 2.1$$

$$\sigma_x^2 = \sum (x - \mu)^2 p(x) = (1 - 2.1)^2(.2) + (2 - 2.1)^2(.5) + (3 - 2.1)^2(.3)$$

$$= 0.49$$

The mean and variance of the random variable $\bar{x}$ are computed as follows:

$$\mu_{\bar{x}} = E(\bar{x}) = \sum \bar{x} p(\bar{x}) = 1.0(.04) + 1.5(.20) + 2.0(.37) + 2.5(.30) + 3.0(.09)$$

$$= 2.1$$

$$\sigma_{\bar{x}}^2 = \sum (\bar{x} - \mu_{\bar{x}})^2 p(\bar{x})$$
$$= (1.0 - 2.1)^2(.04) + (1.5 - 2.1)^2(.20) + (2.0 - 2.1)^2(.37)$$
$$+ (2.5 - 2.1)^2(.30) + (3.0 - 2.1)^2(.09)$$
$$= 0.245$$

As you can see,

$$\mu_{\bar{x}} = \mu_x = 2.1$$

and

$$\sigma_{\bar{x}}^2 = \sigma_x^2/n = 0.49/2 = 0.245$$

Example 8.2

Suppose a random sample of 100 observations is drawn from a normal population whose mean is 600 and whose variance is 2,500. Find the following probabilities:

a) $P(590 < x < 610)$
b) $P(590 < \bar{x} < 610)$
c) $P(x > 650)$
d) $P(\bar{x} > 650)$

Solution

a) X is normally distributed with mean $\mu_x = 600$ and variance $\sigma_x^2 = 2,500$. We standardize x by subtracting $\mu_x = 600$ and dividing by $\sigma_x = 50$. Therefore,

$$P(590 < x < 610) = P\left(\frac{590 - 600}{50} < \frac{x - \mu_x}{\sigma_x} < \frac{610 - 600}{50} \right)$$

$$= P(-.2 < z < .2) = .1586$$

b) We know that $\bar{x}$ is normally distributed with $\mu_{\bar{x}} = \mu_x = 600$ and $\sigma_{\bar{x}}^2 = \sigma_x^2/n = 2,500/100 = 25$. Thus, $\sigma_{\bar{x}} = 5$. Hence,

$$P(590 < \bar{x} < 610) = P\left(\frac{590 - 600}{5} < \frac{\bar{x} - \mu_{\bar{x}}}{\sigma_{\bar{x}}} < \frac{610 - 600}{5} \right)$$

$$= P(-2 < z < 2) = .9544$$

c) $P(x > 650) = P\left(\frac{x - \mu_x}{\sigma_x} > \frac{650 - 600}{50} \right)$

$$= P(z > 1) = .1587$$

d) $P(\bar{x} > 650) = P\left(\dfrac{\bar{x} - \mu_{\bar{x}}}{\sigma_{\bar{x}}} > \dfrac{650 - 600}{5}\right)$

$= P(z > 10) = 0$

Example 8.3

Refer to Example 8.2. Suppose a random sample of 100 observations produced a mean of $\bar{x} = 650$. What does this imply about the statement that $\mu = 600$ and $\sigma^2 = 2,500$?

Solution

From Example 8.2 part d), we found that

$P(\bar{x} > 650) = 0$

Therefore, it is quite unlikely that we could observe a sample mean of 650 in a sample of 100 observations drawn from a population whose mean is 600 and whose variance is 2,500.

Question: What purpose does the sampling distribution serve? In particular, why do we need to calculate probabilities associated with the sample mean?

Answer: (in reverse order) We are not terribly interested in making probability statements about $\bar{x}$. Since knowledge of μ and σ^2 is required in order to compute the probability that $\bar{x}$ falls into some specific interval, we acknowledge that this procedure is quite unrealistic. However, the sampling distribution will eventually allow us to infer something about an unknown population mean from a sample mean. This process, called statistical inference, will be the main topic throughout the rest of the textbook.

EXERCISES

8.1   If 64 observations are taken from a population with $\mu = 100$ and $\sigma = 40$, find $P(102 < \bar{x} < 112)$.

8.2 A normally distributed random variable has a mean of 20 and a standard deviation of 10. If a random sample of 25 is drawn from this population, find $P(\bar{x} > 23)$.

8.3 Given the probability distribution of x below, find all samples of size 3, the sampling distribution of $\bar{x}$, the mean, and the variance of $\bar{x}$.

x	$p(x)$
0	.7
1	.3

Appendix 8.A
Simulation Experiments: Creating Sampling Distributions by Computer Simulation

In Chapter 8 of the textbook, we described how the sampling distribution can be created theoretically. We also pointed out that sampling distributions can be created empirically, but that the effort can be extremely time-consuming. In this appendix, we use the computer and our two software packages to create sampling distributions empirically. We believe that by doing so you will gain a deeper understanding of sampling distributions.

Both Minitab and Excel possess random number generators that can produce data from a variety of distributions. In Chapter 5, we discussed how to generate random numbers from a discrete uniform distribution to choose which members of a population to include in a sample. In this appendix, we will generate data from other distributions, including the normal, binomial, continuous uniform, and the exponential. Because of the importance of the normal distribution, you will find it useful to learn the similarities and differences among these populations. Before we proceed, let's discuss what we mean by simulation experiments.

SIMULATION EXPERIMENTS

Anyone who plans to use statistical techniques must have an understanding of the concepts and principles that underlie the statistical procedures. Most students attempt to learn these principles by reading a textbook or listening to their professor. The simulation experiments presented in this book provide an alternative. We believe that most theoretical ideas are comprehended more easily by active experimentation. Just as in chemistry or physics, performing experiments, observing results, and reporting conclusions provide a deeper insight into the subject than is possible by only reading books or passively attending class. This appendix, together with Appendixes 9.A and 10.A, describe a variety of experiments that students of statistics can perform using either Minitab or Excel that will allow them to make "discoveries" about the underlying principles of statistics.

There are differences between the kind of experiment one performs in chemistry or physics and the kind one performs in statistics. In a chemistry or physics experiment, if we repeat the procedures precisely we will observe exactly the same result (except for relatively small measurement errors). For example, dropping an object in a vacuum in the same location and measuring its speed after one second will produce the same speed no matter how frequently we do it. However, the very nature of probability and statistics makes identical results from the same experiment almost impossible. For example, if our experiment consists of tossing a fair die 60 times and counting the number of ones, the results will probably be somewhere between 6 and 14 ones. If we perform that experiment twice, seeing the same number of ones in both experiments is unlikely. Because of the randomness that is part of the type of experiments that we conduct in statistics, it is necessary for us to repeat that experiment a number of times in order to draw the correct conclusion. Thus, if we toss the die 60 times and observe 6 ones, we may erroneously conclude that the probability of observing a one on the toss of a fair die is 10%. However, if we repeat the experiment 60,000 times and count the number of sixes, we'd see a number around 10,000. Performing the experiment a large number of times would allow us to confirm that the probability of a one is 1/6.

Just as in a chemistry course, you will be expected to summarize what you have learned from each experiment. For each experiment you will be asked specific questions to complete your report.

In Appendixes 9.A and 10.A, we describe a number of experiments that will provide insights into some aspects of statistics.

NORMAL AND NONNORMAL POPULATIONS

The normal distribution is the most important distribution in statistics because so many of the inferential techniques are based on it. However, in practical applications, populations may not be normally distributed. Statisticians need to know whether the nonnormality of a population seriously affects the validity of the technique. In the section above, we pointed out that the sampling distribution of the mean is normal when the population is normal, but it is only approximately normal for nonnormal populations and appropriate sample sizes. In the experiments described, below you will discover whether the approximation is good for various sample sizes and for populations that are normal, moderately nonnormal, and extremely nonnormal. We will use the continuous uniform distribution to represent moderately nonnormal populations. The graph of the continuous uniform appears as a rectangle. Because it is symmetric (like the normal) but far from bell-shaped, we consider this distribution to be moderately nonnormal. We use the exponential distribution to represent an example of extreme nonnormality. Because it is very skewed, data taken from the exponential distribution constitute an extremely nonnormal population. (Excel does not generate the exponential distribution; we will use another method to produce highly skewed data.)

The first three experiments in this appendix generate random numbers from three types of populations; normal, continuous uniform and exponential (Minitab only). For each, the software package will be called on to calculate the mean and standard deviation and draw the histogram.

Using Minitab

All of the experiments can be performed using the Minitab random-number generator. As we explained in Chapter 5, the command

RANDOM 100 C1

causes Minitab to create 100 random numbers and store them in column 1. We specify the distribution from which the numbers are to be drawn using the appropriate subcommand. (Incidentally, if we don't type a subcommand, the random numbers will be generated from a normal distribution with mean 0 and standard deviation 1.) Here is a list of distributions and Minitab subcommands that we will use in our simulation experiments.

Discrete Uniform Distribution

The random variable takes on a countable number of values all of which have the same probability. The subcommand

INTEGER K1 K2

generates integer values between K1 and K2.

Normal Distribution

The subcommand

NORMAL K1 K2

generates random numbers drawn from a normal distribution whose mean is K1 and whose standard deviation in K2.

Continuous Uniform Distribution

The shape of this distribution is a rectangle. The subcommand

UNIFORM K1 K2

produces numbers from a continuous uniform distribution than ranges from K1 to K2. The mean and standard deviation of a continuous uniform distribution that ranges from K1 to K2 is

$$\mu = \frac{K1 + K2}{2}$$

$$\sigma = \frac{(K2 - K1)}{\sqrt{12}}$$

Exponential Distribution

The subcommand

EXPONENTIAL K1

generates values from an exponential distribution whose mean is K1. Incidentally, the standard deviation of an exponential distribution is equal to its mean.

Binomial Distribution

We can use the binomial distribution to create data from a variety of distribution shapes. With $p = .5$, we produce approximately normal populations. With $p = .01$ (or .99), the data are highly skewed creating extremely nonnormal results. Values of p around .2 (or .8) create moderately nonnormal random numbers. The subcommand

BINOMIAL K1 K2

generates random numbers from a binomial distribution with $n = K1$ and $p = K2$.

Don't forget to end each command with a semicolon if you intend to use a subcommand. The subcommand must end with a period.

Using Excel

All of the experiments can be performed using the Excel random-number generator. (Be prepared to wait; Excel generates data quite slowly.) To do so, proceed as follows.

1. Click **Tools, Data Analysis …,** and **Random Number Generation**.
2. Specify the **Number of Variables** and the **Number of Random Numbers**. (We will discuss what numbers you specify later.)
3. Click the distribution from which the random numbers are to be drawn. For the purposes of the simulation experiments, we will use one of **Discrete, Uniform, Normal,** or **Binomial**. The uniform distribution will generate moderately nonnormal data and the binomial will generate approximately normal (using $p = .5$) and extremely nonnormal (using $p = .01$) data. (Excel does not generate numbers from an exponential distribution and for reasons explained below, we sometimes prefer to use the binomial to replace the normal.)

EXPERIMENT 8.1

Objective: To show what the data generated from a normal distribution look like.

Experiment: We will generate 1,000 observations from a normal distribution whose mean and standard deviation are 50 and 5, respectively, draw the histogram of the data, and output some descriptive statistics.

Minitab Instructions

Menu Command	Session Commands
1. Click **Calc, Random Data,** and **Normal ….**	*RANDOM 1000 C1;*
2. Type 1000 to generate 1,000 **rows of data**.	*NORMAL 50 5.*
3. Hit tab and type C1 to store the data in column 1.	*DESCRIBE C1*
4. Hit tab and type 50 (**Mean**).	*HISTOGRAM C1*
5. Hit tab and type 5 (**Standard deviation**).	
6. Click **Stat, Basic Statistics,** and **Descriptive Statistics ….**	
7. Type C1 and click **OK**.	

8. Click **Graph** and **Histogram ....**

9. Type C1 and click **OK**.

These commands generate 1,000 normally distributed numbers with mean 50 and standard deviation 5. The descriptive statistics and the histogram are drawn.

Excel Instructions

1. Click **Tools, Data Analysis ..., Random Number Generation**.

2. Type 1 to specify the **Number of Variables**.

3. Hit tab and type 1000 to specify the **Number of Random Numbers**.

4. Use the cursor and click the **Normal** distribution.

5. Use the cursor to move to the **Parameters** box. Type 50 to specify the **Mean**.

6. Hit tab and type 5 to specify the **Standard Deviation**. Click **OK**.

7. Calculate the descriptive statistics (see Chapter 4 in the textbook).

8. Draw the histogram (see Chapter 2).

Report for Experiment 8.1

1. Does the histogram look the way you expected?
2. Why doesn't the histogram appear exactly bell-shaped?
3. Are the mean and standard deviation computed in this experiment what you anticipated? Explain.

EXPERIMENT 8.2

Objective: To show what the data generated from a continuous uniform distribution look like.

Experiment: We will generate 1,000 observations from a continuous uniform distribution that ranges from 0 to 10, draw the histogram of the data, and output some descriptive statistics.

Minitab Instructions

Menu Commands	Session Commands
Repeat Experiment 8.1 with the following changes.	Repeat Experiment 8.1 with the following change.
Click **Uniform ...** instead of **Normal ....**	Type *UNIFORM 0 10.* instead of *NORMAL 50 5.*
Type 0 to specify **Lower endpoint**.	
Type 10 to specify **Upper endpoint**.	

Excel Instructions

Repeat Experiment 8.1 with the following changes.

Click the **Uniform** distribution instead of the **Normal** distribution.

Type 0 and 10 to specify that the uniform random variable lies **Between 0 and 10.**

Report for Experiment 8.2

1. Does the histogram look the way you expected it to look?
2. Why doesn't the histogram appear exactly as in Figure 8.6?
3. Are the mean and variance computed in this experiment what you anticipated? Explain.

EXPERIMENT 8.3

Objective: To show what the data generated from a distinctly nonnormal distribution look like.

Experiment: Minitab will generate 1,000 observations from an exponential distribution whose mean is 1 (and whose standard deviation is 1). Excel will generate data from a binomial distribution with $n = 100$ and $p = .01$. The mean and standard deviation are 1.

Minitab Instructions

Menu Commands

Repeat Experiment 8.1 with the following changes.

Click **Exponential ...** instead of **Normal ....**

Type 1 to specify the **Mean**.

Session Commands

Repeat Experiment 8.1 with the following change.

Type *EXPONENTIAL 1.* instead of *NORMAL 50 5.*

Excel Instructions

Repeat Experiment 8.1 with the following changes.

Click the **Binomial** distribution.

Type .01 to specify the **p Value**.

Type 100 to specify the **Number of Trials**.

Report for Experiment 8.3

1. Does the histogram look the way you expected it to look?
2. Are the mean and standard deviation computed in this experiment what you anticipated? Explain.

SAMPLING DISTRIBUTIONS

Random number generators can be used to demonstrate how sampling distributions are created, what they look like, and what their parameters are. Let's begin with the sampling distribution of the mean of a sample of two tosses of a fair die described in Section 8.2 We will create 2 columns of 1,000 numbers where the numbers are drawn from a discrete uniform distribution whose integer values fall between 1 and 6 (just like the toss of a die). Both Minitab and Excel will be instructed to treat each *row* of the array of random numbers as a sample of size 2. We will then compute the means and store them in a third column. We can examine the sampling distribution by drawing a histogram and calculating descriptive statistics for the sample means.

EXPERIMENT 8.4

Objective: To simulate tossing two dice 1,000 times and determine the distribution of the mean of the two tosses.

Experiment: The experiment will generate 1,000 integers between 1 and 6 in each of 2 columns. A third column stores the sample means from each row. The sampling distribution of the mean is described numerically and graphically.

Minitab Instructions

Menu Commands	Session Commands
1. Click **Calc, Random Data,** and **Integer ....**	*RANDOM 100 C1 C2;*
2. Type 1000 (**rows of data**).	*INTEGER 1 6.*
3. Hit tab and type C1 C2 (**Store in column(s)**).	*RMEAN C1 C2 C3*
4. Hit tab and type 1 to specify **Minimum value**.	*DESCRIBE C3*
5. Hit tab and type 6 to specify **Maximum Value**. Click **OK**.	*HISTOGRAM C3;*
6. Click **Calc** and **Row Statistics ....**	*MIDPOINTS 1 1.5 2 2.5 3 3.5 4*
7. Use the cursor to specify **Mean**.	*4.5 5 5.5 6.*
8. Hit tab and type C1 C2 (**Input variables**).	
9. Hit tab and type C3 to **Store result in** column 3. Click **OK**.	

10. Calculate the descriptive statistics of the sample means stored in C3.

11. Draw the histogram of C3 with midpoints 1, 1.5, 2, 2.5, 3, 3.5, 4, 4.5, 5, 5.5, 6. In the session window, type

   HISTOGRAM C3;
   MIDPOINTS 1 1.5 2 2.5 3 3.5 4 4.5 5 5.5 6.

The command *RMEAN C1 C2 C3* (or equivalently *C1–C3*) (Menu command steps 6–9) instructs Minitab to calculate the mean of the data in columns 1 and 2 and place it in column 3. To satisfy yourself that these commands work, examine columns 1, 2 and 3.

Excel Instructions

1. In column A store the numbers 1, 2, 3, 4, 5, 6.

2. In column B store the number .16667 in each of the first 4 cells and .16666 for each of the last two cells. (Excel checks to ensure that the sum of the probabilities is 1. If not, it will send an error message. Thus, if we placed the probability .16667 in each cell Excel would not run the program.) Now columns A and B contain the discrete distribution representing the toss of a fair die.

3. Click **Tools, Data Analysis …, Random Number Generation**.

4. Type 2 to specify the **Number of Variables**.

5. Hit tab and type 1000 to specify the **Number of Random Numbers**. Steps 5 and 6 generate an array of random numbers. The array consists of 2 columns (**Number of Variables:** 2) and 1,000 rows (**Number of Random Numbers:** 1,000). If Excel responds **"Selection too large. Continue without undo?"**, click **OK**.

6. Click the **Discrete** distribution.

7. Use the cursor to move to the **Parameters** box. Type A1:B6 to specify the **Value and Probability Input Range** of the distribution.

8. Specify the output range: C1 (or any other column).

9. Click **OK**. Columns C and D will now fill with the random numbers you generated from the discrete distribution.

10. Go to the next available column, which is column E and create the means column. Type
    =Average (C1:D1)

    Excel will calculate the mean of the numbers in C1 and D1 and store it in E1.

11. Drag column E from E1 to E1000. That is place the pointer in the lower right-hand corner of cell E1 (a + will appear), depress the mouse button, and hold while moving down the column until you reach E1000. Column E will contain the 1,000 averages of two die tosses.

12. Calculate the descriptive statistics of the sample means (row averages).

13. Draw the histogram of the sample means using bins 1.0, 1.5, 2.0, 2.5, 3.0, 3.5, 4.0, 4.5, 5.0, 5.5, and 6.0.

Report for Experiment 8.4

1. Compare the histogram that was drawn in this experiment with the theoretical sampling distribution described in this chapter. Are they similar?
2. What did you anticipate seeing when the computer printed the mean and standard deviation of the sampling distribution of the mean?
3. What did you actually observe when the computer printed the mean and standard deviation of the sampling distribution of the mean?
4. Discuss the significance of the results of this experiment.

COMPARING THE SAMPLING DISTRIBUTIONS WITH THE NORMAL DISTRIBUTION

The central limit theorem tells us that under certain conditions the sampling distribution of the mean is approximately normal. We want to compare the sampling distributions created under differing conditions to the normal. To facilitate this comparison, Minitab will output the percentage of observations that fall into each of the intervals,

$$z < 3, -3 \leq z < -2, -2 \leq z < -1, -1 \leq z < 0, 0 \leq z < 1, 1 \leq z < 2, 2 \leq z < 3, z \geq 3$$

Excel will calculate the number of observations in the intervals,

$$z \leq 3, -3 < z \leq -2, -2 < z \leq -1, -1 < z \leq 0, 0 < z \leq 1, 1 < z \leq 2, 2 < z \leq 3, z > 3$$

The only differences between the Minitab and Excel intervals is the way in which the end points are included. We will refer to these intervals as *standard intervals*.

You can compare these percentages with the following probabilities computed from the standard normal distribution.

$P(z < -3) = .0013$

$P(-3 < z < -2) = .0215$

$P(-2 < z < -1) = .1359$

$P(-1 < z < 0) = .3413$

$P(0 < z < 1) = .3413$

$P(1 < z < 2) = .1359$

$P(2 < z < 3) = .0215$

$P(z > 3) = .0013$

EXPERIMENT 8.5

Objective: To simulate tossing n dice 1,000 times and determine the distribution of the mean of the n tosses.

Experiment: The experiment will generate 1,000 integers between 1 and 6 in each of n columns. In another column the sample means of each row are computed and stored. The output includes the mean and standard deviation of the sampling distribution of the mean. Also outputted are the histogram of the standardized values and the proportion of sample means that fall in the standard intervals. Run the experiment with $n = 5$, 10, and 25.

Minitab Instructions

Menu Commands	Sessions Commands
1. Click **Calc, Random Data,** and **Integer ….**	*RANDOM 1000 C1 C2;*
2. Type 1000 (**rows of data**).	*INTEGER 1 6.*
3. Hit tab and type C1 – C5 (**Store in column(s)**).	*RMEAN C1 – C5 C30*
4. Hit tab and type 1 to specify **Minimum value.**	*DESCRIBE C30*
5. Hit tab and type 6 to specify **Maximum Value.** Click **OK.**	*LET C31 = (C30 – 3.5)/(1.71/SQRT(5))*
6. Click **Calc** and **Row Statistics ….**	*HISTOGRAM C31;*
7. Use the cursor to specify **Mean.**	*CUTPOINTS –3 –2 –1 0 1 2 3 4.*
8. Hit tab and type C1 – C5 (**Input variables**).	See step 18 below.

9. Hit tab and type C30 to **Store result in** column 30. Click **OK.**

10. Calculate the descriptive statistics of the sample means stored in C30. (Click **Stat, Basic Statistics,** and **Descriptive Statistics ….**)

11. Click **Calc** and **Mathematical Expression ….**

12. Type C31 to store **Variable (new or modified),** hit tab twice and type

$(C30 – 3.5)/(1.71/SQRT(5))$

Click **OK.**

13. Click **Graph** and **Histogram ….**

14. Type C31 and click **Options ….**

15. Use the cursor to specify **Frequency, Cutpoint,** and **Midpoint/cutpoint positions:**

16. Hit tab and type –3 –2 –1 0 1 2 3 4

17. Click **OK** twice.

18. Calculate the percentage of values of C31 that are in the standard intervals by typing in the session window

    CODE (–9: –3)1(–3: –2)2(–2: –1)3(–1:0)4(0:1)5(1:2)6(2:3)7(3:9)8 C31 C32

    TALLY C32;

    PERCENT.

Column 30 contains the sample means. The output includes the mean and standard deviation of the sampling distribution of the mean. Column 31 stores the standardized values $z = (\bar{x} – \mu)/(\sigma/\sqrt{n})$ and Minitab draws the histogram using the standard intervals. However, we would like to know precisely the percentage that fall into the standard intervals. For this purpose, we use the CODE command. Here's how it works.

The numbers in column 31 are examined. If the number falls between –9 and –3 (this interval is equivalent to "less than 3", but Minitab demands that we specify a lower and upper limit on all intervals), the code 1 is placed in column 32. If the number is between –3 and –2, the code 2 is stored in column 32, and so on. Incidentally, if the value in column 31 is exactly –3, because the first interval in the CODE command is (–9: –3), the code is 1. However, because the next interval includes –3, the code is changed to 2. Thus, the observations that fall on the upper limits of the intervals are assigned the higher codes. Here is a summary of the codes.

If $z < –3$, code = 1

If $–3 \le z < –2$, code = 2

If $–2 \le z < –1$, code = 3

If $–1 \le z < 0$, code = 4

If $0 \le z < 1$, code = 5

If $1 \le z < 2$, code = 6

If $2 \le z < 3$, code = 7

If $z \ge 3$, code = 8

Minitab is instructed to output the percentages of each code. In this way, we print the observed percentages in each standard interval. Compare these percentages to the theoretical ones to gauge how closely this sampling distribution resembles the normal distribution.

Note that there are menu commands that code the data. However, because of limitations, it is easier to code using a session command.

Repeat experiment with $n = 10$. Generate the data into columns 1 to 10. Standardize the sample means in column 30 using the formula

(C30 – 3.5)/(1.71/SQRT(10))

Repeat experiment with $n = 25$. Generate the data into columns 1 to 25. Standardize the sample means in column 30 using the formula

(C30 – 3.5)/(1.71/SQRT(25))

Excel Instructions

1. In column A store the numbers 1, 2, 3, 4, 5, 6.

2. In column B store the number .16667 in each of the first 4 cells and .16666 for each of the last two cells.

3. Click **Tools, Data Analysis ..., Random Number Generation**.

4. Type 5 to specify the **Number of Variables**.

5. Hit tab and type 1000 to specify the **Number of Random Numbers**.

6. Click the **Discrete** distribution.

7. Use the cursor to move to the **Parameters** box. Type A1:B6 to specify the **Value and Probability Input Range** of the distribution.

8. Specify the output range: C1 (or any other column). Click **OK**.

9. Go to the next available column and calculate the sample means.

10. Calculate the descriptive statistics of the sample means. (Click **Tools, Data Analysis ...**, and **Descriptive Statistics**.)

11. In the next available column standardize the sample means using the formula

$$z = \frac{\bar{x} - \mu}{\sigma / \sqrt{n}} = \frac{\bar{x} - 3.5}{1.71 / \sqrt{5}} = \frac{\bar{x} - 3.5}{.7647}$$

12. Draw the histogram of the standardized values using bins 1.0, 1.5, 2.0, 2.5, 3.0, 3.5, 4.0, 4.5, 5.0, 5.5, and 6.0.

Repeat experiment with $n = 10$. In step 4 type 10 to specify **Number of Variables**. Standardize the sample means using

$$z = \frac{\bar{x} - 3.5}{1.71/\sqrt{10}} = \frac{\bar{x} - 3.5}{.5407}$$

Repeat experiment with $n = 25$. In step 4 type 25 to specify **Number of Variables**. Standardize the sample means using

$$z = \frac{\bar{x} - 3.5}{1.71/\sqrt{25}} = \frac{\bar{x} - 3.5}{.342}$$

Depending on the computer you're using you may find that generating 1,000 random numbers is too time consuming. In that case reduce the **Number of Random Numbers** to 400 or perhaps less. The output should still be reasonably good estimates of the theoretical results.

Report for Experiment 8.5

Answer the following questions for each value of n.

1. What values for the mean and standard deviation did you anticipate seeing?
2. What is the value of the observed mean of the sampling distribution of the mean?
3. What is the value of the observed standard deviation of the sampling distribution of the mean?

After running the experiment with $n = 5$, 10, and 25 compare the histograms drawn in the three experiments. Discuss the similarities and differences.

SAMPLING DISTRIBUTION OF THE MEAN: NORMAL AND NONNORMAL POPULATIONS

We know from the discussion in the chapter that if the population is normal, the sampling distribution of the mean is also normal. If the population is nonnormal, the sample mean will be approximately normally distributed, provided that the sample size is sufficiently large. The size of the sample required to make $\bar{x}$ approximately normally distributed depends on how nonnormal the population is. This issue will be the focus of the next three experiments.

EXPERIMENT 8.6

Objective: To examine the sampling distribution of the mean when the population is normal.

Experiment: We will generate 1,000 samples of size 2, 5, 10, and 25 from a normal population with mean 50 and standard deviation 5. We then compute the sample means, draw the histogram of the sample means and compute the descriptive statistics.

Minitab Instructions

Repeat Experiment 8.5 using a normal distribution with mean 50 and standard deviation 5 and sample sizes 2, 5, 10, and 25. Standardize the sample means with $z = \dfrac{\bar{x} - 50}{5/\sqrt{n}}$.

Excel Instructions

Repeat Experiment 8.5 using a binomial distribution with **p Value** = .5 and **Number of Trials** = 100 and sample sizes n = 2, 5, 10, and 25. (Because Excel generates normal data so slowly, we will use binomial data with 100 trials and probability of success = .5, which is very nearly normally distributed with mean 50 and standard deviation 5.) Standardize the sample means with $z = \dfrac{\bar{x} - 50}{5/\sqrt{n}}$.

Report for Experiment 8.6

Answer the following questions for each value of n.

1. What are the mean and standard deviation of the population from which we're sampling?
2. Draw the distribution of the population from which we're sampling.
3. Use the central limit theorem to determine the mean and standard deviation of the sampling distribution of the sample mean calculated by drawing samples of size n from a normal population whose mean is 50 and whose standard deviation is 5.
4. What are the mean and standard deviation of the sampling distribution created in this experiment?
5. Does the histogram produced in this experiment appear to be bell shaped?
6. Does this experiment confirm the central limit theorem and what you anticipated seeing when the mean and standard deviation of the sampling distribution of the mean were computed? Explain.

EXPERIMENT 8.7

Objective: To see what happens to the sampling distribution of the mean when the population is moderately nonnormal.

Experiment: We generate 1,000 samples of size 2, 5, 10, and 25 from a uniform distribution that ranges from 0 to 10. (Such a distribution has a mean of $\mu = 5$ and a standard deviation of $\sigma = 2.887$.) The sampling distribution of the mean is then created.

Minitab Instructions

Repeat Experiment 8.6 using a uniform distribution that ranges from 0 to 10. Standardize the sample means with $z = \dfrac{\bar{x} - 5}{2.887/\sqrt{n}}$.

Excel Instructions

Repeat Experiment 8.6 using a uniform distribution that ranges from 0 to 10. Standardize the sample means with $z = \dfrac{\bar{x} - 5}{2.887 / \sqrt{n}}$.

<u>Report for Experiment 8.7</u>

Answer the following questions for each value of n.

1. What are the mean and standard deviation of the population from which we're sampling?
2. Draw the distribution of the population from which we're sampling.
3. Use the central limit theorem to determine the mean and standard deviation of the sampling distribution of the sample mean calculated by drawing samples of size n from a population whose mean is 5 and whose standard deviation is 2.887.
4. What are the mean and standard deviation of the sampling distribution created in this experiment?
5. Does the histogram produced in this experiment appear to be bell shaped?
6. Discuss the effect of increasing the sample size.
7. Does this experiment confirm the central limit theorem and what you anticipated seeing when the mean and standard deviation of the sampling distribution of the mean were computed? Explain.

EXPERIMENT 8.8

Objective: To see what happens to the sampling distribution of the mean when the population is extremely nonnormal.

Experiment: We generate 1,000 samples of size 2, 5, 10, and 25 from an extremely nonnormal distribution whose mean is 1 (and whose standard deviation is 1). The sampling distribution of the mean is then created.

Minitab Instructions

Repeat Experiment 8.6 using an exponential distribution whose mean (and standard deviation) is 1. Standardize with $z = \dfrac{\bar{x} - 1}{1 / \sqrt{n}}$.

Excel Instructions

Repeat Experiment 8.6 using a binomial distribution with **p Value** = .01 and **Number of Trials** = 100. This produces a highly skewed distribution whose mean and standard deviation are 1. Standardize with $z = \dfrac{\bar{x} - 1}{1 / \sqrt{n}}$.

Report for Experiment 8.8

Answer the following questions for each value of *n*.

1. What are the mean and standard deviation of the population from which we're sampling?
2. Draw the distribution of the population from which we're sampling.
3. Use the central limit theorem to determine the mean and standard deviation of the sampling distribution of the sample mean calculated by drawing samples of size *n* from a population whose mean is 1 and whose standard deviation is 1.
4. What are the mean and standard deviation of the sampling distribution created in this experiment?
5. Does the histogram produced in this experiment appear to be bell shaped?
6. Discuss the effect of increasing the sample size.
7. Does this experiment confirm the central limit theorem and what you anticipated seeing when the mean and standard deviation of the sampling distribution of the mean were computed? Explain.

SAMPLING DISTRIBUTION OF THE MEDIAN AND THE VARIANCE

The sampling distribution of the mean is only one of many sampling distributions encountered in a typical statistics course. We can develop the sampling distribution of any sample statistic. Experiments 8.9 and 8.10 create the sampling distributions of the median and the variance, respectively.

Statisticians have proved that the sample median is approximately normally distributed with mean μ and standard deviation $1.2533\sigma / \sqrt{n}$ where μ and σ are the mean and standard deviation, respectively of the population from which we're sampling.

EXPERIMENT 8.9

Objective: To develop the sampling distribution of the median when the population is normally distributed.

Experiment: The computer will generate 1,000 samples of size n (n = 2, 5, 10, and 25) from a normal population whose mean and standard deviation are 50 and 5, respectively. For each sample, we compute the median. We then draw the histogram and calculate descriptive statistics of the sampling distribution.

Minitab Instructions

Repeat Experiment 8.6 calculating the row **Median** rather than the row **Mean**. Standardize the sample medians with $z = \dfrac{\text{median} - 50}{1.2533\sigma / \sqrt{n}}$.

Excel Instructions

Repeat Experiment 8.6 computing the row median rather than the row average. (Type =median(A1:E1) to compute the median of the data in columns A through E.) Standardize the sample medians with $z = \dfrac{median - 50}{1.2533\sigma / \sqrt{n}}$.

Report for Experiment 8.9

Answer the following questions for each value of n.

1. What are the mean and standard deviation of the population from which we're sampling?
2. Determine the mean and standard deviation of the sampling distribution of the sample median calculated by drawing samples of size n from a normal population whose mean is 50 and whose standard deviation is 5.
3. What are the mean and standard deviation of the sampling distribution created in this experiment?
4. Does the histogram produced in this experiment appear to be bell shaped?
5. Does this experiment confirm that the sample median is approximately normally distributed with mean 50 and standard deviation $1.2533 \times 5/\sqrt{n}$? Explain.

EXPERIMENT 8.10

Objective: To develop the sampling distribution of the variance when the population is normally distributed.

Experiment: The computer will generate 1,000 samples of size 25 from a normal population whose mean and standard deviation are 50 and 5, respectively. For each sample, we compute the variance. We then draw the histogram and calculate descriptive statistics of the sampling distribution.

Minitab Instructions

Repeat Experiment 8.9 calculating the row variance instead of the row median. (Compute the standard deviation of each row and then square to produce the variance.) Do not standardize when drawing the histogram. Do not calculate the percentages in the standard intervals.

Excel Instructions

Repeat Experiment 8.9 calculating the row variance instead of the row median. (Type Variance instead of Median.) Do not standardize when drawing the histogram. Do not calculate the percentages in the standard intervals.

Report for Experiment 8.10

1. What are the mean and standard deviation of the population from which we're sampling?
2. What are the mean and standard deviation of the sampling distribution created in this experiment?
3. Does the histogram produced in this experiment appear to be bell shaped?
4. Does it appear that the central limit theorem applies to the sample variance? Explain.

Chapter 9: Introduction to Estimation

9.1 Introduction

This chapter introduced estimation, a form of statistical inference. Make certain that you understand the sampling distribution of the mean before proceeding.

At the completion of this chapter, you are expected to know the following:

1. Understand the fundamental concepts of estimation.
2. How to produce confidence interval estimates of the population mean.
3. How to interpret confidence interval estimates.
4. How to determine the sample size to estimate a population mean.

9.2 Concepts of Estimation

This section dealt with the fundamental concepts of estimation. You are expected to know the meaning of the terms introduced in this chapter and understand why estimation is necessary in most practical situations.

EXERCISES

9.1 What is the difference between an estimator and an estimate?

9.2 Define each of the following terms:

   a) Unbiased estimator

   b) Consistent estimator

9.3 Explain why $\bar{x}$ is an unbiased estimator of μ.

9.4 Explain why s^2 is an unbiased estimator of σ^2.

9.5 Explain why $\bar{x}$ is a consistent estimator of μ.

9.3 Estimating the Population Mean Value When the Population Variance Is Known

We presented the technique to produce a confidence interval estimate of a population mean when the population variance is known. The confidence interval estimator of μ is

$$\bar{x} \pm z_{\alpha/2}\, \sigma/\sqrt{n}$$

It is assumed that the population variance is known. The confidence level is equal to $1 - \alpha$, and from this value you need to be able to determine $z_{\alpha/2}$. Other than plugging the numbers into the formula, no other arithmetic skills are required.

Question:　How can I tell when the population variance is known?

Answer:　The question must state explicitly that the population variance σ^2 is known, and it must also specify the value.

Question:　How do I find $z_{\alpha/2}$?

Answer:　The question will specify the confidence level $1 - \alpha$. From the confidence level, determine a and divided it by 2. For example, if the confidence level is .84, then since $1 - \alpha = .84$ it follows that $\alpha = .16$ and $\alpha/2 = .08$. To find $z_{\alpha/2} = z_{.08}$, we need to find the value of z such that the area to its right is .08.

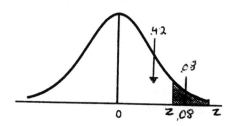

Since Table 3 is designed to provide the areas between 0 and z, we need to subtract .08 from .5 to produce .42. (Notice that we can get .42 more directly by dividing the confidence level by 2.) Now in Table 3 find the area closest to .42 (.4200). As you should be able to see, the area between 0 and 1.40 is .4192 and the area between 0 and 1.41 is .4207. Since the latter area is closer to .4200, we find $z_{.08} = 1.41$.

Example 9.1

A statistician would like to estimate the mean number of cars making legal right turns on the red light at a particular busy intersection. She observes 25 red light sequences and counts the number of legal right turns. She finds the mean to be 7.3. If it is known that the population standard deviation is 1.8, find the 98% confidence interval estimate of the mean number of legal right turns made per sequence.

Solution

The confidence interval estimator of μ is

$$\bar{x} \pm z_{\alpha/2}\, \sigma / \sqrt{n}$$

The confidence level is specified as 98%. Thus,

$$1 - \alpha = .98$$

or

$$\alpha = .02$$

and

$$\alpha/2 = .01$$

We need to find $z_{\alpha/2} = z_{.01}$. From Table 3 in Appendix B, we find $z_{.01} = 2.33$. The population standard deviation is $\sigma = 1.8$. Thus, the 98% confidence interval estimate of μ is

$$\bar{x} \pm z_{\alpha/2}\, \sigma / \sqrt{n} = 7.3 \pm 2.33\,(1.8) / \sqrt{25} = 7.3 \pm .84$$

The lower confidence limit (LCL) is 6.46, and the upper confidence level (UCL) is 8.14.

Question: Does this result mean that there is a 98% probability that the population mean falls between 6.46 and 8.14?

Answer: No. The interval estimate in this case is LCL = 6.46 and UCL = 8.14. If we applied this technique repeatedly, 98% of the samples would produce interval estimates that include the actual population mean and 2% would exclude it. For the sample of 25 in this application, we do not know if this estimate includes μ or excludes it.

EXERCISES

9.6 In a random sample of 50 observations drawn from a normal population whose standard deviation is 250, the sample mean was found to be 1,275.

 a) Find the 95% confidence interval estimate of μ.

 b) Find the 92.5% confidence interval estimate of μ.

9.7 Given the following observations from a normal population whose variance is 25, find the 99% confidence interval estimate of the population mean.

 8, 12, 15, 3, 8, 10, 12, 18

9.8 In a time and motion study, the amount of time required to paint a 10-foot by 10-foot room is measured for 15 painters. The sample mean is calculated and found to be $\bar{x} = 73$. If we assume that the population standard deviation is 8 minutes, find the 95% confidence interval estimate of the mean time for all painters to paint a 10-foot by 10-foot room.

9.4 Selecting the Sample Size

In this section, we discussed how to determine the sample size necessary to produce a confidence interval estimate of the population mean. In order to calculate n, we need to know the confidence level and the error bound. Once these are known, the calculation is quite simple. We use the formula

$$n = \left[\frac{z_{\alpha/2}\sigma}{B} \right]^2$$

Question:	Where do I get σ from?
Answer:	The population standard deviation may be known from previous experiments. (The question will state that.) It can also be approximated from the range. That is,
	$$\sigma \approx \frac{\text{Range}}{4}$$
	Recall that the range is the difference between the largest and smallest observations.

Question:	Where do I get B from?
Answer:	The exercise will state that we wish to estimate μ (or p) with a certain degree of confidence to within a specified amount. The specified amount is the value of B.

Example 9.2

A research scientist would like to estimate the tensile strength of a newly created synthetic fiber. She would like to estimate the mean strength to within 2 pounds with 90% confidence. In a preliminary study, she observed a tensile strength as low as 220 and one as high as 360. What sample size should the research scientist use?

Solution

The confidence level is 90%. Thus,

$$1 - \alpha = .90$$

and

$$z_{\alpha/2} = z_{.05} = 1.645$$

Because we wish to estimate μ to within 2, we have

$$B = 2$$

Finally, we're told that the range is $360 - 220$, so

$$4\sigma \approx \text{Range} = 140$$

and

$$\sigma \approx 35$$

Thus,

$$n = \left[\frac{z_{\alpha/2}\sigma}{B} \right]^2 = \left[\frac{1.645(35)}{2} \right]^2 = 829$$

EXERCISES

9.9   Determine the sample size necessary to estimate μ to within 10 with 99% confidence and $\sigma = 200$.

9.10 Repeat Exercise 9.9 with $\sigma = 2{,}000$.

9.11 A dietician would like to estimate the mean weight loss of a new type of diet. He would like to estimate the parameter to within 1/2 pound with 95% confidence. From past experience, he believes that the population standard deviation is about 10 pounds. How large a sample of dieters should he draw?

Appendix 9.A
Simulation Experiments

In this appendix we continue the use of Minitab and Excel to demonstrate a variety of statistical concepts. The first five experiments focus on the definition of unbiased estimators. Experiments 9.6 and 9.7 deal with interval estimators.

EXPERIMENT 9.1

Objective: To illustrate that $\bar{x}$ is an unbiased estimator of μ.

Experiment: We generate 1,000 samples of size 10 from a normal population whose mean is 50 (and whose standard deviation is 5). We compute the sample means and the mean of the sample means. The mean of the sample means is outputted.

Minitab Instructions

Menu Commands	Session Commands
1. Click **Calc, Random Data,** and **Normal ....**	*RANDOM 1000 C1 – C10*
2. Type 1000 to generate 1000 **rows of data**.	*NORMAL 50 5.*
3. Hit tab and type C1 – C10 to store the data in columns 1 to 10.	*RMEAN C1 – C11*
4. Hit tab and type 50 (**Mean**).	*MEAN C11*
5. Hit tab and type 5 (**Standard deviation**). Click **OK.**	
6. Click **Calc,** and **Row Statistics ....**	
7. Use the cursor to specify **Mean**.	

8. Hit tab and type C1 – C10 (**Input variables**).

9. Hit tab and type C11 to **Store result in** column 11.

10. Click **Calc** and **Column Statistics**.

11. Use the cursor to specify **Mean**.

12. Hit tab and type C11 (**Input variable**). Click **OK**.

Excel Instructions

1. Click **Tools, Data Analysis ..., Random Number Generation**.

2. Type 10 to specify the **Number of Variables**.

3. Hit tab and type 1000 to specify the **Number of Random Numbers**.

4. Click the **Binomial** distribution. (Recall that we use the binomial distribution with 100 trials and probability of success = .5 to approximate a normal distribution with $\mu = 50$ and $\sigma = 5$.

5. Type .5 to specify the p **Value**.

6. Type 100 to specify the **Number of Trials**.

7. Go to the next available column and calculate the sample means (row averages).

8. Calculate the average of the sample means.

Report for Experiment 9.1

1. If the sample mean is an unbiased estimator of the population mean, what did you anticipate that the computer would print?
2. What did the computer print?
3. Does it appear reasonable to believe that the sample mean is an unbiased estimator of the population mean? Explain.

EXPERIMENT 9.2

Objective: To illustrate the sample median is an unbiased estimator of the population mean when the population is normal.

Experiment: The computer will generate 1,000 samples of size 10 from a normal population whose mean is 50 (and whose standard deviation is 5). The sample medians and the mean of the sample medians will then be computed.

Minitab Instructions

Repeat Experiment 9.1 computing the same (row) medians rather than the means. Print the mean of the sample medians.

Excel Instructions

Repeat Experiment 9.1 computing the sample (row) medians rather than the averages. Print the average of the sample medians.

Report for Experiment 9.2

1. If the sample median is an unbiased estimator of the population mean, what output did you anticipate that the computer would print?
2. What did the computer print?
3. Why did we instruct the computer to print the *mean* of the sample medians.
4. Does it appear that the sample median is an unbiased estimator of the population mean? Explain.

The next two experiments examine whether the sample variance s^2 is an unbiased estimator of the population variance σ^2. Recall that s^2 is defined in the following way.

$$\frac{\sum(x_i - \bar{x})^2}{n-1}$$

When you first encountered this formula, you may have wondered why the denominator was $n - 1$ rather than the seemingly more logical value of n. We divide by $n - 1$ because by doing so we produce an estimator that is an unbiased estimator of the population variance σ^2. Experiments 9.3 and 9.4 will demonstrate this point.

EXPERIMENT 9.3

Objective: To illustrate that the sample variance s^2 is an unbiased estimator of the population variance σ^2.

Experiment: Generate 1,000 samples of size 4 from a normal population whose variance is 25 (standard deviation is 5) and whose mean is 50. Calculate the sample variances and the mean of the sample variances.

Minitab Instructions

Repeat Experiment 9.1 with samples of size 4 and computing the sample (row) variances instead of the means. Because Minitab does not compute the row variance directly, calculate the sample standard deviations and square them to produce the sample variances. Print the mean of the sample variances.

Excel Instructions:

Repeat Experiment 9.1 with samples of size 4 and computing the sample (row) variances instead of the means. Print the average of the sample variances.

Report for Experiment 9.3

1. If the sample variance is an unbiased estimator of the population variance, what did you anticipate that the computer would print?
2. What did the computer print?
3. Does it appear that the sample variance defined as

$$s^2 = \frac{\sum(x_i - \bar{x})^2}{n-1}$$

is an unbiased estimator of the population variance? Explain.

EXPERIMENT 9.4

Objective: To illustrate that the statistic

$$\frac{\sum(x_i - \bar{x})^2}{n}$$

is a biased estimator of the population variance.

Experiment: The computer will generate 1,000 samples of size 4 from a normal population whose variance is 25 (standard deviation is 5) and whose mean is 50. In each sample we compute the statistic

$$\frac{\sum(x_i - \bar{x})^2}{n}$$

and print the mean value of the 1,000 samples.

Minitab Instructions

Repeat Experiment 9.3 with the following difference. Multiply the sample (row) variances by $n - 1$ and divide by n. That is, multiply by 3 and divide by 4. Print the mean of these statistics.

Excel Instructions

Repeat Experiment 9.3 with the following difference. Multiply the sample (row) variances by $n - 1$ and divide by n. That is, multiply by 3 and divide by 4. Print the average of these statistics.

1. If the quantity

$$\frac{\sum (x_i - \bar{x})^2}{n}$$

is an unbiased estimator of the population variance, what value do you anticipate the computer printing?

2. What did the computer print?

3. Does it appear that the quantity

$$\frac{\sum (x_i - \bar{x})^2}{n}$$

is an unbiased estimator of the population variance? Explain.

4. Why do you suppose we specified a sample size of only 4 in this experiment?

EXPERIMENT 9.5

Objective: To illustrate that the sample standard deviation is a *biased* estimator of the population standard deviation.

Experiment: Generate 1,000 samples of size 4 from a normal population whose standard deviation is 5 and whose mean is 50. The computer will calculate the mean of the sample standard deviations.

Minitab Instructions

Repeat Experiment 9.1 computing the sample (row) standard deviations. Print the mean of the sample standard deviations.

Excel Instructions:

Repeat Experiment 9.1 computing the sample (row) standard deviations. Print the average of the sample standard deviations.

Report for Experiment 9.5

1. If the sample standard deviation is an unbiased estimator of the population standard deviation, what did you anticipate that the computer would print?

2. What did the computer print?

3. Does it appear that the sample standard deviation is an unbiased estimator of the population standard deviation? Explain.

ESTIMATING THE POPULATON MEAN WHEN THE POPULATION VARIANCE IS KNOWN

The confidence interval estimator of μ developed in this chapter is

$$\bar{x} \pm z_{\alpha/2} \frac{\sigma}{\sqrt{n}}$$

One of the fundamental concepts of statistical inference is that the confidence interval estimate does not always include the value of the parameter we're trying to estimate. That means, for example, that the process that produces 95% confidence intervals will produce intervals that contain the true value of the parameter 95% of the time. The remaining 5% of the time, the interval estimate will be incorrect.

EXPERIMENT 9.6

Objective: To show that confidence interval estimates are correct most, but not all, of the time.

Experiment: We will generate 1,000 samples of 9 observations from a normal population with mean 50 and standard deviation 5. For each sample we will compute the 90% confidence interval estimator, which is

$$\bar{x} \pm 1.645 \frac{\sigma}{\sqrt{n}} = \bar{x} \pm 1.645 \frac{5}{\sqrt{9}} = \bar{x} \pm 2.74$$

The computer will then be instructed to count the number of intervals that include the true value of the population mean, which is $\mu = 50$.

Minitab Instructions

Menu Commands	Session Commands
1. Click **Calc, Random Date,** and **Normal ....**	*RANDOM 1000 C1 – C9;*
2. Type 1000 to generate 1000 **rows of data**.	*NORMAL 50 5.*
3. Hit tab and type C1 – C9 to store the data in columns 1 to 9.	*RMEAN C1 – C10*
4. Hit tab and type 50 (**Mean**).	*LET C11 = C10 – 2.74*
5. Hit tab and type 5 (**Standard deviation**).	*LET C12 = C10 + 2.74*
6. Click **Calc,** and **Row Statistics ....**	*LET C13*
7. Use the cursor to specify **Mean.**	*(C11 < 50) AND (C12 > 50)*
8. Hit tab and type C1 – C9 (**Input variables**).	*TALLY C13;*
9. Hit tab and type C10 to **Store result in** column 10.	*PERCENT.*

128

10. Click **Calc** and **Mathematical Expressions ....**

11. Type C11 (**Variable (new or modified)**).

12. Hit tab twice and type *C10 – 2.74.*

13. Click **Calc** and **Mathematical Expressions ....**

14. Type C12 (**Variable (new or modified)**).

15. Hit tab twice and type *C10 + 2.74.*

16. Click **Calc** and **Mathematical Expressions ....**

17. Type C13 (**Variable (new or modified)**).

18. Hit tab twice and type *(C11 < 50) AND (C12 > 50).*

19. Click **Stat, Tables**, and **Tally ....**

20. Type C13 and use the cursor to specify **Percents**. Click **OK**.

Columns 11 and 12 contain the lower and upper confidence limits, respectively. Column 13 uses comparison and logical operators to count the number of interval estimates that are correct. If the value in column 11 (lower confidence limit) is less than 50 and the value in column 12 (upper confidence limit) is greater than 50, a 1 will be recorded in column 13. If not, a 0 will be recorded. Thus, a 1 in column 13 indicates an interval estimate that includes the true value of μ, which is 50. The *TALLY C13* command and its subcommand counts the number of 1s and 0s in column 13 and prints the percentages.

Excel Instructions

1. Click **Tools, Data Analysis ..., Random Number Generation**.

2. Type 9 to specify the **Number of Variables**.

3. Hit tab and type 1000 to specify the **Number of Random Numbers**.

4. Click the **Binomial** distribution.

5. Type .5 to specify the **p Value**.

6. Type 100 to specify the **Number of Trials**.

7. Go to the next available column and calculate the sample means (row averages).

8. In column J calculate the lower confidence limit LCL = $\bar{x}$ – 2.74.

9. In column K calculate the upper confidence limit; UCL = $\bar{x}$ + 2.74.

10. In column L type

=AND(K1 < 50, J1 > 50)

If K1 (lower confidence limit) is less than 50 and J1 (upper confidence limit) is greater than 50, the word TRUE will be recorded in column M. If not, the word FALSE will be recorded.

11. Perform the same operation on the other rows.

12. Click **f$_x$**, **Statistical**, **COUNTIF**, and **Next>**.

13. Specify the range of the column where the words TRUE and FALSE are stored: L1:L1000

14. Specify the criteria: TRUE

15. Click **Finish**.

Steps 11 through 15 count the number of times the word TRUE appears in the last column. Thus, it counts the number of intervals that include the true value of μ.

Report for Experiment 9.6

1. What is the number of intervals containing the true population mean you anticipated seeing?
2. What is the number of intervals containing the true population mean observed in this experiment?
3. What conclusions can you draw from this experiment?

EXPERIMENT 9.7

Objective: To demonstrate what happens when the confidence level is raised to 95%.

Experiment: We repeat Experiment 9.6 using a confidence level of 95%. The 95% confidence interval estimator is

$$\bar{x} \pm z_{\alpha/2} \frac{\sigma}{\sqrt{n}} = \bar{x} \pm 1.96 \frac{5}{\sqrt{9}} = \bar{x} \pm 3.27$$

Minitab Instructions

Repeat Experiment 9.6 with the following change. The lower confidence limit is $\bar{x}$ - 3.27 and the upper confidence limit is $\bar{x}$ + 3.27.

Excel Instructions

Repeat Experiment 9.6 with the following change.

In column J calculate the lower confidence limit $\bar{x} - 3.27$.

In column K calculate the upper confidence limit $\bar{x}$ + 3.27.

<u>Report for Experiment 9.7</u>

1. What is the number of intervals containing the true population mean you anticipated seeing?
2. What is the number of intervals containing the true popluation mean observed in this experiment?
3. What conclusions can you draw from this experiment?

Chapter 10: Introduction to Hypothesis Testing

10.1 Introduction

This chapter introduced hypothesis testing, the central topic of a statistics course. Almost every chapter following this one uses the concepts, terminology, and notation discussed here. As a result, your understanding of the material in this chapter is critical to your mastery of the subject. We cannot state this too strongly. If you do not have a strong grasp of this material, you will not be capable of applying statistical techniques with any degree of success. We recommend that you spend as much time as possible on this chapter. You will find it to be a worthwhile investment.

At the completion of this chapter you are expected to know the following:

1. Understand the fundamental concepts of hypothesis testing.
2. How to test hypotheses about the population mean.
3. How to set up the null and alternative hypotheses.
4. How to interpret the results of a test of hypothesis.
5. How to compute the p-value of a test when the sampling distribution is normal.
6. How to interpret the p-value of a test.
7. How to calculate the probability of a Type II error and interpret the results.
8. That there are five problem objectives and three types of data addressed in the book and that for each combination there are one or more statistical techniques that can be employed.
9. Understand that the format of the statistical techniques introduced in subsequent chapters is identical to those presented in this chapter and that the real challenge of this subject lies in identifying the correct statistical technique to use.

10.2 Concepts of Hypothesis Testing

In this section, we presented the basic concepts of hypothesis testing. You are expected to know that meaning of the new terms introduced in the section.

EXERCISES

10.1   Define the following terms:

   a) Type I error

   b) Type II error

   c) Rejection region

10.2   What do we call the probability of committing a Type I error?

10.3   What do we call the probability of committing a Type II error?

10.4   What is the significance level of a test?

10.5   What is the basis of the test statistic for a test of μ?

10.3 Testing the Population Mean When the Population Variance Is Known

This section is extremely important because it demonstrates how to test a hypothesis and because the method described here is repeated throughout Chapters 11 to 24. There are three critical elements that you must understand:

1. How to set up the null and alternative hypotheses.
2. How to perform the required calculations, which include the determination of the rejection region and the computation of the value of the test statistic.
3. The interpretation of the results of the test.

Of these elements, the first is usually the most difficult to grasp. As we repeatedly point out in the text, the null hypothesis must always specify that the parameter is equal to some particular value. Since we cannot establish equality by using statistical methods, it falls to the alternative hypothesis to answer the question. Hence, in order to specify the alternative hypothesis, you must determine what the question asks. If it asks (either implicitly or explicitly) if there is sufficient evidence to conclude that μ is not equal to (or is different from) a specific value (say, 100), then

$H_A: \mu \neq 100$

and of course it automatically follows that

$H_0: \mu = 100$

If the question asks if there is sufficient evidence to conclude that μ is greater than 100, then

$H_A: \mu > 100$

and

$H_0: \mu = 100$

If the question asks if there is sufficient evidence to conclude that μ is less than 100, then

$$H_A: \mu < 100$$

and

$$H_0: \mu = 100$$

It should be noted that even though in the formal hypothesis test the null hypothesis precedes the alternative hypothesis, we determine the alternative hypothesis first, and the null hypothesis automatically follows.

The second element requires little more than arithmetic to determine the value of the test statistic, which is

$$z = \frac{\bar{x} - \mu}{\sigma / \sqrt{n}}$$

The value of μ in the test statistic comes from the null hypothesis.

Some care must be exercised in setting up the rejection region. Bear in mind that the probability that the test statistic falls into the rejection region is α. That means that in a two-tail test the rejection region is

$$z > z_{\alpha/2} \text{ or } z < -z_{\alpha/2}$$

or, represented another way,

$$|z| > z_{\alpha/2}$$

In a one-tail test with

$$H_0: \mu = 100$$
$$H_A: \mu > 100$$

the rejection region is

$$z > z_{\alpha}$$

Notice that we z_{α} (rather than $z_{\alpha/2}$) because the entire rejection region is located in only one tail of the sampling distribution. Similarly, if we test

$$H_0: \mu = 100$$
$$H_A: \mu < 100$$

the rejection region is

$$z < -z_{\alpha}$$

Don't forget the minus sign—this is a very common mistake.

The third element is the interpretation. There are only two possible conclusions of a test. If the test statistic falls into the rejection region, we reject the null hypothesis and conclude that there is sufficient evidence to conclude that the alternative hypothesis is true. If the test statistic does not fall into the rejection region, we do not reject the null hypothesis and conclude that there is not sufficient evidence to conclude that the alternative hypothesis is true. Notice that in either case the conclusion is based on the alternative hypothesis. That is, there is either enough evidence (reject H_0) or not enough evidence (do not reject H_0) to support the alternative hypothesis.

Example 10.1

A statistical analyst who works for a large insurance company is in the process of examining several pension plans. Because the length of life of the pension plan holders is critical to the plans' integrity, the analyst needs to know if the mean age has changed. In the last census (1991), suppose the mean age of retirees is 67.5. To determine whether the mean age has increased, the analyst selects a random sample of 100 retirees and finds that $\bar{x} = 68.2$. If we assume that the population standard deviation is $\sigma = 3.1$, can we conclude with $\alpha = .05$ that there is evidence to indicate the mean age of retirees has increased since 1991?

Solution

The question asks if there is sufficient evidence to conclude that μ (the mean age at present) is greater than the mean age in 1991 (67.5). As a result, the alternative hypothesis is

$H_A: \mu > 67.5$

It follows that the null hypothesis is

$H_0: \mu = 67.5$

The test statistic is

$$z = \frac{\bar{x} - \mu}{\sigma / \sqrt{n}}$$

We wish to reject the null hypothesis in favor of the alternative hypothesis only if the test statistic is too large. Since the probability of rejecting the null hypothesis when it is true is $\alpha = .05$, the rejection region is

$z > z_\alpha = z_{.05} = 1.645$

Finally, the value of the test statistic is

$$z = \frac{\bar{x} - \mu}{\sigma / \sqrt{n}} = \frac{68.2 - 67.5}{3.1 / \sqrt{100}} = 2.26$$

Since 2.26 > 1.645, the test statistic falls into the rejection region. As a result, we reject the null hypothesis and conclude that there is sufficient evidence to indicate that $\mu > 67.5$.

Question: Why must the null hypothesis specify one single value for the parameter?

Answer: Because we must substitute one single value of the parameter when calculating the test statistic. Thus, if we specify

H_0: $\mu = 100$

we substitute $\mu = 100$ when computing the test statistic

$$z = \frac{\bar{x} - \mu}{\sigma / \sqrt{n}}$$

If we had specified

H_0: $\mu \neq 100$

what value of μ would we use to calculate the test statistic?

Question: What does it mean to reject the null hypothesis?

Answer: When we reject the null hypothesis, we do so because there is enough statistical evidence (based on the value of a) to indicate that the value of the parameter specified in the null hypothesis is not correct. We conclude that there is enough evidence to support the alternative hypothesis.

Example 10.2

It is important for airlines to know the approximate total weight of the baggage carried on each airplane. An airline researcher believes that the mean baggage weight for each adult is 60 pounds. To test his belief, he draws a random sample of 50 adult passengers and weighs their baggage. He finds the sample mean to be 57.1 pounds. If he knows that the population standard deviation is 10 pounds, can he conclude at the 5% significance level that his belief is incorrect?

Solution

The researcher wants to know if the statistical result ($\bar{x} = 57.1$) is sufficient for him to conclude that his belief that $\mu = 60$ is untrue. As a result, the alternative hypothesis is

H_A: $\mu \neq 60$

and the null hypothesis is

H_0: $\mu = 60$

Notice that the question did not ask if there was sufficient evidence to support his belief. That's because there cannot be enough statistical evidence (except knowledge of the whole population) to conclude that $\mu = 60$. The test statistic is

$$z = \frac{\bar{x} - \mu}{\sigma / \sqrt{n}}$$

If the value of the test statistic is either too large or too small, we intend to reject H_0. Thus, the rejection region is

$$|z| > z_{\alpha/2} = z_{.025} = 1.96$$

The value of the test statistic is

$$z = \frac{\bar{x} - \mu}{\sigma / \sqrt{n}} = \frac{57.1 - 60}{10 / \sqrt{50}} = -2.05$$

Since $|-2.05| = 2.05 > 1.96$, we reject the null hypothesis and conclude that there is enough statistical evidence to indicate that the belief that $\mu = 60$ is wrong.

Question: How do I know when to use a one-tail or a two-tail test?

Answer: Always remember that the alternative hypothesis is set up to answer the question. If the question asks us to determine whether there is enough statistical evidence to conclude that the mean is not equal to 100, then we specify

$$H_A: \mu \neq 100$$

and we perform a two-tail test. If the question asks us to determine whether there is enough statistical evidence to conclude that the mean is greater than 100, then we specify

$$H_A: \mu > 100$$

and we perform a one-tail test. Similarly, we perform a one-tail test if we specify

$$H_A: \mu < 100$$

Question:	Why do we change the decision rule (and the rejection region) for different alternative hypotheses?
Answer:	The rejection region must always have a probability of α. Thus, if we perform a two-tail test, the rejection region is

$$|z| > z_{\alpha/2}$$

which is a shortcut way of saying

$$z > z_{\alpha/2} \text{ or } z < -z_{\alpha/2}$$

In this test the rejection region is divided in half. In a one-tail test, the entire rejection region is located in one tail of the sampling distribution. Consequently, we reject the null hypothesis if

$$z > z_{\alpha} \text{ (when } H_A: \mu > 100)$$

and

$$z < -z_{\alpha} \text{ (when } H_A: \mu < 100)$$

Question:	Why is it misleading to say that we accept the null hypothesis when the value of the test statistic does not fall into the rejection region?
Answer:	If we say that we accept the null hypothesis, it implies that there is enough statistical evidence to infer that the parameter is actually equal to the value specified in the null hypothesis. In Example 7.3, we would state that since x = 58.1, there is enough evidence to conclude that $\mu = 60$. This is, of course, an absurd conclusion. Consequently, when we do not reject the null hypothesis, we conclude that there is not enough evidence to support the alternative hypothesis.

EXERCISES

10.6 Find the rejection region for each of the following tests:

a) $H_0: \mu = 55$
   $H_A: \mu \neq 55$
   $\sigma = 10 \quad n = 100 \quad \alpha = .05$

b) $H_0: \mu = 125$
   $H_A: \mu > 125$
   $\sigma = 18 \quad n = 27 \quad \alpha = .01$

c) H_0: $\mu = 6$

H_A: $\mu < 6$

$\sigma = 1$ $n = 15$ $\alpha = .10$

10.7 Test each of the following:

a) H_0: $\mu = 28$

H_A: $\mu > 28$

$\sigma = 5$ $n = 75$ $\alpha = .05$ $\bar{x} = 32$

b) H_0: $\mu = 225$

H_A: $\mu \neq 225$

$\sigma = 15$ $n = 30$ $\alpha = .01$ $\bar{x} = 218$

10.8 The director of the M.B.A. program at a large university informs incoming students that they are expected to devote more than 25 hours per week to homework. She decides to examine the extent to which students listen to her advice by taking a random sample of 15 students and calculating the mean number of hours per week of homework. Set up the null and alternative hypotheses and the rejection region if the director wants to know whether there is enough statistical evidence to indicate that the students have accepted her advice. (Assume that σ^2 is known.) Use $\alpha = .05$.

10.9 Repeat Exercise 10.8, supposing that the director wants to know whether there is enough statistical evidence to indicate that the students have not accepted her advice.

10.10   Complete the test described in Exercise 10.9 given $\sigma = 5$ and $\bar{x} = 22.9$.

   H_0:

   H_A:

   Test statistic:

   Rejection region:

   Value of the test statistic:

   Conclusion:

10.11   A pizza parlor boasts that it can deliver pizzas on the average in less than 33 minutes. A random sample of 25 delivery times yields a sample mean of 31.2 minutes. If we assume that the population standard deviation is $\sigma = 4$ minutes, can we conclude at the 10% significance level that the pizza parlor is correct?

   H_0:

   H_A:

   Test statistic:

   Rejection region:

   Value of the test statistic:

   Conclusion:

10.4 The *p*-Value of a Hypothesis Test

The *p*-value of a test is another method of presenting the results of the test. You are expected to know how to interpret and how to calculate a *p*-value.

The interpretation of the p-value is quite straightforward. The smaller the p-value, the greater the statistical evidence to reject the null hypothesis. That means that if a statistician judges that a *p*-value is small then the conclusion of the test is to reject the null hypothesis. The definition of a small *p*-value is subjective. That is, everyone must judge for himself whether a *p*-value is small enough. That choice usually is somewhere between 1% and 10%. For example, if the *p*-value of the test is .0372 and the statistician decides that for this test anything less than .05 is small enough, he would reject the null hypothesis. Another statistician who decides that the *p*-value must be less than .01 to reject would not reject the null hypothesis.

The calculation of the *p*-value is quite similar to the normal probability questions encountered in Chapter 7. If the test statistic is normally distributed (z-statistic), the *p*-value is simply the probability that appears in one or both tails of the standard normal curve. Whether it's one-tail or two-tail (and if one-tail, which one) depends on the rejection region. For example, in a two-tail test where the test statistic is $z = 2.0$ and the rejection region is $z > z_{\alpha/2}$ or $z < -z_{\alpha/2}$,

$p\text{-value} = P(z > 2.0) + P(z < -2.0) = .0228 + .0228 = .0456$

If the rejection region is $z > z_\alpha$ and $z = 2.0$, then

$p\text{-value} = P(z > 2.0) = .0228$

Finally, if the rejection region is $z < {\sim}z_a$ and $z = 2.0$, then

$p\text{-value} = P(z < 2.0) = .9772$

If this last calculation seems strange, remember that the direction of the inequality in the probability statement is based completely on the rejection region.

Example 10.3

In testing the hypotheses

$H_0: \mu = 150$

$H_A: \mu > 150$

with $n = 64$ and $\sigma = 16$, find the *p*-value if $\bar{x}$ equals a) 152, b) 160, c) 145.

Solution

a) With $\bar{x} = 152$,

$$z = \frac{\bar{x} - \mu}{\sigma/\sqrt{n}} = \frac{152 - 150}{16/\sqrt{64}} = 1.0$$

$p\text{-value} = P(z > 1.0) = .1587$

b) With $\bar{x} = 160$,

$$z = \frac{\bar{x} - \mu}{\sigma / \sqrt{n}} = \frac{160 - 150}{16 / \sqrt{64}} = 5.0$$

p-value $= P(z > 5.0) = 0.0$

c) With $\bar{x} = 145$,

$$z = \frac{\bar{x} - \mu}{\sigma / \sqrt{n}} = \frac{145 - 150}{16 / \sqrt{64}} = -2.5$$

p-value $= P(z > -2.5) = .9938$

EXERCISES

10.12 Suppose that you, as a statistician (amateur, at this point) decide that for a series of hypothesis tests the level of significance should be .05. For each of the tests described below, determine the tests' conclusions.

a) H_0: $\mu = 25$
    H_A: $\mu \neq 25$

    p-value $= .0499$

b) H_0: $\mu = 70$
    H_A: $\mu > 70$

    p-value $= .0522$

c) H_0: $\mu = 200$
    H_A: $\mu < 200$

    p-value $= .9860$

10.13 In testing the hypotheses

H_0: $\mu = 700$
H_A: $\mu > 700$

with $\sigma = 200$ and $n = 100$, we found $\bar{x} = 720$. Find the p-value of the test.

10.14 Repeat Exercise 10.13 with $\bar{x} = 700$.

10.15 Repeat Exercise 10.13 with $\bar{x} = 650$.

10.16 Find the *p*-value of the test for each given value of the test statistic *z* for the hypotheses

   H_0: $\mu = 25$
   H_A: $\mu > 25$

   a) $z = 1.0$

   b) $z = 2.0$

   c) $z = 3.0$

   d) $z = 4.0$

10.5 Calculating the Probability of a Type II Error

This section presented the method by which we calculate the probability of a Type II error. For you, the statistics student, the calculation of β provides insights into how the hypothesis test works and how the significance level is selected. It is particularly important for you to realize that, for a fixed value of *n*, α and β have an inverse relationship. That is, increasing α decreases β, and vice versa. For a fixed α, increasing *n* decreases β, so by increasing the sample size we can improve the test. Additionally, the calculation of β allows the statistician to judge how well a test performs. For example, if for a specific value of the parameter the statistician determines that β is too large, corrective action is called for. The statistician can either increase α or increase *n*.

Students often have some difficulty in calculating β. It is important to remember that the process involves two stages. Stage 1 expresses the rejection region in terms of the unstandardized test statistic. This requires some algebraic manipulation to solve an inequality. Stage 2 calculates the probability that the unstandardized test statistic falls into the acceptance region given that the parameter is equal to some specific value.

Example 10.4

In testing the hypotheses

H_0: $\mu = 100$

H_A: $\mu > 100$

where $\sigma = 30$, we choose $n = 36$ and $\alpha = .05$. Find β when $\mu = 110$.

Solution

The standardized test statistic is

$$z = \frac{\bar{x} - \mu}{\sigma / \sqrt{n}}$$

and the rejection region is

$$z > z_\alpha = z_{.05} = 1.645$$

To determine the rejection region for $\bar{x}$, we solve the inequality

$$z = \frac{\bar{x} - \mu}{\sigma / \sqrt{n}} > 1.645$$

or

$$\frac{\bar{x} - 100}{30 / \sqrt{36}} > 1.645$$

or

$$\bar{x} > 108.225$$

Notice that in solving this inequality we use the value of $\mu = 100$ from the null hypothesis. The reason for this is that α is the probability of a Type I error, which assumes that the null hypothesis is true. This completes stage 1. In stage 2, we calculate the probability that $\bar{x}$ falls into the acceptance region. Hence,

$$\beta = P(\bar{x} < 108.225 \text{ given } \mu = 110)$$

Since $\bar{x}$ is normally distributed, we standardize $\bar{x}$ by subtracting its mean (which is now assumed to be $\mu = 110$) and dividing by its standard deviation ($\sigma / \sqrt{n} = 30 / \sqrt{36}$).

$$\beta = P\left(\frac{\bar{x} - \mu}{\sigma / \sqrt{n}} < \frac{108.225 - 110}{30 / \sqrt{36}}\right) = P(z < -.36) = .3594$$

Example 10.5

Suppose that in Example 10.4 we decide that β is too large. We decide to increase the sample size to 100. What is the new value of β?

Solution

Stage 1: $z = \dfrac{\bar{x} - \mu}{\sigma / \sqrt{n}} > 1.645$

or

$$\frac{\bar{x} - 100}{30 / \sqrt{100}} > 1.645$$

or

$$\bar{x} > 104.935$$

Stage 2: $\beta = P(\bar{x} < 104.935 \text{ given } \mu = 110)$

$$= \left(\frac{\bar{x} - \mu}{\sigma / \sqrt{n}} < \frac{104.935 - 110}{30 / \sqrt{100}}\right) = P(z < -1.69) = .0455$$

Thus, by increasing the sample size from 36 to 100, we decrease β from .3594 to .0455 (with $\sigma = 30$, $\alpha = .05$, and the actual value of μ assumed to be 110).

EXERCISES

10.17 For the hypothesis test below set up the rejection region in terms of x.

$H_0: \mu = 200$
$H_A: \mu < 200$

$\sigma = 20 \quad n = 25 \quad \alpha = .01$

10.18 Find β if in Exercise 10.17 μ is actually equal to 195.

10.19 Find β if in Exercise 10.17 μ is actually equal to 188.

10.20 A supermarket manager boasts that the average customer waits no more than 10 minutes at the checkout counter. A dissatisfied customer decides to show that there is statistical evidence that the manager is wrong. She decides to perform a test with $n = 100$ customers and $\alpha = .05$. Calculate the probability of erroneously concluding that the customer is not correct when in actual fact the average waiting time is 11.5 minutes. (Assume that $\sigma = 5$.)

Appendix 10.A
Simulation Experiments

The simulation experiments in this appendix examine Type I and Type II errors and the factors that affect them.

EXPERIMENT 10.1

Objective: To illustrate that when testing a true null hypothesis, Type I errors will be committed at a rate equal to the significance level.

Experiment: We will generate 1,000 samples of size 4 from a normal population whose mean and standard deviation are 50 and 5, respectively. For each sample we will conduct the following test of hypotheses.

$H_0: \mu = 50$

$H_A: \mu \neq 50$

The test will be conducted three times with different significant levels; $\alpha = .10, .05,$ and $.01$. We will assume that $\sigma = 5$. The test statistic and the rejection region are

Test statistic: $z = \dfrac{\bar{x} - \mu}{\sigma / \sqrt{n}}$

Rejection region: $|z| > z_{\alpha/2}$

With $\alpha = .10$: Rejection region: $|z| > z_{.05} = 1.645$

With $\alpha = .05$: Rejection region: $|z| > z_{.025} = 1.96$

With $\alpha = .01$: Rejection region: $|z| > z_{.005} = 2.575$

Since the null hypothesis is true, σ is equal to 5, and n is equal to 4, the value of the test is

$$z = \frac{\bar{x} - \mu}{\sigma / \sqrt{n}} = \frac{\bar{x} - 50}{5 / \sqrt{4}} = \frac{\bar{x} - 50}{2.5}$$

Minitab Instructions

Menu Commands	Session Commands
1. Click **Calc, Random Data,** and **Normal ....**	*RANDOM 1000 C1 – C4;*
2. Type 1000 to generate 1000 **rows of data**.	*NORMAL 50 5.*
3. Hit tab and type C1 – C4 to store the data in columns 1 to 4.	*RMEAN C1 – C5*

4. Hit tab and tyupe 50 (**Mean**).

5. Hit tab and type 5 (**Standard deviation**). Click **OK**.

6. Click **Calc** and **Row Statistics**.

7. Use the cursor to specify **Mean**.

8. Hit tab and type C1 – C4 (**Input variables**).

9. Hit tab and type C5 to **Store results** in column 5.

10. Click **Calc** and **Mathematical Expressions ....**

11. Type C6 (**Variable (new or modified)**).

12. Hit tab twice and type $(C5 – 50)/2.5$

13. Click **Calc** and **Mathematical Expressions ....**

14. Type C7 (**Variable (new or modified)**).

15. Hit tab twice and type $(C6 < 1.645)$ OR $(C6 > 1.645)$.

16. Click **Stat, Tables**, and **Tally ....**

17. Type C7 and use the cursor to specify **Percents**. Click **OK**.

$LET\ C6 = (C5 – 50)/2.5$

$LET\ C7 =$

$(C6 < –1.645)\ OR\ (C6 > 1.645)$

$TALLY\ C7;$

$PERCENT.$

Column 6 stores the values of the test statistics and column 7 records a "1" when the test statistic falls into the rejection region and a "0" when it does not. Since the null hypothesis is true, a "1" represents a Type I error. Minitab outputs the percentage of 0s and 1s in column 7. The percentage of 1s is an estimate of the probability of a Type I error.

Repeat experiment with $\alpha = .05$ (rejection region $|z| > 1.96$) and with $\alpha = .01$ (rejection region $|z| > 2.575$). Change step 15 accordingly.

Excel Instructions

1. Click **Tools, Data Analysis ..., Random Number Generation**.

2. Type 4 to specify the **Number of Variables**.

3. Type 1000 to specify the **Number of Random Numbers**.

4. Click the **Binomial** Distribution. (Recall that we use the binomial distribution with 100 trials and probability of success = .5 to generate normal data.)

5. Type .5 to specify the **p Value**.

6. Type 100 to specify the **Number of Trials**.

7. Go to column E and calculate the sample means (row averages)

8. Go to column F and calculate the test statistics. $z = \dfrac{\bar{x} - 50}{2.5}$

9. Go to Column G and type

     = OR (F1 < −1.645, F1 > 1.645)

   Complete G2 to G1000 in the same way.

10. Go to H1 and click f_x, **Statistical**, **COUNTIF**, and **Next>**.

11. Specify the range: G1:G1000.

12. Specify the criteria: TRUE. Click **Finish**.

Column F stores the values of the test statistics and column G records whether the test statistic falls into the rejection region. (TRUE = falls into the rejection region and FALSE = does not.) Excel outputs the number of tests where a Type I error occurred.

Repeat the experiment with $\alpha = .05$ (rejection region $|z| > 1.96$) and with a = .01 (rejection region $|z| > 2.575$). Change step 9 accordingly.

Report for Experiment 10.1

1. For each value of α, indicate the anticipated percentage of Type I errors and the observed percentage of Type I errors.

   $\alpha = .10$:   Anticipated percentage of Type I errors

                          Observed percentage of Type I errors

   $\alpha = .05$:   Anticipated percentage of Type I errors

                          Observed percentage of Type I errors

   $\alpha = .01$:   Anticipated percentage of Type I errors

                          Observed percentage of Type I errors

2. Explain why, when a Type I error is committed, it is not necessarily because of some mistake the statistician made.

As we discussed above, it is possible to make two types of error when conducting a test of hypothesis. A Type II error occurs when we do not reject a false null hypothesis. Consider the example discussed in Experiment 10.1. The null and alternative hypotheses were

   $H_0: \mu = 50$

   $H_A: \mu \neq 50$

When the test was conducted at the 10% significance level, the rejection region was

$$|z| > 1.645$$

The next three experiments address the issue of calculating the probability of a Type II error under different conditions.

Suppose that we want to compute the probability of a Type II error when μ is actually equal to 5.25.

EXPERIMENT 10.2

Objective: To illustrate the occurrence of Type II errors and to illustrate the effect of the sample size on the probability of Type II errors.

Experiment: We will generate 1,000 samples of size n (where $n = 4$, 9, and 25) from a normal population with mean of 52.5 and a standard deviation of 5. Using these data, we will test the following hypotheses at the 5% significance level.

H_0: $\mu = 50$

H_A: $\mu \neq 50$

The test statistic is

$$z = \frac{\bar{x} - \mu}{\sigma / \sqrt{n}} = \frac{\bar{x} - 50}{5 / \sqrt{n}}$$

and the rejection region is

$$|z| > 1.645$$

Since the null hypothesis is false (μ is really equal to 52.5), any values of the test statistic that do not lead to the rejection of the null hypothesis will result in Type II errors.

Minitab Instructions

Repeat Experiment 10.1 (with $\alpha = .10$) with the following change. Generate random data from a normal distribution whose mean is 52.5 (and whose standard deviation is 5). Since the null hypothesis is false ($\mu = 52.5$) a 1 in column 7 indicates a correct decision. Minitab will output the percentage of 1s and 0s. The percentage of 0s is the proportion of Type II errors.

Repeat for sample sizes $n = 9$ and 25. Use appropriate column numbers and test statistics (step 12).

Excel Instructions

Repeat Experiment 9.1 (with $\alpha = .10$) with the following change. Generate random data from a binomial distribution where the number of trials is 100 and where the probability of success = .525 (approximating a normal distribution with $\mu = 52.5$ and $\sigma \cong 5$). At step 12 specify FALSE instead of TRUE. Since the null hypothesis is false ($\mu = 52.5$) Excel will print the number of tests where the test statistic does not fall into the rejection region. Divide this number by the number of random numbers generated to estimate the probability of a Type II error.

Repeat for sample sizes $n = 9$ and 25. Use appropriate columns and test statistics (step 8).

Report for Experiment 10.2

1. For each value of n report the observed percentage of Type II errors.

   $n = 4$

   $n = 9$

   $n = 25$

2. What effect does increasing the sample size have on the probability of a Type II error?

EXPERIMENT 10.3

Objective: In concert with Experiment 10.2, to illustrate the effect of changing the significance level on the probability of a Type II error.

Experiment: We will repeat Experiment 10.2 (with $n = 4$ only) using $\alpha = .05$ and .01. The rejection region is

$$|z| > z_{\alpha/2}$$

With $\alpha = .05$: Rejection region: $|z| > z_{.05} = 1.96$

With $\alpha = .10$: Rejection region: $|z| > z_{.005} = 2.575$

Minitab Instructions

Repeat Experiment 10.1 with $\alpha = .05$ and .01; rejection regions $|z| > 1.96$ and $|z| > 2.575$, respectively (step 15).

Excel Instructions

Repeat Experiment 10.1 with $\alpha = .05$ and .01; rejection regions $|z| > 1.96$ and $|z| > 2.575$, respectively (step 9).

1. For each value of α (including form Experiment 10.2 with $n = 4$), report the observed percentage of Type II errors.

   $\alpha = .10$

   $\alpha = .05$

   $\alpha = .01$

2. What effect does the significance level have on the probability of a Type II error?

EXPERIMENT 10.4

Objective: To illustrate the effect of changing the actual value of μ on the probability of a Type II error.

Experiment: We repeat Experiment 10.2 (with $n = 4$ and $\alpha = .05$) using the following values of μ: 45.0, 47.5, 50.0, 52.5, 55.0

Minitab Instructions

Repeat Experiment 10.2 generating data from normal distributions with mean $\mu = 45$, 47.5, 50, 52.5, and 55 (one at a time), and with standard deviation 5 (step 4).

Excel Instructions

Repeat Experiment 10.2 generating data from binomial distributions with 100 trials and probability of success = .45, .475, .5, .525, and .55 (one at a time) (approximating normal distributions with mean $\mu = 45$, 47.5, 50, 52.5, and 55 and $\sigma \cong 5$) (step 5).

Report for Experiment 10.4

$\mu=45$: Observed percentage of Type II errors

$\mu=47.5$: Observed percentage of Type II errors

$\mu=50$: Observed percentage of Type II errors

$\mu=52.5$: Observed percentage of Type II errors

$\mu=55$: Observed percentage of Type II errors

Discuss what effect the value of μ has on the probability of making a Type II error.

Chapter 11: Inference About the Description of a Single Population

11.1 Introduction

In this chapter, we presented the statistical inference methods used when the problem objective is to describe a single population. Sections 11.2 and 11.3 addressed the problem of drawing inferences about a single population when the data are quantitative. In Section 11.2, we introduced the confidence interval estimator and the test statistic for drawing inferences about a population mean. This topic was covered earlier in Sections 9.3 and 10.3. However, in Chapters 9 and 10 we operated under the unrealistic assumption that the population variance was known. In this chapter, the population variance was assumed to be unknown. Section 11.3 presented the methods used to make inferences about a population variance. Finally, in Section 11.4 we addressed the problem of describing a single population when the data are qualitative.

At the completion of this chapter, you are expected to know the following:

1. How to apply the concepts and techniques of estimation and hypothesis testing introduced in Chapters 9 and 10, including:
   a) setting up the null and alternative hypotheses
   b) calculating the test statistic (by hand or using a computer)
   c) setting up the rejection region
   d) interpreting statistical results
2. How to recognize when the parameter of interest is a population mean.
3. How to recognize when to use the Student t distribution to estimate and test a population mean and when to use the standard normal distribution.
4. How to recognize when the parameter of interest is a population variance.
5. How to recognize when the parameter of interest is a population proportion.

11.2 Inference About Population Mean When the Population Variance Is Unknown

We presented the statistical techniques used when the parameter to be tested or estimated is the population mean under the more realistic assumption that the population variance is unknown. Thus, the only difference between this section and Sections 9.3 and 10.3 is that when the population variance σ^2 is known we use the z-statistic as the basis for the inference, whereas when σ^2 is unknown we use the t-statistic.

The formula for the confidence interval estimator of the population mean when the population variance is unknown is

$$\bar{x} \pm t_{\alpha/2} \frac{s}{\sqrt{n}}$$

The test statistic is

$$t = \frac{\bar{x} - \mu}{s / \sqrt{n}}$$

The number of degrees of freedom of this Student t distribution is $n - 1$.

Question: How do I determine $t_{\alpha/2}$?

Answer: The degrees of freedom are $n - 1$, where n is the sample size. Turn to Table 4 in Appendix B and locate the degrees of freedom in the left column. Pick one of $t_{.100}$, $t_{.050}$, $t_{.025}$, $t_{.010}$ or $t_{.005}$ depending on the confidence level $1 - \alpha$. The value of $t_{\alpha/2}$ is at the intersection of the row of the degrees of freedom and the column of the value of $\alpha/2$.

Question: Which interval estimator do I use when the degrees of freedom are greater than 200?

Answer: If σ^2 is unknown, the interval estimator of μ is

$$\bar{x} \pm t_{\alpha/2} \frac{s}{\sqrt{n}}$$

regardless of the sample size. The fact that $t_{\alpha/2}$ is approximately equal to $z_{\alpha/2}$ for d.f. > 200 does not change the interval estimator.

Example 11.1

The mean monthly sales of insurance agents in a large company is $72,000. In an attempt to improve sales, a new training program has been devised. Ten agents are randomly selected to participate in the program. At its completion, the sales of the agents in the next month are recorded as follows (in $1,000):

63, 87, 95, 75, 83, 78, 69, 79, 103, 98

a) Do these data provide sufficient evidence at the 10% significance level to indicate that the program is successful?

b) Estimate with 95% confidence the mean monthly sales for those agents who have taken the new training program.

Solution

The problem objective is to describe the population of monthly sales, which is a quantitative variable. Thus, the parameter of interest is μ. We have no knowledge of the population variance σ^2. As a result we must calculate s (as well as $\bar{x}$) from the data. Hence, the basis of the statistical inference is the t-statistic.

a) To establish that the program is successful, we must show that there is enough evidence to conclude that μ is greater than \$72 (thousand). Thus, the alternative hypothesis is

$$H_A: \mu > 72$$

and the null hypothesis is

$$H_0: \mu = 72$$

The test statistic is

$$t = \frac{\bar{x} - \mu}{s / \sqrt{n}}$$

which is Student t distributed with $n - 1$ degrees of freedom. The rejection region is

$$t > t_{\alpha,\, n-1} = t_{.10,\, 9} = 1.383$$

From the data, we compute

$$\bar{x} = 83.0$$

and

$$s = 12.85$$

The value of the test statistic is

$$t = \frac{\bar{x} - \mu}{s / \sqrt{n}} = \frac{83.0 - 72}{12.85 / \sqrt{10}} = 2.71$$

Since $2.71 > 1.383$, we reject H_0 and conclude that there is enough evidence to show that $\mu > 72$ (thousand) and hence that the program is successful.

b) Once we've determined that the parameter to be estimated is μ and that the population variance is unknown, we identify the confidence interval estimator as

$$\bar{x} \pm t_{\alpha/2}\, s / \sqrt{n}$$

The specified confidence level is .95. Thus,

$$1 - \alpha = .95$$

or

$\alpha = .05$

and

$\alpha/2 = .025$

From Table 4 in Appendix B, we find

$t_{.025, 9} = 2.262$

The 95% confidence interval estimate of μ is

$\bar{x} \pm t_{\alpha/2} s / \sqrt{n} = 83.0 \pm 2.262(12.85) / \sqrt{10} = 83.0 \pm 9.19$

EXERCISES

11.1   Find each of the following values:

    a) $t_{.05, 17}$

    b) $-t_{.01, 28}$

    c) $t_{.10, 40}$

11.2   A statistician wants to test the hypotheses below. If the sample size is 17 and the significance level is 5%, find the rejection region.

    $H_0: \mu = 1$
    $H_A: \mu < 1$

11.3   Repeat Exercise 11.2 assuming a sample of size 41.

11.4   The following seven observations were drawn from a normal population. Estimate the population mean with 99% confidence.

    3, 9, 0, −2, 5, 8, 5

11.5 In a random sample of 13 observations from a normal population the sample mean and sample standard deviation are 57.3 and 6.8, respectively. Find the 98% confidence interval estimate of the population mean.

11.6 Repeat Exercise 11.5 assuming we know that the population standard deviation σ is equal to 6.8.

11.7 A random sample of 100 observations yielded the following statistics:

$\bar{x} = 1,550$

$s = 125$

a) Estimate μ with 90% confidence.

b) Do these statistics provide sufficient evidence to indicate that ~ is not equal to 1500? Test with $\alpha = .01$.

H_0:
H_A:

Test statistic:

Rejection region:

Value of the test statistic:

Conclusion:

11.8 An oil refiner has developed a new type of oil that is supposed to not only reduce engine wear but also increase gas mileage. A random sample of 50 cars that have a mean gas mileage of 24 miles per gallon is selected. When the new oil is put into the cars, each is driven until the gas tank is dry. The mileage was recorded. The mean and standard deviation of the 50 observations are $\bar{x} = 26.3$ and $s = 7.6$. At the 5% significance level; can we conclude that the new type of oil is effective in increasing gas mileage?

H_0:

H_A:

Test statistic:

Rejection region:

Value of the test statistic:

Conclusion:

11.9 Estimate with 99% confidence the mean gas mileage for the data in Exercise 11.8.

11.10 A random sample of the wholesale price of a dozen eggs in New York is shown below. Find the 95% confidence interval estimate of the mean price of eggs in New York.

58.4, 55.3, 55.6, 56.4, 51.7, 52.8, 57.6, 53.0, 50.0, 53.2, 52.8, 57.8

11.3 Inference About a Population Variance

This section presented the methods used to estimate and test the population variance. As in the previous sections, you are expected to be able to identify the parameter of interest, calculate the confidence interval estimate, or perform the hypothesis test. If you've been able to handle the techniques of estimation and hypothesis testing of μ, your only challenge will be in correctly identifying the parameter. All examples and exercises in this section deal with problems whose objective is to describe a single population of quantitative data. Furthermore, the descriptive measure of interest is variability. As a result, each question refers to terms such as variability, variance, and standard deviation. Questions may also refer to stability and consistency, which are measured by the variance.

The confidence interval estimator of σ^2 is

$$LCL = \frac{(n-1)s^2}{\chi^2_{\alpha/2}}$$

$$UCL = \frac{(n-1)s^2}{\chi^2_{1-\alpha/2}}$$

The test statistic is

$$\chi^2 = \frac{(n-1)s^2}{\sigma^2}$$

The degrees of freedom of this χ^2-statistic are $n-1$.

Example 11.2

Because all the spark plugs in a car are usually changed at the same time, there are advantages if the spark plugs all wear out at about the same time. A spark plug manufacturer has developed a new spark plug whose length of life is supposed to be more consistent. In extensive studies of the current type of spark plug, it is known that the population standard deviation is 1,200 miles. In a random sample of 20 of the new spark plugs, it was found that the sample standard deviation was 800 miles. Can we conclude at the 5% significance level that the new spark plug has a more consistent length of life than the current type?

Solution

The problem objective is to describe the population of length of life of the new spark plug, a variable that is quantitative. Because we want to learn something about its consistency, the parameter of interest is σ^2. Furthermore, since we want to know if the statistical evidence is sufficient for us to conclude that the standard deviation is less than 1,200, the alternative hypothesis is

H_A: $\sigma^2 < 1,200^2$

and the null hypothesis is

H_0: $\sigma^2 = 1,200^2$

The test statistic is

$$\chi^2 = \frac{(n-1)s^2}{\sigma^2}$$

and the rejection region is

$$\chi^2 < \chi^2_{1-\alpha, n-1} = \chi^2_{.95, 19} = 10.1170$$

The value of the test statistic is

$$\chi^2 = \frac{(n-1)s^2}{\sigma^2} = \frac{19(800^2)}{1,200^2} = 8.44$$

We reject H_0 and conclude that the length of life of the new spark plug is more consistent than the current type.

Example 11.3

Estimate with 99% confidence the population variance of the length of life of the new spark plug.

Solution

$$LCL = \frac{(n-1)s^2}{\chi^2_{\alpha/2}} = \frac{19(800^2)}{38.5822} = 315,171$$

$$UCL = \frac{(n-1)s^2}{\chi^2_{1-\alpha/2}} = \frac{19(800^2)}{6.84398} = 1,776,744$$

EXERCISES

11.11   Find the rejection region for each of the following tests:

   a) H_0: $\sigma^2 = 50$
        H_A: $\sigma^2 \neq 50$

        $n = 30$ $\alpha = .10$

   b) H_0: $\sigma^2 = 125$
        H_A: $\sigma^2 > 125$

        $n = 91$ $\alpha = .01$

   c) H_0: $\sigma^2 = 10$
        H_A: $\sigma^2 < 10$

        $n = 25$ $\alpha = .05$

11.12 Given the following observations drawn from a normal population, can we conclude with $\alpha = .05$ that σ^2 is not equal to 200?

22, 53. 17, 61, 44, 36, 18

H_0:

H_A:

Test statistic:

Rejection region:

Value of the test statistic:

Conclusion:

11.13 A random sample of 18 observations from a normal population yielded the statistic $s^2 = 57.3$. Does this statistic permit us to conclude at the 1% significance level that σ^2 is less than 75.0?

H_0:

H_A:

Test statistic:

Rejection region:

Value of the test statistic:

Conclusion:

11.14 A contract for the delivery of 2 million steel shafts specifies that the variance must be no more than .012 mm^2. Before shipping out the shafts, the manufacturer samples 30 shafts and calculates the sample variance, which she finds to be $s^2 = .018$ mm^2. Can she conclude at the 10% significance level that the contract has been violated?

H_0:

H_A:

Test statistic:

Rejection region:

Value of the test statistic:

Conclusion:

11.15   Estimate the population variance in Exercise 11.14 with 95% confidence.

11.4 Inference About a Population Proportion

When the data are qualitative, the only legitimate calculation is to count the number of each type of outcome and compute proportions. It follows then that when the problem objective is to describe a single population of qualitative data, the parameter of interest is the population proportion p. In this section, we addressed the problem of drawing inferences about p.

The estimator of p is the sample proportion $\hat{p}$. Since $\hat{p} = x/n$ (where x is the number of successes in a sample of size n) and x is a binomial random variable, $\hat{p}$ is a binomial random variable. For inference purposes, however, we use the normal approximation to the binomial, a method discussed in Chapter 7. Thus, the sampling distribution of $\hat{p}$ is approximately normal. From this sampling distribution, we produce the test statistic and confidence interval estimator. The test statistic is

$$z = \frac{\hat{p} - p}{\sqrt{pq / n}}$$

The confidence interval estimator is

$$\hat{p} \pm z_{\alpha / 2} \sqrt{\hat{p}\hat{q} / n}$$

Example 11.4

A supplier of tomato seeds boasts that at least 95% of her tomato seeds will eventually produce tomato plants. A farmer decides to test the claim. He takes a random sample of 400 seeds and plants them. After two weeks he finds that there are only 368 plants. Can the farmer conclude at the 1% significance level that the supplier is wrong?

Solution

The problem objective is to describe the population of tomato plants produced from the supplier's seeds. The data are qualitative since there are only two possible values of the random variable—the seed produces a plant, or the seed does not produce a plant. Therefore, the parameter of interest is p. Since we wish to know if we can conclude that the supplier's boast is wrong, we test to determine if p is less than .95. We test

$H_0: p = .95$

$H_A: p < .95$

Test statistic: $z = \dfrac{\hat{p} - p}{\sqrt{pq / n}}$

Rejection region: $z < -z_\alpha = -z_{.01} = -2.33$

Value of the test statistic:

$\hat{p} = 368/400 = .92$

$z = \dfrac{.92 - .95}{\sqrt{(.95)(.05) / 40}} = -2.75$

Conclusion: Reject H_0.

There is sufficient evidence to indicate that $p < .95$ and that the supplier is wrong.

Example 11.5

Find the p-value of the test in Example 11.4.

Solution

Because the test statistic is approximately normally distributed, we can compute the p-value of the test. The alternative hypothesis was $H_A: p < .95$, and $z = -2.75$. Thus,

p-value $= p(z < -2.75) = .0030$

Example 11.6

A large department store located in a shopping center wanted to know what proportion of shopping center customers entered the department store. In a sample of 1,000 shopping center patrons, 361 entered the department store. Find the 99% confidence interval estimate of the proportion.

Solution

The problem objective is to describe the population of shopping center customers, and the data are qualitative. Therefore, the parameter to be estimated is p. The confidence interval estimate is

$$\hat{p} \pm z_{\alpha/2}\sqrt{\hat{p}\hat{q}/n} = .361 \pm 2.575 \sqrt{(.361)(.639)/1,000}$$

$$= .361 \pm .039$$

Question:	I'm a bit confused about identifying qualitative data. For example, suppose I'm told that in a sample of 1,000, there were 361 successes. Doesn't this mean that we're dealing with quantitative data?
Answer:	No. To identify the type of data, you must think about the actual observations and not the summarized results. The experiment referred to in the question clearly indicates that each of the 1,000 patrons in the sample was categorized as either a success (entered the department store) or a failure (did not enter the department store). Thus, the data are qualitative. The number of successes (361) is the way in which this type of data is summarized (much like the mean and variance summarize quantitative data).

Selecting the Sample Size to Estimate a Proportion

To determine the sample size necessary to estimate p to within B, we use the formula

$$n = \left[\frac{z_{\alpha/2}\sqrt{\hat{p}\hat{q}}}{B} \right]^2$$

If we have no knowledge about a likely value for $\hat{p}$, we let $\hat{p}$ equal .5 (and since $\hat{q} = 1 - \hat{p}$, $\hat{q}$ also equals .5).

Example 11.7

Suppose that in Example 8.6, we wanted to estimate the proportion of shopping center customers who entered the store to within .02 with 99% confidence. Find the sample size.

Solution

If we have no information about the value of the sample proportion, we let $\hat{p} = \hat{q} = .5$. Because the error bound $B = .02$ and $z_{\alpha/2} = z_{.005} = 2.575$, we find

$$n = \left[\frac{z_{\alpha/2}\sqrt{\hat{p}\hat{q}}}{B} \right]^2 = \left[\frac{2.575\sqrt{(.5)(.5)}}{.02} \right]^2 = 4{,}145$$

Thus, it would require a sample of 4,145 customers to estimate the proportion who enter the department store to within .02 with 99% confidence.

Incidentally, if we were quite certain that the sample proportion would be no larger than .40, the sample size would equal

$$n = \left[\frac{z_{\alpha/2}\sqrt{\hat{p}\hat{q}}}{B} \right]^2 = \left[\frac{2.575\sqrt{(.4)(.6)}}{.02} \right]^2 = 3{,}979$$

EXERCISES

11.16 Explain why $\hat{p}$ is an unbiased estimator of p.

11.17 Explain why $\hat{p}$ is a consistent estimator of p.

11.18 Test to determine if a finding of 12 defectives in a sample of 250 is sufficient evidence to conclude that the population proportion of defectives is more than 3%. Use $\alpha = .05$.

H_0:

H_A:

Test statistic:

Rejection region:

Value of the test statistic:

Conclusion:

11.19 Find the p-value of the test in Exercise 11.18.

164

11.20 Estimate the proportion of defectives in Exercise 11.18 with 95% confidence.

11.21 The RIDE Program (Reduce Impaired Driving Everywhere) is a series of police spot checks checking drivers at random to apprehend drunk drivers. It is believed that the program reduces the incidence of impaired driving. Prior to its inception, the proportion of drunk drivers was known to be 4%. One month after the RIDE Program began, a random sample of 628 drivers was selected. Seventeen drivers were found to be impaired. Is this statistical result sufficient evidence at the 10% significance level to allow the police to conclude that the RIDE Program is successful?

H_0:

H_A:

Test statistic:

Rejection region:

Value of the test statistic:

Conclusion:

11.22 Find the p-value of the test in Exercise 11.21.

11.23 In a sample of 100 high school students, 12 said that they regularly smoke cigarettes. Find the 95% confidence interval estimate of the proportion of all high school students who smoke.

11.24 Find the sample size necessary to estimate p with 95% confidence to within .05 of the true value if we have no idea about the value of $\hat{p}$.

11.25 Repeat Exercise 11.24 if we know that $\hat{p}$ will be at least .80.

11.26 Repeat Exercise 11.24 if we know that $\hat{p}$ will be less than .10.

Chapter 12: Inference About The Comparison Of Two Populations

12.1 Introduction

The methods of drawing inferences when comparing two populations were discussed in this chapter. When the data are quantitative and we want to compare measures of location, the parameter of interest is the difference between two means, $\mu_1 - \mu_2$. When the descriptive measure is variability, we draw inferences about the ratio of two variances σ_1^2 / σ_2^2. In problems where the data are qualitative, the parameter of interest is the difference between two proportions, $p_1 - p_2$.

Because three new parameters were introduced in this chapter, the importance of being capable of identifying the correct technique to use is growing. As you work your way through each example and exercise below, make certain that you understand how we determine what the parameter is and what statistical technique needs to be employed.

You are expected to know the following by the time you finish this chapter:

1. How to apply the concepts and techniques of estimation and hypothesis testing introduced in Chapters 9 and 10.
2. How to recognize when the parameter of interest is the difference between two population means.
3. How to recognize when the samples were independently drawn and when they were taken from a matched pairs experiment.
4. How to determine when to use the equal-variances and unequal variances t-test and estimator of $\mu_1 - \mu_2$.
5. How to recognize when the parameter of interest is the ratio of two population variances.
6. How to recognize when the parameter of interest is the difference between two proportions.
7. How to determine when to use the Case 1 test statistic and when to use the Case 2 test statistic when testing hypotheses about the difference between two proportions.

12.2 Inference About the Difference Between Two Means: Independent Samples

In this section, the problem objective was to compare two populations. The data are quantitative, the descriptive measure is location, and the samples are independently drawn. Hence, the parameter we estimate and test is $\mu_1 - \mu_2$.

There are two sets of formulas used to make inferences about $\mu_1 - \mu_2$. The formulas and the conditions that tell us when they are used are listed below.

1. When the population variances are unknown and equal ($\sigma_1^2 = \sigma_2^2$), the test statistic is

$$t = \frac{(\bar{x}_1 - \bar{x}_2) - (\mu_1 - \mu_2)}{\sqrt{s_p^2\,(1/n_1 + 1/n_2)}} \qquad \text{d.f.} = n_1 + n_2 - 2$$

The confidence interval estimator is

$$(\bar{x}_1 - \bar{x}_2) \pm t_{\alpha/2}\sqrt{s_p^2\,(1/n_1 + 1/n_2)}$$

2. In problems where the population variances are unknown and unequal, the test statistic is

$$t = \frac{(\bar{x}_1 - \bar{x}_2) - (\mu_1 - \mu_2)}{\sqrt{s_1^2/n_1 + s_2^2/n_2}} \qquad \text{d.f.} = \frac{(s_1^2/n_1 + s_2^2/n_2)^2}{\dfrac{(s_1^2/n_1)^2}{n_1 - 1} + \dfrac{(s_2^2/n_2)^2}{n_2 - 1}}$$

The confidence interval estimate is

$$(\bar{x}_1 - \bar{x}_2) \pm t_{\alpha/2}\sqrt{s_1^2/n_1 + s_2^2/n_2}$$

Example 12.1

A study of the scholastic aptitude test (SAT) revealed that in a random sample of 100 males the mean SAT score was 431.5 with a standard deviation of 93.7. A random sample of 100 female SAT scores produced a mean of 423.9 with a standard deviation of 88.6. Can we conclude at the 1% significance level that male and female scores differ?

Solution

The problem objective is to compare male and female SAT scores, a quantitative variable. Therefore, the parameter of interest is $(\mu_1 - \mu_2)$. The sample standard deviations are similar, making it reasonable to assume that $\sigma_1^2 = \sigma_2^2$. Thus, we employ the equal-variances t-test. The complete test follows.

H_0: $(\mu_1 - \mu_2) = 0$
H_A: $(\mu_1 - \mu_2) \neq 0$

Rejection region: $|t| > t_{\alpha/2, n1+n2-2} = t_{.005,198} \approx 2.601$

Test statistic: $t = \dfrac{(\bar{x}_1 - \bar{x}_2) - (\mu_1 - \mu_2)}{\sqrt{s_p^2\left(\dfrac{1}{n_1} + \dfrac{1}{n_2}\right)}} = \dfrac{(431.5 - 423.9) - 0}{\sqrt{8315\left(\dfrac{1}{100} + \dfrac{1}{100}\right)}} = .59$

Conclusion: Do not reject H_0.

There is not enough evidence to conclude that male and female SAT scores differ.

Example 12.2

Estimate the difference between male and female mean SAT scores (in Example 12.1) with 90% confidence.

Solution

The confidence interval estimate is

$$(\bar{x}_1 - \bar{x}_2) \pm t_{\alpha/2} \sqrt{s_p^2\left(\frac{1}{n_1} + \frac{1}{n_2}\right)} = (431.5 - 423.9) \pm 1.653\sqrt{8315\left(\frac{1}{100} + \frac{1}{100}\right)}$$

$$= 7.6 \pm 21.3$$

Example 12.3

A statistician wants to compare the relative success of two large department store chains. She decides to measure the sales per square foot. She takes a random sample of five stores from chain 1 and five stores from chain 2. The gross sales per square foot are shown below. Do these data provide sufficient evidence to indicate that the two chains differ? (Test with $\alpha = .10$.)

Chain 1	Chain 2
65.50	82.50
72.00	63.50
103.00	68.00
93.50	70.00
82.60	66.50

Solution

The problem objective is to compare the population of sales per square foot of one chain with the population of sales per square foot of another chain. As a result, the parameter of interest is $\mu_1 - \mu_2$. The sample variances are quite different; we can assume that $\sigma_1^2 \neq \sigma_2^2$. The appropriate technique is the unequal variances t-test of $\mu_1 - \mu_2$.

H_0: $(\mu_1 - \mu_2) = 0$
H_A: $(\mu_1 - \mu_2) \neq 0$

Test statistic: $t = \dfrac{(\bar{x}_1 - \bar{x}_2) - (\mu_1 - \mu_2)}{\sqrt{s_1^2/n_1 + s_2^2/n_2}}$

d.f. $= \dfrac{(s_1^2/n_1 + s_2^2/n_2)^2}{\dfrac{(s_1^2/n_1)^2}{n_1 - 1} + \dfrac{(s_2^2/n_2)^2}{n_2 - 1}}$

Rejection region: $|t| > t_{\alpha/2, d.f.} \approx t_{.05, 6} = 1.943$

Value of the test statistic:

$$\bar{x}_1 = 83.32 \qquad \bar{x}_2 = 70.10$$

$$s_1^2 = 234.29 \qquad s_2^2 = 53.67$$

$$\text{d.f.} = \frac{(234.29/5+53.67/5)^2}{\dfrac{(234.29/5)^2}{4}+\dfrac{(53.67/5)^2}{4}}$$

$$= 5.7 \approx 6$$

$$t = \frac{(\bar{x}_1-\bar{x}_2)-(\mu_1-\mu_2)}{\sqrt{s_p^2(1/n_1+1/n_2)}} = \frac{(83.32-70.10)-0}{\sqrt{234.29/5+53.67/5}} = 1.74$$

Conclusion: Do not reject H_0.

There is not enough evidence to indicate that the mean sales per square foot differ between the two chains.

EXERCISES

12.1   Test to determine if there is enough evidence to indicate that μ_1 exceeds μ_2 for the following situation. (Use $\alpha = .05$)

$$\begin{array}{ll} \bar{x}_1 = 28 & \bar{x}_2 = 20 \\ s_1 = 10 & s_2 = 12 \\ n_1 = 50 & n_2 = 40 \end{array}$$

H_0:

H_A:

Test statistic:

Rejection region:

Value of the test statistic:

Conclusion:

12.2 Estimate $\mu_1 - \mu_2$ with 95% confidence using the results of Exercise 12.1.

12.3 A statistician found that in a random sample of 43 cans of paint produced by one manufacture the mean drying time was $\bar{x}_1 = 185$ minutes, with a standard deviation of 20 minutes. In a random sample of 40 cans of paint produced by another manufacturer, the mean drying time was $\bar{x}_2 = 201$ minutes, with a standard deviation of 57 minutes. Do these data allow us to conclude at the 10% significance level that the mean drying times of the two kinds of paints differ?

H_0:

H_A:

Test statistic:

Rejection region:

Value of the test statistic:

Conclusion:

12.4 Estimate the difference between mean drying times with 99% confidence for the data in Exercise 12.3.

12.5 Find the 95% confidence interval estimate of $\mu_1 - \mu_2$ for Example 12.3.

12.6 An automobile parts manufacturer has been experimenting with a new type of spark plug designed to improve gas mileage. In order to determine if the new spark plug is effective, eight cars are randomly selected. The conventional spark plug is installed in four of the cars, and the new experimental spark plug is installed in the other four. The gas mileage is measured and reported below. Can we conclude at the 5% significance level that the new experimental spark plug is effective in increasing gas mileage?

Experimental Spark Plug	Conventional Spark Plug
23	25
28	29
36	26
24	20

H_0:

H_A:

Test statistic:

Rejection region:

Value of the test statistic:

Conclusion:

12.7 Find the 99% confidence interval estimate of $(\mu_1 - \mu_2)$ for Exercise 12.6.

12.4 Inference About the Difference Between Two Means: Matched Pairs Experiment

The greatest difficulty encountered by students in this section is recognizing when an experiment has been conducted using matched pairs. If you are such a student, bear in mind that a matched pairs experiment has been conducted when, because of the way in which the samples were selected, there is a direct connection between an observation in one sample and an observation in the second sample. That direct connection may be very strong, such as when one group of people is used to measure the effectiveness of a sleeping pill or when one set of cars is used to measure the gas mileage of each of two different gasolines. The connection can be fairly weak, such as comparing the amount of traffic at two intersections when the times of the day or the days of the week are matched. In any situation where a direct connection exists between each pair of observations (one from the first sample and one from the second sample), the experiment is matched pairs.

The test statistic is

$$t = \frac{\bar{x}_D - \mu_D}{s_D / \sqrt{n_D}}$$

with d.f. $= n_D - 1$.

The confidence interval estimator is

$$\bar{x}_D \pm t_{\alpha/2}\, s_D / \sqrt{n_D}$$

Example 12.4

A plant that operates two shifts would like to know if the two shifts differ in productivity. The number of units that each shift produces in each of the 5 days is counted and recorded below. Can we conclude that the two shifts differ in the mean number of units per shift? Test with $\alpha = .10$.

Day	Shift 1	Shift 2
Monday	263	265
Tuesday	288	278
Wednesday	290	277
Thursday	275	268
Friday	255	244

Solution

The problem objective is to compare two populations where the data are quantitiative. The experiment is matched pairs, because each observation for shift 1 is matched by the day of the week with an observation for shift 2. That is, sample 1 and sample 2 are connected by the days of the week. Hence, the appropriate statistical technique is the t-test of μ_D.

$H_0: \mu_D = 0$

$H_A: \mu_D \neq 0$

Test statistic: $t = \dfrac{\bar{x}_D - \mu_D}{s_D / \sqrt{n_D}}$

Rejection region: $|t| > t_{\alpha/2,\, n_D-1} = t_{.05,\, 4} = 2.132$

Value of the test statistic:

$D = x_1 - x_2 = -2,\ 10,\ 13,\ 7,\ 11$

$\bar{x}_D = 7.80$

$s_D = 5.89$

$t = \dfrac{\bar{x}_D - \mu_D}{s_D / \sqrt{n_D}} = \dfrac{7.80 - 0}{5.89 / \sqrt{5}} = 2.96$

Conclusion: Reject H_0.

There is enough evidence to indicate that the two shifts differ in the mean number of units per shift.

EXERCISES

12.8   An accountant is in the process of investigating the consequences of switching to another method of depreciating assets. In particular, she would like to know if the switch will result in a decrease in after-tax profit. To help decide, she randomly selects six firms and calculates the after-tax profits using both depreciation methods. The results (rounded to the nearest million) are shown below. Do these data provide sufficient evidence to indicate that the adoption of method 2 results in a lower after-tax profit? Test with $\alpha = .05$.

Company	Method 1	Method 2
A	87	84
B	18	19
C	66	64
D	112	105
E	77	74
F	27	25

H_0:

H_A:

Test statistic:

Rejection region:

Value of the test statistic:

Conclusion:

12.9   Find the 99% confidence interval estimate of the mean difference in Exercise 12.8.

12.10 Find the 99% confidence interval estimate of the mean difference in Example 12.4.

12.11 The automotive parts manufacturer referred to in Exercise 12.6 concluded that the reason his product was not shown to be superior was because of too much variation between cars. To eliminate that variation, he decided to redo the experiment by selecting four cars. Each is operated for a set number of miles with the experimental spark plug and again with the conventional spark plug. (The order is randomly determined.) The results are shown below. Do these data provide sufficient evidence at the 5% significance level to conclude that the experimental spark plug is effective in increasing gas mileage?

Car	Experimental Spark Plug	Conventional Spark Plug
1	36	34
2	25	22
3	29	28
4	20	19

H_0:

H_A:

Test statistic:

Rejection region:

Value of the test statistic:

Conclusion:

12.13   Find the 95% confidence interval estimate of the mean difference in Exercise 12.11.

12.5 Inference About the Ratio of Two Variances

We test and estimate the parameter σ_1^2 / σ_2^2 in cases where we want to compare two populations of quantitative data and the descriptive measurement is variability. The test statistic use to test σ_1^2 / σ_2^2 is

$$F = s_1^2 / s_2^2$$

which is F-distributed with v_1 and v_2 degrees of freedom where $v_1 = n_1 - 1$ and $v_2 = n_2 - 1$. The confidence interval estimator is

$$LCL = \left(\frac{s_1^2}{s_2^2} \right) \frac{1}{F_{\alpha/2, v_1, v_2}}$$

$$UCL = F_{\alpha/2, v_2, v_1}$$

It is assumed that the populations from which we've sampled are normally distributed.

Example 12.5

A statistician wanted to perform a t-test of $\mu_1 - \mu_2$ with $n_1 = 16$ and $n_2 = 25$. One of the requirements of this test is that the two unknown population variances are equal. She found that $s_1^2 = 56$ and $s_2^2 = 18$. Can she conclude with $\alpha = .10$ that the assumption of equal variances is not valid?

Solution

H_0: $\sigma_1^2 / \sigma_2^2 = 1$

H_A: $\sigma_1^2 / \sigma_2^2 \neq 1$

Test statistic: $F = s_1^2 / s_2^2$

Rejection region: $F > F_{\alpha/2, v_1, v_2} = F_{.05, 15, 24} = 2.11$

$$\text{or } F < F_{1-\alpha/2, v_1, v_2} = F_{.95, 15, 24} = \frac{1}{F_{.05, 24, 15}} = \frac{1}{2.29} = .437$$

Value of the test statistic: $F = 56/18 = 3.11$

Conclusion: Reject H_0.

There is sufficient evidence to indicate that the assupmption of equal variances is invalid.

Example 12.6

In Example 12.5, estimate σ_1^2 / σ_2^2 with 95% confidence.

Solution

$$\text{LCL} = \left(\frac{s_1^2}{s_2^2}\right) \frac{1}{F_{\alpha/2, v_1, v_2}} = (3.11)\frac{1}{F_{.025, 15, 24}} = \frac{3.11}{2.44} = 1.27$$

$$\text{UCL} = \left(\frac{s_1^2}{s_2^2}\right) F_{\alpha/2, v_2, v_1} = (3.11)F_{.025, 24, 15} = (3.11)(2.70) = 8.40$$

EXERCISES

12.14   In random samples of 8 and 10 from two normal populations, it was found that $s_1^2 = 128$ and $s_2^2 = 45$, respectively. Do these statistics allow us to conclude that the variance of population 1 exceeds the variance of population 2? Use $\alpha = .05$.

H_0:

H_A:

Test statistic:

Rejection region:

Value of the test statistic:

Conclusion:

12.15   In Exercise 12.14, estimate σ_1^2 / σ_2^2 with 98% confidence.

12.16   An educational statistician wanted to determine whether the scholastic aptitude test (SAT) scores achieved by children living in cities was less variable than scores achieved by children living in the suburbs. A random sample of 25 SAT scores of city children yielded a variance of $s_1^2 = 7,814$. A random sample of 25 SAT scores of suburban children produced a variance of $s_2^2 = 9,258$. At the 5% significance level, can we conclude that the city SAT score variance is less than the suburban SAT score variance?

H_0:

H_A:

Test statistic:

Rejection region:

Value of the test statistic:

Conclusion:

12.17   In Exercise 12.16, estimate σ_1^2 / σ_2^2 with 95% confidence.

12.6 Inference About the Difference Between Two Proportions

When the problem objective is to compare two populations and the data are qualitative, the parameter we make inferences about is the difference between two population proportions. There are two test statistics. The choice of which to use is made on the basis of the null hypothesis. If the null hypothesis states that the two proportions are identical (H_0: $p_1 - p_2 = 0$), the test statistic is

$$\text{Case 1: } z = \frac{(\hat{p}_1 - \hat{p}_2)}{\sqrt{\hat{p}\hat{q}\,(1/n_1 + 1/n_2)}}$$

If the null hypothesis states that the difference between the two proportions is a value other than zero (H_0: $p_1 - p_2 = .10$), the test statistic is

$$\text{Case 2: } z = \frac{(\hat{p}_1 - \hat{p}_2) - (p_1 - p_2)}{\sqrt{\hat{p}_1\hat{q}_1/n_1 + \hat{p}_2\hat{q}_2/n_2}}$$

The confidence interval estimator is

$$(\hat{p}_1 - \hat{p}_2) \pm z_{\alpha/2}\sqrt{\hat{p}_1\hat{q}_1/n_1 + \hat{p}_2\hat{q}_2/n_2}$$

> *Question:* How do I determine whether a particular problem is Case 1 or Case 2?
>
> *Answer:* If the question asks if there is enough evidence to conclude that p_1 is not equal to p_2, greater than p_2, or less than p_2, the problem is Case 1. If we're asked to show that the difference between p_1 and p_2 is not equal to, greater than, or less than a specific value, the problem is Case 2.

Example 12.7

A police detective is examining the crime rates in two different areas of the city. One area is middle class, while the second area is quite affluent. The detective believes that the proportion of burglarized homes in the middle-class area is greater than the proportion of burglarized homes in the affluent area. From random samples of 1,000 homes in each area, he finds that last year there were 32 burglaries in the middle-class area and 14 in the affluent area. At the 1% significance level, can we conclude that the detective's belief is correct?

Solution

The problem objective is to compare two populations—the population of homes in the middle-class area and the population of homes in the affluent area. The data are qualitative since the values of the variable are "the home was burglarized" and "the home was not burglarized." Finally, because we want to determine if one proportion is greater than a second proportion, the null and alternative hypotheses are

H_0: $(p_1 - p_2) = 0$
H_A: $(p_1 - p_2) > 0$

where p_1 = proportion of burglarized homes in the middle-class area, and

p_2 = proportion of burglarized homes in the affluent area

This is a situation described by Case 1, so that

Test statistic: $z = \dfrac{(\hat{p}_1 - \hat{p}_2)}{\sqrt{\hat{p}\hat{q} \, (1/n_1 + 1/n_2)}}$

Rejection region: $z > z_\alpha = z_{.01} = 2.33$

Value of the test statistic:

$\hat{p}_1 = 32/1{,}000 = .032$

$\hat{p}_2 = 14/1{,}000 = .014$

$\hat{p} = (32+14)/(1{,}000+1{,}000) = .023$

$z = \dfrac{(.032-.014)}{\sqrt{(.023)(.977)(1/1{,}000+1/1{,}000)}} = 2.69$

Conclusion: Reject H_0.

There is sufficient evidence to conclude that the detective's belief is correct.

Example 12.8

In Example 12.7, estimate $p_1 - p_2$ with 90% confidence.

Solution

There is only one confidence interval estimator of $p_1 - p_2$. It is

$(\hat{p}_1 - \hat{p}_2) \pm z_{\alpha/2} \sqrt{\hat{p}_1\hat{q}_1 / n_1 + \hat{p}_2\hat{q}_2 / n_2}$
$= (.032 - .014) \pm 1.645\sqrt{(.032)(.968) / 1{,}000 + (.014)(.986) / 1{,}000}$
$= .018 \pm .011$

Example 12.9

Suppose that in Example 12.7 the detective believes that the proportion of burglarized homes in the middle-class area is more than 1% higher than the proportion of burglarized homes in the affluent area. Once again, test the detective's belief at the 1% significance level.

Solution

The null and alternative hypotheses are

H_0: $(p_1 - p_2) = .01$
H_A: $(p_1 - p_2) > .01$

Because the null hypthesis indicates a value other than zero, this situation is described as Case 2. Therefore,

Test statistic: $z = \dfrac{(\hat{p}_1 - \hat{p}_2) - (p_1 - p_2)}{\sqrt{\hat{p}_1\hat{q}_1 / n_1 + \hat{p}_2\hat{q}_2 / n_2}}$

Rejection region: $z > z_\alpha = z_{.01} = 2.33$

Value of the test statistic:

$$z = \frac{(.032 - .014) - .01}{\sqrt{(.032)(.968) / 1,000 + (.014)(.986) / 1,000}} = 1.20$$

Conclusion: Do not reject H_0.

There is not enough evidence to conclude that the proportion of burglarized middle-class homes exceeds the proportion of burglarized affluent homes by more than 1%.

EXERCISES

12.18 Test with $\alpha = .05$ to determine if the following data allow us to conclude that p_1 is less than p_2.

$$x_1 = 200 \quad n_1 = 1,000$$
$$x_2 = 300 \quad n_2 = 1,200$$

H_0:

H_A:

Test statistic:

Rejection region:

Value of the test statistic:

Conclusion:

12.19 A random sample of 250 units from one production line produced 25 defectives. In a random sample of 400 units from a second production line, 80 were found to be defective. Can we conclude at the 1% significance level that the defective rate from the second production line exceeds the proportion defective from the first production line by more than 5%?

H_0:

H_A:

Test statistic:

Rejection region:

Value of the test statistic:

Conclusion:

12.20 For Exercise 12.19, estimate $p_1 - p_2$ with 90% confidence.

12.21 In July 1987, the Candian parliament debated the reinstatement of the death penalty. One of the factors in this debate was the amount of public support for the death penalty. In 1982, a sample of 1,500 Canadians revealed that 70% favored the death penalty. In 1987, 61% in a sample of 1,500 supported the death penalty. Do these data provide sufficient evidence at the 1% significance level to indicate that support has fallen between 1982 and 1987?

H_0:

H_A:

Test statistic:

Rejection region:

Value of the test statistic:

Conclusion:

12.22 Referring to Exercise 12.21, can we conclude with $\alpha = .01$ that support for the death penalty has fallen by more than 5 percentage points?

H_0:

H_A:

Test statistic:

Rejection region:

Value of the test statistic:

Conclusion:

12.23 In Exercise 12.21, estimate the difference in public support for the reinstatement of the death penalty between 1982 and 1987 with 95% confidence.

12.24 A company that produces an insect repellant is constantly looking for ways to improve the product. Each time a new formula is developed, it is tested by taking a random sample of 1,000 people. Five hundred people have the existing product sprayed on their arms, while the remaining 500 have the new formula sprayed on their arms. Each person then sits for 5 minutes with only their arms exposed in a room full of mosquitoes. The number of people who have at least one mosquito bite is recorded. Suppose that for one such experiment it was found that 45 people who used the existing product and 29 people who used the new formula suffered at least one mosquito bite. Do these results indicate at the 5% significance level that the new formula is better than the existing product?

H_0:
H_A:

Test statistic:

Rejection region:

Value of the test statistic:

Conclusion:

12.25 In Exercise 12.24, estimate $p_1 - p_2$ with 90% confidence.

Chapter 13: Statistical Inference: A Review of Chapters 11 And 12

13.1   Introduction

This chapter was much more than a review of the statistical techniques presented in the previous three chapters. As we've repeatedly said, the most difficult challenge facing statistics students is the problem of choosing the correct method. At this point, we think it is necessary for you to look back and check to see whether you can select the appropriate inferential procedure from the dozen or so already presented. Obviously, if you cannot identify the right technique now, you will be unable to perform that task later (in a real-world setting, in another course, or on the final exam in this course) when two or three times as many methods have been covered.

In this chapter, we provide 10 exercises whose solution requires the use of one of the statistical techniques introduced in Chapters 11 and 12. We recommend that you use the flowchart exhibited in the textbook (Figure 13.1). For each exercise, proceed through the flowchart answering all questions in order to eventually identify the method to use. Then specify the null and alternative hypotheses and the rejection region. Although in our solutions appearing at the back of this study guide we've shown complete solutions, including the calculation of the test statistic, we suggest that this last step is not absolutely necessary for you. It is far more important that you concentrate on technique identification than on the simple arithmetic needed to produce the value of the test statistic. If you're short of time, do not compute the test statistic.

For an illustration of how the flowchart is to be used, examine the following example.

Example 13.1

Several years ago, two adjacent counties elected school boards with diametrically different philosophies of education. Each school board established its own curriculums and standards. To determine whether differences exist between the two counties in terms of the success of their high school students, a preliminary study was launched. Random samples of 100 20-year-olds were drawn from each county. The respondents were asked the following questions.

a)   Did you complete high school?

   1. Yes   0. No

b)   How many years of high school did you complete?

The data are not shown. (Assume that they were stored on a data disk.)

Determine the statistical techniques and specify the null and alternative hypotheses, the test statistic, and the rejection region (using $\alpha = 5\%$) to conclude that differences between the two counties exist in terms of dropout rates and years of high school completed.

Solution

For help in answering these questions, we turn to the flowchart.

<u>Dropouts</u>

The first question in the flowchart asks us to determine the problem objective. We want to compare two populations (the records of the two counties). Next we're asked to ascertain the type of data. The data are qualitative, because the responses are "Yes, I completed high school" and "No, I did not complete high school." The flowchart does not require the answers to any other questions to determine the correct method to use. It is the z-test of $p_1 - p_2$. The hypotheses and the test statistic are as follows:

$H_0: (p_1 - p_2) = 0$
$H_A: (p_1 - p_2) \neq 0$

Test statistic:

$$(\text{Case 1}) \; z = \frac{(\hat{p}_1 - \hat{p}_2)}{\sqrt{\hat{p}\hat{q} \; (1/n_1 + 1/n_2)}}$$

<u>Years of High School completed</u>

The problem objective is the same—to compare two populations. The data are quantitative, because in this case we're working with real numbers that were not arbitrarily assigned—years of high school completed. For this combination of problem objective and data type, the flowchart has more questions. The next question asks for the descriptive measurement. We're interested in comparing the population locations to determine if one county is more successful than the other in persuading students to stay in high school. Next we're asked to identify the experimental design. The experiment did not require any matching between the two samples. Accordingly, we specify that the samples are independent. Next, we're asked whether the data are normal. Drawing histograms of each group would provide some insight. Let us suppose that the histograms are bell-shaped. The flowchart then asks if the population variances are equal. We can conduct an F-test of σ_1^2 / σ_2^2 to answer. We'll assume that they are. At this point, the flowchart tells us that the appropriate technique is the equal-variances test of $\mu_1 - \mu_2$. The test would be conducted in the following way:

$H_0: (\mu_1 - \mu_2) = 0$
$H_A: (\mu_1 - \mu_2) \neq 0$

Test statistic:

$$t = \frac{(\bar{x}_1 - \bar{x}_2) - (\mu_1 - \mu_2)}{\sqrt{s_p^2 \left(\frac{1}{n_1} + \frac{1}{n_2} \right)}}$$

The computer could be used to produce the values of the test statistic and draw conclusions.

EXERCISES

13.1 In the game of squash, it is quite common for the ball to attain speeds in excess of 100 mph. As a result, squash balls do not last very long. In an effort to improve the longevity of squash balls, a sporting goods manufacturer has been experimenting with a new type of squash ball construction. To assess the results, 50 squash balls made the conventional way and another 50 made the experimental way are distributed to amateur squash players. Each player is told to use the squash balls until they split and record the number of complete games for which the balls were used. The statistical results are as follows:

Conventional Squash Ball	Experimental Squash Ball
$\bar{x}_1$ = 13.6 games	$\bar{x}_2$ = 14.7 games
s_1 = 3.9 games	s_2 = 1.8 games

Do these statistics allow the manufacturer to conclude at the 5% significance level that the experimental squash ball is superior? (Assume that the data are normal.)

H_0:

H_A:

Test statistic:

Rejection region:

Value of the test statistic:

Conclusion:

13.2   A distributor of low-priced jewelry sells most of his product by mail order. In his newspaper and magazine advertising, he offers a money-back guarantee if the customer is not satisfied with the purchase. The distributor has calculated that if more than 15% of his customers return their purchases he will be in financial trouble. In a random sample of 512 purchasers, it was found that 101 returned their purchases and demanded their money back. Do these data indicate, with $\alpha = .10$, that the distributor is in financial trouble?

H_0:

H_A:

Test statistic:

Rejection region:

Value of the test statistic:

Conclusion:

13.3   An oil exploration company is in the process of deciding in which of two large geographic regions it intends to drill a series of exploratory wells. In the past two years, region 1 has produced 12 oil wells and 27 dry holes. During the same period, region 2 has produced 19 oil wells and 32 dry holes. The company would prefer to drill in region 1 because it costs less to explore that region. However, if it can be shown that region 2 is more likely to produce a successful well, that region will be selected. With $\alpha = .10$, what should the company do?

H_0:

H_A:

Test statistic:

Rejection region:

Value of the test statistic:

Conclusion:

13.4 A spokesman for the gasoline retailers in a large state claims that the price charged for a gallon of gasoline is less variable in his state than in all the surrounding states. To test his claim, a random sample of 15 service stations in his state and 25 stations in the surrounding states is taken. In his state, he found the statistics $\bar{x}_1 = 103\cent$ and $s_1 = 3.5\cent$. In the other states, he found $\bar{x}_2 = 102.5\cent$ and $s_2 = 5.6\cent$. Do these statistics provide sufficient evidence at the 5% significance level to support the spokesman's claim? (Assume that the data are normal.)

H_0:

H_A:

Test statistic:

Rejection region:

Value of the test statistic:

Conclusion:

13.5 A diet doctor claims that dieting alone is not effective in reducing weight and maintaining any weight losses. She claims that a moderate diet with at least 30 minutes of exercise per day is considerably more effective. To test her belief, she selects 12 overweight women at random. She places 6 of them on a standard diet and the other 6 on a diet and exercise program. Each person is weighed at the start of the experiment and again 10 weeks later. The results are shown in the accompanying table. Can we conclude at the 5% significance level that the doctor is correct? (Assume that the data are normal.)

Diet Alone		Diet Plus Exercise	
Weight at Start	Weight After 10 Weeks	Weight at Start	Weight After 10 Weeks
170	170	177	167
192	186	166	155
206	201	209	189
166	166	193	188
153	150	198	181
188	172	152	144

H_0:

H_A:

Test statistic:

Rejection region:

Value of the test statistic:

Conclusion:

13.6   As a safety measure, wood paneling is made as nonflammable as possible. A wood product manufacturer would like to make its product less flammable by coating it with a special new chemical solution. However, because of the chemical's cost, it will not be used unless it can be shown to improve the product. As an experiment, six different types of wood paneling are selected. Each piece is split into two halves, with one half being treated with the chemical solution. Each half is then placed over an open flame, and the number of seconds until the panel bursts into flame is recorded. The results are exhibited below. Do these data provide sufficient evidence at the 5% significance level to conclude that the chemical solution is effective? (Assume that the data are normal.)

Panel Type	Treated	Untreated
1	73	70
2	52	53
3	47	41
4	81	72
5	66	60
6	79	70

H_0:

H_A:

Test statistic:

Rejection region:

Value of the test statistic:

Conclusion:

13.7   A soft drink manufacturer would like to know if there is a difference between men and women in terms of their preference for its product. In a survey of a random sample of 325 men, 58 expressed a preference for the soft drink. In a sample of 412 women, 88 preferred the soft drink. Can we conclude, with $\alpha = .05$, that a difference exits between men and women in their soft drink preference?

H_0:
H_A:

Test statistic:

Rejection region:

Value of the test statistic:

Conclusion:

13.8　University bookstores are often accused of having inflated prices for textbooks. To examine this issue, a representative of the student council at a large university randomly selected eight books that are required reading. She found the prices of the books at the university bookstore and the prices charged at an off-campus bookstore. The results are shown below. Do these data allow the representative to conclude at the 5% significance level that the campus bookstore is more expensive than the off-campus bookstore? (Assume that the data are nonnormal.)

Book	Campus Bookstore Price	Off-campus Bookstore Price
1	$27.50	$26.00
2	33.45	31.95
3	19.25	22.50
4	25.65	24.90
5	23.70	24.00
6	19.20	18.50
7	29.30	27.10
8	38.50	35.00

H_0:

H_A:

Test statistic:

Rejection region:

Value of the test statistic:

Conclusion:

13.9 The loan manager of a new bank branch believes that the average loan request will be higher at her branch than the average at the other branches of the bank. The mean loan request at all branches is known to be \$3,600. A random sample of 20 loan requests at the new branch yielded the statistics $\bar{x} = \$3,915$ and $s = \$502$. At the 5% significance level, can we conclude that the loan manager is correct?

H_0:

H_A:

Test statistic:

Rejection region:

Value of the test statistic:

Conclusion:

13.10 In recent years, the post office has been criticized for slow service and lost mail. In response, the post office claims that its loss rate of less than one item per thousand is unchanged. In a random sample of 8,000 items, it was found that 16 were lost. Can we conclude at the 5% significance level that the post office's claim is incorrect?

H_0:

H_A:

Test statistic:

Rejection region:

Value of the test statistic:

Conclusion:

Chapter 14: Analysis of Variance

14.1   Introduction

In this chapter, we introduced the analysis of variance technique, which deals with problems whose objective is to compare two or more populations of quantitative data. You are expected to learn how to do the following:

1. Recognize when the analysis of variance is to be employed.
2. Recognize which of the two models introduced in this chapter is to be used.
3. How to interpret the ANOVA table.

14.2   Single-Factor (One-Way) Analysis of Variance: Independent Samples

When the k samples are drawn independently of each other, we partition the total sum of squares into two sources of variability: sum of squares for treatment and sum of squares for error. The F-test is then used to complete the technique.

The important formulas are

$$SS(\text{Total}) = \sum_{j=1}^{k} \sum_{i=1}^{n_j} (x_{ij} - \overline{\overline{x}})^2$$

$$SST = \sum_{j=1}^{k} n_j (\overline{x}_j - \overline{\overline{x}})^2 = n_1(\overline{x}_1 - \overline{\overline{x}})^2 + n_2(\overline{x}_2 - \overline{\overline{x}})^2 + \dots + n_k(\overline{x}_k - \overline{\overline{x}})^2$$

$$SSE = \sum_{j=1}^{k} \sum_{i=1}^{n_j} (x_{ij} - \overline{x}_j)^2$$

$$= \sum_{i=1}^{n_1} (x_{i1} - \overline{x}_1)^2 + \sum_{i=1}^{n_2} (x_{i2} - \overline{x}_2)^2 + \dots + \sum_{i=1}^{n_k} (x_{ik} - \overline{x}_k)^2$$

$$= (n_1 - 1)s_1^2 + (n_2 - 1)s_2^2 + \dots + (n_k - 1)s_k^2$$

$$MST = \frac{SST}{k - 1}$$

$$MSE = \frac{SSE}{n - k}$$

$$F = \frac{MST}{MSE}$$

The ANOVA table for the completely randomized design is shown below.

Source	d.f.	Sums of Squares	Mean Squares	F-ratio
Treatments	$k - 1$	SST	MST	F
Error	$n - k$	SSE	MSE	
Total	$n - 1$	SS(Total)		

Example 14.1

A major computer manufacturer has received numerous complaints concerning the short life of its disk drives. Most need repair within two years. Since the cost of repairs often exceeds the cost of a new disk drive, the manufacturer is concerned. In his search for a better disk drive, he finds three new products. He decides to test these three plus his current disk drive to determine if differences in lifetimes exist among the products. He takes a random sample of five disk drives of each type and links it with a computer. The number of weeks until the drive breaks down is recorded and is shown below. Do these data allow us to conclude at the 5% significance level that there are differences among the disk drives?

Type 1	Type 2	Type 3	Current Product
78	125	143	101
92	110	125	96
101	116	133	88
105	88	108	125
98	128	121	128
$\bar{x}_1 = 94.8$	$\bar{x}_2 = 113.4$	$\bar{x}_3 = 126.0$	$\bar{x}_4 = 107.6$
$s_1^2 = 110.7$	$s_2^2 = 252.8$	$s_3^2 = 171.9$	$s_4^2 = 320.4$

Solution

The problem objective is to compare the populations of lifetimes of the four disk drives, and the data are quantitative. Because the samples are independent, the appropriate technique is the completely randomized design of the analysis of variance. The null and alternative hypotheses automatically follow.

H_0: $\mu_1 = \mu_2 = \mu_3 = \mu_4$

H_A: At least two means differ.

The rejection region is

$$F > F_{\alpha, k-1, n-k} = F_{.05, 3, 16} = 3.24$$

The test statistic is computed as follows:

$$n_1 = n_2 = n_3 = n_4 = 5$$

$$\overline{\overline{x}} = \frac{5(94.80) + 5(113.4) + 5(126.0) + 5(107.6)}{20} = \frac{2,209}{20} = 110.45$$

$$\text{SST} = 5(94.8 - 110.45)^2 + 5(113.4 - 110.45)^2 + 5(126.0 - 110.45)^2 + 5(107.6 - 110.45)^2$$

$$= 2,517.75$$

$$\text{SSE} = 4(110.7) + 4(252.8) + 4(171.9) + 4(320.4) = 3,423.2$$

$$\text{MST} = \frac{2,517.75}{3} = 839.25$$

$$\text{MSE} = \frac{3,423.2}{16} = 213.95$$

$$F = \frac{839.25}{213.95} = 3.92$$

The complete ANOVA table follows.

Source	d.f.	Sums of Squares	Mean Squares	F-ratio
Treatments	3	2,517.75	839.25	3.92
Error	16	3,423.2	213.95	
Total	19	5,940.95		

Since the F-ratio (3.92) exceeds $F_{\alpha, k-1, n-k}$ (3.24), we reject H_0 and conclude that at least two means differ.

EXERCISES

14.1   Complete the ANOVA table and F-test with $\alpha = .05$.

Source	d.f.	Sums of Squares	Mean Squares	F-ratio
Treatments	5			
Error		3,000		
Total	20	3,500		

14.2   Develop the ANOVA table from the following information and perform the F-test with $\alpha = .01$.

SS(Total)   =   150

SST   =   90

SSE   =   60

k = 5

$n_1 = 7$ $n_2 = 5$ $n_3 = 8$ $n_4 = 9$ $n_5 = 4$

ANOVA Table

Source	d.f.	Sums of Squares	Mean Squares	F-ratio

14.3 Test the hypotheses (with $\alpha = .10$)

H_0: $\mu_1 = \mu_2 = \mu_3$
H_A: At least two means differ.

given the following statistics:

$\bar{x}_1 = 25$	$\bar{x}_2 = 22$	$\bar{x}_3 = 31$
$s_1 = 6$	$s_2 = 11$	$s_3 = 9$
$n_1 = 5$	$n_2 = 8$	$n_3 = 10$

ANOVA Table

Source	d.f.	Sums of Squares	Mean Squares	F-ratio

14.4 Perform the analysis of variance test with $\alpha = .05$ using the following information:

Treatment	1	2	3	4
$\sum x_{ij}$	310	260	540	410
$\sum x_{ij}^2$	9,650	8,520	20,100	14,800
n_j	10	8	15	12

H_0:
H_A:

Rejection region:

Value of the test statistic:

ANOVA Table

Source	d.f.	Sums of Squares	Mean Squares	F-ratio

Conclusion:

14.5 A nationwide real estate chain is in the process of examining condominium prices across the country. The company has hired a statistician who takes a random sample of six sales in each of four cities. The results are recorded to the nearest thousand dollars and are shown below. Can we conclude from these data that there are differences in the selling prices of condominiums among the four cities? (Use $\alpha = .05$.)

New York	Chicago	Dallas	Los Angeles
253	199	273	305
178	256	185	288
212	285	176	266
315	232	203	328
248	277	219	275
296	189	224	244
$\sum x_i = 1{,}502$	$\sum x_i = 1{,}438$	$\sum x_i = 1{,}280$	$\sum x_i = 1{,}706$
$\sum x_i^2 = 388{,}982$	$\sum x_i^2 = 352{,}636$	$\sum x_i^2 = 279{,}076$	$\sum x_i^2 = 489{,}470$

H_0:

H_A:

Rejection region:

Value of the test statistic:

ANOVA Table

Source	d.f.	Sum of Squares	Mean Squares	F-ratio

Conclusion:

14.4 Single-Factor Analysis of Variance: Randomized Blocks

If the experimental design is randomized block, the total variation as measured by SS(Total) must be partitioned into three sources of variation: treatments (measured by SST), blocks (measured by SSB), and error (measured by SSE). The general form of the ANOVA table is shown below.

ANOVA Table for Randomized Block Design

Source	d.f.	Sums of Squares	Mean Squares	F-ratio
Treatments	$k-1$	SST	MST	$F = \text{MST/MSE}$
Blocks	$b-1$	SSB	MSB	$F = \text{MSB/MSE}$
Error	$n-k-b+1$	SSE	MSE	
Total	$n-1$	SS(Total)		

The rejection region for testing the treatment means is

$$F > F_{\alpha,\, k-1,\, n-k-b+1}$$

The rejection region for testing the block means is

$$F > F_{\alpha,\, b-1,\, n-k-b+1}$$

Example 14.2

The statistician in Exercise 14.5 decides to redo the experiment to eliminate the variation among condominium prices. In each city, the selling prices of a 1,000-square-foot, a 1,500-square-foot, a 2,000-square-foot, a 2,500-square-foot and a 3,000-square-foot condominium are randomly selected. The results are shown below.

Condominium Size	New York	Chicago	Dallas	Los Angeles
1,000 square feet	165	185	173	200
1,500 square feet	198	193	181	196
2,000 square feet	251	215	197	278
2,500 square feet	312	268	229	332
3,000 square feet	405	381	294	446

The following statistics were computed:

SST = 15,190.9

SSB = 107,157.7

SSE = 8,360.3

Complete the ANOVA table to determine if we can conclude at the 5% significance level that there are differences in condominium prices among the four cities.

Solution

We test the hypotheses

H_0: $\mu_1 = \mu_2 = \mu_3 = \mu_4$

H_A: At least two treatment means differ.

Rejection region: $F > F_{\alpha, k-1, n-k-b+1} = F_{.05,3,12} = 3.49$

Value of the test statistic: From the table below, we find $F = 7.3$.

Source	d.f.	Sums of Squares	Mean Squares	F-ratio
Treatments	3	15,190.9	5,063.6	7.3
Blocks	4	107,157.7	26,789.4	38.5
Error	12	8,360.3	696.7	
Total	19	130,708.9		

Conclusion: Reject H_0.

There is sufficient evidence to conclude that there are differences in condominium prices among the four cities.

EXERCISES

14.6 Complete the following ANOVA table (randomized block design).

Source	d.f.	Sums of Squares	Mean Squares	F-ratio
Treatments	5	300		
Blocks	8			
Error		400		
Total	53	1,000		

14.7 Refer to Exercise 14.6. Test to determine if there are differences among the treatment means with $\alpha = .01$.

14.8 Refer to Exercise 14.6. Test to determine if there are differences among the block means with $\alpha = .01$.

14.9 A large catalogue chain store has been experimenting with several methods of advertising its extensive variety of bicycles. Three kinds of catalogues have been prepared. In one, a side view of each bicycle is shown. In another, each bicycle's excellent record of longevity is extolled. In the third, pictures of the bicycles with their riders are shown. The company's management would like to know if there are differences in sales among the stores that use the different catalogues. The monthly sales of bicycles of three randomly selected stores, each using a different catalogue, are shown below. Do these data allow us to conclude that there are differences in bicycle sales among the stores using the three catalogues? Use $\alpha = .10$.

Monthly Bicycle Sales

Month	Catalogue		
	1	2	3
March	17	28	14
April	25	29	20
May	120	127	188
June	217	195	241
July	283	261	303
August	185	215	161
September	90	138	85
October	21	52	14

SST(Catalogues) = 523

SSB(Months) = 205,135

SS(Total) = 214,018

H_0:

H_A:

Rejection region:

Value of the test statistic:

ANOVA Table

Source	d.f.	Sums of Squares	Mean Squares	*F*-ratio

Conclusion:

Chapter 15: Additional Tests for Qualitative Data

15.1   Introduction

This chapter introduced two popular statistical procedures that use the chi-squared distribution to conduct tests on qualitative data. At the completion of this chapter, you are expected to know the following:

1. How to conduct a goodness-of-fit test on data that have been generated by a multinomial experiment.
2. How to conduct a test on data arranged in a contingency table to determine if two classifications of qualitative data are statistically independent.

15.2   Chi-Squared Test of a Multinomial Experiment

This section introduced an extension of the binomial experiment called the multinomial experiment, in which the outcome of each trial of the experiment can be classified as belonging to one of k categories, called cells. The goodness-of-fit test described in this section allows us to test hypotheses concerning the values of the probabilities p_i ($i = 1, 2, \ldots, k$), which represent the proportions of observations that belong to each of the k cells. The null and alternative hypotheses might, for example, be

H_0: $p_1 = .2, p_2 = .3, p_3 = .5$

H_A: At least one p_i is not equal to its specified value.

After a multinomial experiment has been conducted, the test involves a comparison of the observed frequencies (o_i) of outcomes that fall into each of the k cells with the frequencies (e_i) that are expected for each cell. For a multinomial experiment consisting of n trials, the expected frequencies are calculated from the hypothesized probabilities p_i:

$e_i = np_i$, for $i = 1, 2, \ldots, k$

The test statistic used to compare the observed and expected frequencies is

$$\chi^2 = \sum_{i=1}^{k} \frac{(o_i - e_i)^2}{e_i},$$

which has an approximate chi-squared distribution with $k - 1$ degrees of freedom. Since only relatively large values of the differences ($o_i - e_i$), and thus of χ^2, would cause us to suspect that the values specified in the null hypothesis are incorrect, the rejection region is always located in the right tail of the chi-squared distribution.

The rule of five requires that the expected frequency (e_i) for each cell be at least 5. Where necessary, cells should be combined so that this condition is satisfied.

Example 15.1

The records of an investment banking firm show that, historically, 60% of its clients were primarily interested in the stock market, 36% in the bonds market, and 4% in the futures market. A recent sample of 200 clients showed that 132 were primarily interested in stocks, 52 in bonds, and 16 in futures. Is there sufficient evidence to conclude, at the 1% level of significance, that there has been a shift in the primary interest of clients?

Solution

The problem objective is the description of a single population (the population of primary interests of clients), and the data are qualitative, consisting of three categories. The parameters of interest are the following:

p_1 = proportion of clients primarily interested in stocks

p_2 = proportion of clients primarily interested in bonds

p_3 = proportion of clients primarily interested in futures

Since we want to determine whether these proportions have changed from their historic levels, the null and alternative hypotheses are

H_0: $p_1 = .60$, $p_2 = .36$, $p_3 = .04$

H_A: At least one p_i is not equal to its specified value.

The test statistic is

$$\chi^2 = \sum_{i=1}^{3} \frac{(o_i - e_i)^2}{e_i}, \text{ with d.f.} = (k-1) = (3-1) = 2$$

Since the rejection region for this goodness-of-fit test is always in the right tail of the chi-squared distribution, the rejection region is

$$\chi^2 > \chi^2_{\alpha, k-1} = \chi^2_{.01, 2} = 9.21034$$

In order to evaluate the test statistic, we need to find the expected frequencies. Assuming that the null hypothesis is true, the expected numbers of clients interested in stocks, bonds, and futures (respectively) are

$e_1 = np_1 = (200)(.60) = 120$

$e_2 = np_2 = (200)(.36) = 72$

$$e_3 = np_3 = (200)(.04) = 8$$

Finally, the value of the test statistic is

$$\chi^2 = \frac{(132 - 120)^2}{120} + \frac{(52 - 72)^2}{72} + \frac{(16 - 8)^2}{8} = 14.76$$

Since $14.76 > 9.21034$, the value of the test statistic falls into the rejection region. As a result, we reject H_0 and conclude that there is sufficient evidence to state that there has been a shift in the primary interest of clients.

When solving this type of problem on your own, you may find it convenient to use a table such as the one below to compute the value of the test statistic.

Market	Observed Frequency o_i	Expected Frequency e_i	$(o_i - e_i)^2$	$\dfrac{(o_i - e_i)^2}{e_i}$
Stock	132	120	144	1.20
Bond	52	72	400	5.56
Futures	16	8	64	8.00
Total	200	200		$14.76 = \chi^2$

Example 15.2

Refer to Example 15.1. What would you conclude if the sample had consisted of only 100 clients, of whom 66 were primarily interested in stocks, 26 in bonds, and 8 in futures? Use $\alpha = .10$.

Solution

At first sight, it would appear that the hypotheses, the test statistic and the rejection region, remain the same as in Example 15.1, with only the value of the test statistic and the conclusion requiring a change. Notice, however, that the new expected frequencies are

$$e_1 = (100)(.60) = 60$$

$$e_2 = (100)(.36) = 36$$

$$e_3 = (100)(.04) = 4$$

Since $e_3 < 5$, the rule of five requires that we combine the third cell with one of the other two. Let's choose to combine bonds with futures, leaving us with $k = 2$ cells. The p_2 is redefined to be

p_2 = proportion of clients primarily interested in bonds or futures

Thus, $p_2 = .36 + .04 = .40$. The test now becomes

H_0: $p_1 = .60$, $p_2 = .40$

H_A: At least one p_i is not equal to its specified value.

Test statistic: $\chi^2 = \sum_{i=1}^{2} \dfrac{(o_i - e_i)^2}{e_i}$, with d.f. $= (k - 1) = (2 - 1) = 1$

Rejection region: $\chi^2 > \chi^2_{\alpha,\,k-1} = \chi^2_{.10,1} = 2.70554$

Value of the test statistic:

$$\chi^2 = \frac{(66 - 60)^2}{60} + \frac{(34 - 40)^2}{40} = 1.5$$

Conclusion: Do not reject H_0. There is insufficient evidence to conclude that there has been a shift in the primary interest of clients.

Notice that we are now unable to detect a shift in the clients' interests, even though we're using a higher level of significance and the observed frequencies are proportionately the same as in Example 15.1. The reason is that it is more difficult to reject a null hypothesis with a smaller sample, all other things being equal.

Market	Observed Frequency o_i	Expected Frequency e_i	$(o_i - e_i)^2$	$\dfrac{(o_i - e_i)^2}{e_i}$
Stock	66	60	36	.6
Bond	26 } 34	36 } 40	36	.9
Futures	8	4		
Total	100	100		$1.5 = \chi^2$

Example 15.3

Use another statistical technique to solve Example 15.2.

Solution

After combining cells 2 and 3, there are only two cells. When there are only two possible outcomes, the experiment is binomial. Thus, we can use the z-test of p described in Section 11.4. We define (arbitrarily)

p = proportion of clients primarily interested in stocks

The complete test is as follows.

$H_0: p = .60$

$H_A: p \neq .60$

Test statistic: $z = \dfrac{\hat{p} - p}{\sqrt{pq/n}}$

Rejection region: $|z| > z_{\alpha/2} = z_{.05} = 1.645$

Value of the test statistic: Since $\hat{p} = \dfrac{66}{100} = .66$

$$z = \frac{.66 - .60}{\sqrt{(.60)(.40)/100}} = 1.225$$

Conclusion: Do not reject H_0. There is not enough evidence to conclude that there has been a shift in the primary interest of clients.

Notice that the conclusions of Examples 15.2 and 15.3 are identical. To show that the two techniques are identical, we square the value of the test statistic and the critical value of the rejection region.

$z^2 = (1.225)^2 = 1.50$

$(z_{.05})^2 = (1.645)^2 = 2.706$

As you can see when we square the value of the z-statistic and the critical value of the rejection region in Example 15.3, we produce the corresponding χ^2-values in Example 15.2. Mathematical statisticians explain this relationship by proving that $z^2 = \chi^2$ with one degree of freedom. Don't worry about this theoretical discussion. We provided it to show that the multinomial experiment is truly an extension of the binomial experiment. Remember that when the problem objective is to describe a single population of qualitative data, we use the chi-squared test of a multinomial experiment when there are two or more outcomes per trial (categories). The z-test of p is used only when there are two outcomes per trial.

EXERCISES

15.1 Suppose that we want to test the following hypotheses.

H_0: $p_1 = .2$, $p_2 = .3$, $p_3 = .5$
H_A: At least one p_i is not equal to its specified value.

The observed values are

$o_1 = 20$ $o_2 = 30$ $o_3 = 50$

Without calculating the value of the test statistic, determine whether the data support the null or the alternative hypotheses.

15.2 Repeat Exercise 15.1 if the observed values are

$o_1 = 60$ $o_2 = 10$ $o_3 = 30$

15.3 Calculate the values of the test statistics in Exercises 15.1 and 15.2 to confirm your answers.

Value of χ^2 for Exercise 15.1

Cell	Observed Frequency o_i	Expected Frequency e_i	$(o_i - e_i)^2$	$\dfrac{(o_i - e_i)^2}{e_i}$
1				
2				
3				
Total				

Value of χ^2 for Exercise 15.2

Cell	Observed Frequency o_i	Expected Frequency e_i	$(o_i - e_i)^2$	$\dfrac{(o_i - e_i)^2}{e_i}$
1				
2				
3				
Total				

15.4 Repeat Example 15.3 by defining

p = proportion of clients primarily interested in bonds or futures

H_0:
H_A:

Test statistic:

Rejection region:

Value of the test statistic:

Conclusion:

15.5 A certain town has only three gasoline stations (A, B, and C). When the three stations were all self-serve, their shares of the market were equal. But station A converted to full service two months ago in an attempt to improve its market share. A recent survey of 180 residents found that 76 now patronize station A, 54 patronize station B, and 50 patronize station C. Is there reason to believe that the stations' market shares have changed since the conversion of station A? Use $\alpha = .05$.

H_0:

H_A:

Test statistic:

Rejection region:

Value of the test statistic:

Conclusion:

15.6   Refer to Exercise 15.5. What would you conclude if the sample had consisted of only 90 resi-
        dents, of whom 38 patronized station A, 27 patronized station B, and 25 patronized station C?
        Use $\alpha = .05$.

H_0:

H_A:

Test statistic:

Rejection region:

Value of the test statistic:

Conclusion:

15.3 Chi-Squared Test of a Contingency Table

This section described the chi-squared test of independence, which examines the relationship between two qualitative variables. This test is used to determine whether two variables (or classifications of items in a population) are dependent or independent. For example, we could use the test to determine if the method of payment used by shoppers (cash, check, or credit card) is dependent upon sex (male/female). The hypotheses to be tested are

H_0: The two classifications are independent.

H_A: The two classifications are dependent.

Suppose that one classification consists of r categories and the other consists of c categories. In preparation for the test of independence, a random sample is selected from the population. Each item in the sample is then cross-classified according to the two criteria (such as payment method and sex) into one of the $r \times c$ categories, called cells. The observed frequencies (o_i) of items falling into each of these cells are then recorded in a two-way cross-classification table, called a contingency table. These observed frequencies (o_i) are then compared with the expected cell frequencies (e_i), which are the cell frequencies we would expect if H_0 is correct. The test statistic used to compare the observed and expected frequencies is

$$\chi^2 = \sum_{i=1}^{r \times c} \frac{(o_i - e_i)^2}{e_i}$$

Although the form of this test statistic is the same as the one used in the goodness-of-fit test for a multinomial experiment, there are differences. For the test of independence being considered here, the number of degrees of freedom for the approximate chi-squared distribution of the test statistic χ^2 is

d.f. $= (r-1)(c-1)$

Moreover, the computation of the expected cell frequencies, e_i, is somewhat more involved than before. (The expected frequencies should again satisfy the rule of five discussed in the previous section.) Just as with the goodness-of-fit test, however, the rejection region is always located in the right tail of the chi-squared distribution. To be specific, the rejection region for a chi-squared test of independence at the α level of significance is

$\chi^2 > \chi^2_{\alpha,(r-1)(c-1)}$.

Example 15.4

A large jewelry store wishes to determine if there are differences between men and women in their method of payment for purchases. A cross-classification of 400 shoppers according to method of payment and sex is shown in the accompanying contingency table. Do these data indicate that there are differences between men and women in their method of payment? Use $\alpha = .05$.

	Method of Payment			
Sex	Cash	Check	Credit Card	Total
Male	20	70	120	210
Female	24	76	90	190
Total	44	146	210	400

Solution

The 400 shoppers can be treated as a sample from a single population, classified according to both their method of payment and their sex. The data are qualitative. The hypotheses for a chi-squared test to determine if these two classifications are statistically independent are

H_0: The two classifications are independent.

H_A: The two classifications are dependent.

Notice that, alternatively, we can consider that we are dealing with two populations: the populations of methods of payment by men and women. If the two classifications are independent (i.e., not related), then there are no differences in the method of payment by men and women. Similarly, the alternative hypothesis states that method of payment and sex are dependent, or related, meaning that there are differences in the methods of payment between the two populations (men and women).

Since there are $r \times c = 2 \times 3 = 6$ cross-classifications, the test statistic is

$$\chi^2 = \sum_{i=1}^{6} \frac{(o_i - e_i)^2}{e_i}, \text{ with d.f.} = (1)(2) = 2$$

The rejection region, which is always in the right tail of the chi-squared distribution for a test of independence, is

$$\chi^2 > \chi^2_{\alpha,(r-1)(c-1)} = \chi^2_{.05,2} = 5.99147$$

We next need to find the expected frequencies. Assuming the null hypothesis is correct, the expected frequency of the cell in row i and column j of the contingency table is

$$e_{ij} = \frac{(\text{row } i \text{ total}) \cdot (\text{column } j \text{ total})}{\text{sample size}}$$

Thus,

$$e_{11} = \frac{(210)(44)}{400} = 23.10$$

$$e_{21} = \frac{(190)(44)}{400} = 20.90$$

$$e_{12} = \frac{(210)(146)}{400} = 76.65$$

$$e_{22} = \frac{(190)(146)}{400} = 69.35$$

$$e_{13} = \frac{(210)(210)}{400} = 110.25$$

$$e_{23} = \frac{(190)(210)}{400} = 99.75$$

Finally, the value of the test statistic is

$$\chi^2 = \frac{(20 - 23.10)^2}{23.10} + \frac{(24 - 20.90)^2}{20.90} + \cdots + \frac{(90 - 99.75)^2}{99.75}$$

$$= .42 + .46 + \cdots + .95 = 3.91$$

Since $3.91 < 5.99147$, the value of the test statistic does not fall into the rejection region. We cannot reject the hypothesis that the two classifications are independent. That is, there is not sufficient evidence to conclude, at the 5% significance level, that there are differences in methods of payment between male and female shoppers.

Cell	Observed Frequency o_i	Expected Frequency e_i	$(o_i - e_i)^2$	$\dfrac{(o_i - e_i)^2}{e_i}$
1	20	23.10	9.61	.42
2	24	20.90	9.61	.46
3	70	76.65	44.22	.58
4	76	69.35	44.22	.64
5	120	110.25	95.06	.86
6	90	99.75	95.06	.95
Total	400	400.00		$3.91 = \chi^2$

Example 15.5

One of the issues that arose in the most recent election (and is likely to arise in many future elections) is whether it is more important for the government to decrease the deficit by cutting spending or to borrow additional money to "restart" the economy. To determine who supports each of the options, a sample of 250 people was surveyed and asked a variety of questions dealing with the economy and demographics. From these data the following table was created.

	Number of People Who Believe That the Government Should:	
Educational Level	Reduce Deficit	Restart Economy
Completed university or college	55	45
Did not complete university or college	65	85

Can we conclude at the 5% significance level that university/college graduates differ from those who did not graduate from university or college in their support for the two options for the economy?

Solution

The problem objective is to compare two populations (university/college graduates and those who did not graduate from university or college) of qualitative data. Because there are only two responses (reduce deficit or restart economy), we can use either the chi-squared test of a contingency table or the z-test of $p_1 - p_2$. To demonstrate the equivalence of these two techniques, we'll solve this problem both ways. Let's start with the chi-squared test of a contingency table.

H_0: The two classifications are independent.

H_A: The two classifications are dependent.

Test statistic: $\chi^2 = \sum \dfrac{(o_i - e_i)^2}{e_i}$.

Rejection region: $\chi^2 > \chi^2_{\alpha,(r-1)(c-1)} = \chi^2_{.05,1} = 3.84146$.

Value of the test statistic: The observed and expected values (in parentheses) are shown below.

55 (48)	45 (52)
65 (72)	85 (78)

$$\chi^2 = \frac{(55-48)^2}{48} + \frac{(65-72)^2}{72} + \frac{(45-52)^2}{52} + \frac{(85-78)^2}{78}$$

$$= 3.27$$

Conclusion: Do not reject H_0. There is not enough evidence to infer that university and college graduates differ from those who did not complete university or college regarding economic options.

The z-test of $p_1 - p_2$ is applied below. We define

p_1 = proportion of university/college graduates who support deficit reduction.

p_2 = proportion of those who did not complete university or college who support deficit reduction.

H_0: $(p_1 - p_2) = 0$.

H_A: $(p_1 - p_2) \neq 0$.

Test statistic: $z = \dfrac{(\hat{p}_1 - \hat{p}_2)}{\sqrt{\hat{p}\hat{q}(1/n_1 + 1/n_2)}}$.

Rejection region: $|z| > z_{\alpha/2} = z_{.025} = 1.96$.

Value of the test statistic:

$$\hat{p}_1 = \frac{55}{100} = .550$$

$$\hat{p}_2 = \frac{65}{150} = .433$$

$$\hat{p} = \frac{120}{250} = .480$$

$$\hat{q} = 1 - .480 = .520$$

$$z = \frac{(.550 - .433)}{\sqrt{(.480)(.520)(1/100 + 1/150)}} = 1.81$$

Conclusion: Do not reject H_0.

As you can see, we produce the same conclusion in both tests. If we square the value of the z-statistic and the critical value of the rejection region, the results are identical to the χ^2-values (with minor variations due to rounding).

$$z^2 = (1.81)^2 = 3.28$$

$$(z_{.025})^2 = (1.96)^2 = 3.8416$$

Example 15.6

Suppose that in Example 15.5 there were three economic policy options

1. Reduce the deficit by cutting spending
2. Borrow more money to restart the economy
3. Raise taxes

Which technique should be used?

Solution

The problem objective is to compare two populations (university/college graduates and those who did not complete university or college). The data are qualitative, with three possible outcomes or categories. Consequently, we cannot use the z-test of $p_1 - p_2$. (If we attempted to use the z-test of $p_1 - p_2$, how could we define the proportions?) The only choice is to use the chi-squared test of a contingency table.

Question: When we compare two populations of qualitative data with only two categories, we can use the z-test of $p_1 - p_2$ or the chi-squared test of a contingency table. Why do we need the z-test of $p_1 - p_2$ at all?

Answer: The chi-squared test of a contingency table can only be used to infer that differences exist between the two populations. If we want to show that one population proportion exceeds another, we must use the z-test of $p_1 - p_2$. That is, if the alternative hypothesis is

$$H_A: (p_1 - p_2) > 0$$

or

$$H_A: (p_1 - p_2) < 0$$

We cannot use the chi-squared test of a contingency table.

EXERCISES

15.7   In testing the following hypotheses

H_0: The two classifications are independent
H_A: The two classifications are dependent

we created the following contingency table.

	1	2	3	Total
1	50	30	20	100
2	100	60	40	200
Total	150	90	60	

Without calculating the value of the test statistic, determine whether the data support the null or the alternative hypothesis.

15.8   Repeat Exercise 15.7 given the following contingency table.

	1	2	3	Total
1	40	20	40	100
2	50	100	50	200
Total	90	120	90	

15.9 Calculate the values of the χ^2-statistic in Exercises 15.7 and 15.8 to check your answers.

Value of χ^2 for Exercise 15.7

Value of χ^2 for Exercise 15.8

15.10 New drugs are usually tested by giving a randomly selected group of people the drug and another randomly selected group of people a placebo. Each person is then asked whether he or she suffered serious side effects. Suppose that for a new drug used to treat migraine headaches the following table was created.

Medication	Suffered Serious Side Effect	Did Not Suffer Serious Side Effect
New drug	41	165
Placebo	28	161

Use the chi-squared test of a contingency table to determine if we conclude at the 10% significance level that differences exist between the new drug and the placebo in terms of reported side effects.

H_0:
H_A:

Test statistic:

Rejection region:

Value of the test statistic:

Conclusion:

15.11 Repeat Exercise 15.10 using the z-test of $p_1 - p_2$

H_0:
H_A:

Test statistic:

Rejection region:

Value of the test statistic:

Conclusion:

15.12 Suppose that in Exercise 15.10 we recorded the exact nature of the side effect and produced the table below. Can we conclude at the 10% significance level that differences exist between the new drug and the placebo?

| Medication | Side Effects | | Did Not Suffer |
	Nausea	Drowsiness	Serious Side Effect
New drug	32	9	165
Placebo	8	20	161

H_0:

H_A:

Test statistic:

Rejection region:

Value of the test statistic:

Conclusion:

15.13 Divisions in a corporation can be based upon function, product, or project dimensions. A management consulting firm believes that there are differences between American and Canadian firms in terms of their preferences for organizational structures in the workplace. Is there evidence to support this belief, based on the sample data shown in the accompanying contingency table? Use $\alpha = .005$.

Nationality	Preferred Organizational Structure			Total
	Functional	Product	Project	
American	105	95	50	250
Canadian	65	105	80	250
Total	170	200	130	500

H_0:

H_A:

Test statistic:

Rejection region:

Value of the test statistic:

Conclusion:

15.14 In preparation for an upcoming election, a political party conducts a survey of 400 eligible voters. A breakdown of their responses, according to geographical region and attitude toward the party, is shown in the accompanying table. Is there reason to believe that there are differences in attitude among the four geographic regions? Use $\alpha = .01$

	Geographic Region				
Attitude	Northwest	Northeast	Southwest	Southeast	Total
For	64	45	58	43	210
Against	45	34	43	28	150
Undecided	16	46	24	54	140
Total	125	125	125	125	500

H_0:

H_A:

Test statistic:

Rejection region:

Value of the test statistic:

Conclusion:

Chapter 16: Simple Linear Regression and Correlation

16.1   Introduction

This chapter dealt with the problem objective of analyzing the relationship between two variables.

You are expected to know the following:

1. Why the model includes the error variable, ε.
2. How to calculate the sample regression coefficients $\hat{\beta}_0$ and $\hat{\beta}_1$.
3. How to interpret the coefficients.
4. The four required conditions to perform the statistical inference.
5. How to calculate SSE and s_ε
6. How to test and estimate β_1
7. How to calculate and interpret the coefficient of determination.
8. How to distinguish between and calculate the confidence interval estimate of the expected value of y and the prediction interval of y.
9. How to calculate and test the Spearman rank coefficient of correlation.

16.2   Model

In this section, we discussed why the model includes the linear part $y = \beta_0 + \beta_1 x$ plus the error variable, ε. You should have a clear understanding of how the error variable is measured and of the definition of the y-intercept β_0 and the slope β_1.

16.3   Least Squares Method

We calculate the sample regression coefficients using the following formulas:

$$\hat{\beta}_1 = \frac{SS_{xy}}{SS_x}$$

where

$$SS_{xy} = \sum x_i y_i - \frac{(\sum x_i)(\sum y_i)}{n}$$

and

$$SS_x = \sum x_i^2 - \frac{(\sum x_i)^2}{n}$$

$$\hat{\beta}_0 = \bar{y} - \hat{\beta}_1 \bar{x}$$

Example 16.1

An educational economist wants to establish the relationship between an individual's income and education. He takes a random sample of 10 individuals and asks for their income (in $1,000s) and education (in years). The results are shown below. Find the least squares regression line.

x (education)	y (income)
11	25
12	33
11	22
15	41
8	18
10	28
11	32
12	24
17	53
11	26

Solution

Note that we've labeled education x and income y because income is affected by education. Our first step is to calculate the sums, $\sum x_i$, $\sum x_i^2$, $\sum y_i$, $\sum y_i^2$, and $\sum x_i y_i$. The sum $\sum y_i^2$ is not required in the least squares method but is usually needed for other techniques involved with regression. We find

$$\sum x_i = 118$$

$$\sum x_i^2 = 1,450$$

$$\sum y_i = 302$$

$$\sum y_i^2 = 10,072$$

$$\sum x_i y_i = 3,779$$

Next, we compute the sums of squares:

$$SS_{xy} = \sum x_i y_i - \frac{(\sum x_i)(\sum y_i)}{n} = 3{,}779 - \frac{(118)(302)}{10} = 215.4$$

$$SS_x = \sum x_i^2 - \frac{(\sum x_i)^2}{n} = 1{,}450 - \frac{(118)^2}{10} = 57.6$$

Therefore,

$$\hat{\beta}_1 = \frac{SS_{xy}}{SS_x} = \frac{215.4}{57.6} = 3.74$$

$$\hat{\beta}_0 = \bar{y} - \hat{\beta}_1 \bar{x}$$

The least squares regression line is

$$\hat{y} = -13.93 + 3.74x$$

Example 16.2

Interpret the coefficients of Example 16.1.

Solution

The sample slope $\hat{\beta}_1 = 3.74$ tells us that on average for each additional year of education, an individual's income rises by \$3.74 thousand. The y-intercept is $\hat{\beta}_0 = -13.93$. It should be obvious that this value has no meaning. Recall that whenever the range of the observed values of x does not include zero it is usually pointless to try to interpret the meaning of the y-intercept.

Question:	How do I know which is the dependent variable and which is the independent variable?
Answer:	The dependent variable is the one that we want to forecast or analyze. The independent variable is hypothesized to affect the dependent variable. In Example 16.1, we wish to analyze income, and we choose as the variable that most affects income the individual's education. Hence, we label income y and education x.

EXERCISES

16.1 Fifteen observations were taken to estimate a simple regression model. The following summations were produced:

$$\sum x = 50 \quad \sum x^2 = 250 \quad \sum y = 100 \quad \sum y^2 = 1{,}100 \quad \sum xy = 500$$

Find the least squares regression line.

16.2 The manager of a large furniture store wanted to determine the effectiveness of her advertising. The furniture store regularly runs several ads per month in the local newspaper. The manager wanted to know if the number of ads influenced the number of customers. During the past eight months, she kept track of both figures, which are shown below. Find the equation of the regression line.

Month	Number of Ads, x	Number of Customers, y
1	5	528
2	12	876
3	8	653
4	6	571
5	4	556
6	15	1058
7	10	963
8	7	719

16.4 Error Variable: Required Conditions

In order to perform the statistical techniques that follow, we need the following four required conditions about ε to be satisfied:

1. ε is normally distributed
2. $E(\varepsilon) = 0$
3. The variance of ε is σ_ε^2.
4. The errors are independent of each other.

16.5   Assessing the Model

In this section we examined three ways to assess the model's fit; the standard error of estimate, the t-test of the slope, and the coefficient of determination.

Standard Error of Estimate

The estimator of σ_ε^2 is s_ε^2, which is defined as

$$s_\varepsilon^2 = \frac{SSE}{n-2}$$

where SSE is the sum of squares for error, which is calculated by the following shortcut formula.

$$SSE = SS_y - \frac{SS_{xy}^2}{SS_x}$$

where

$$SS_y = \sum y_i^2 - \frac{(\sum y_i)^2}{n}$$

The positive square root of s_ε^2 is called the standard error of estimate.

Example 16.3

Find s_ε^2 and s_ε for Example 16.1 and interpret what they tell you about how well the regression line fits the data.

Solution

Recall from Example 16.1 that

$$SS_{xy} = 215.4$$

and

$$SS_x = 57.6$$

We also found $\sum y_i = 302$ and $\sum y_i^2 = 10{,}072$. Therefore,

$$SS_y = \sum y_i^2 - \frac{(\sum y_i)^2}{n} = 10{,}072 - \frac{(302)^2}{10} = 951.6$$

We can now compute SSE:

$$SSE = SS_y - \frac{SS_{xy}^2}{SS_x} = 951.6 - \frac{(215.4)^2}{57.6} = 146.09$$

Therefore,

$$s_\varepsilon^2 = \frac{SSE}{n-2} = \frac{146.09}{10-2} = 18.26$$

and

$$s_\varepsilon = \sqrt{s_\varepsilon^2} = \sqrt{18.26} = 4.27$$

It is difficult to interpret s_ε^2. However, the value of s_ε can be compared with the mean value of y to provide a rough guide as to whether s_ε is large or small. Since $\bar{y} = 30.2$ and $s_\varepsilon = 4.27$, we would conclude that s_ε is relatively small, which indicates that the regression line fits the data quite well.

Question: Is there another way to interpret s_ε?

Answer: Remember that s_ε is an estimator of a population standard deviation. Given that the errors are normally distributed, we can state that approximately 68% of the errors will fall between $-s_\varepsilon$ and $+s_\varepsilon$ (recall that the mean of the error variable is zero) and that about 95% of the errors will fall between $-2s_\varepsilon$ and $+2s_\varepsilon$.

Testing the Slope

The purpose of this technique is to determine whether or not there is evidence of a linear relationship between x and y. We usually test to determine if β_1 is not equal to zero. The test statistic is

$$t = \frac{\hat{\beta}_1 - \beta_1}{s_{\hat{\beta}_1}}$$

where

$$s_{\hat{\beta}_1} = \frac{s_\varepsilon}{\sqrt{SS_x}}$$

The test statistic is Student t distributed with $(n-2)$ degrees of freedom.

Example 16.4

Is there sufficient evidence at the 5% significance level to indicate that x and y are linearly related in Example 16.1?

Solution

If $\beta_1 = 0$, the regression line is horizontal, indicating that as x increases y is unaffected. Therefore, in order to test for linearity, we test the hypotheses

H_0: $\beta_1 = 0$

H_A: $\beta_1 \neq 0$

The rejection region is

$$|t| > t_{\alpha/2, n-2} = t_{.025, 8} = 2.306$$

The value of the test statistic is determined as follows:

$\hat{\beta}_1 = 3.74$

$s_\varepsilon = 4.27$

$SS_x = 57.6$

Hence,

$$t = \frac{3.74 - 0}{4.27 / \sqrt{57.6}} = 6.65$$

There is sufficient evidence to indicate that x and y are linearly related.

Incidentally, had we wanted to test for a positive linear relationship we would have proceeded in the following way:

H_0: $\beta_1 = 0$

H_A: $\beta_1 > 0$

Rejection region: $t > t_{\alpha/2, n-2} = t_{.05, 8} = 1.860$

Value of the test statistic: $t = 6.65$

Conclusion: Reject H_0.

Question: When we draw the regression line with $\beta_1 = 0$, we draw a straight horizontal line. Isn't this evidence of a linear relationship?

Answer: When we seek evidence of a linear relationship, we're attempting to determine if there is enough evidence to show that the independent variable affects the dependent variable. For this we need to show that $\beta_1 \neq 0$.

Coefficient of Determination

The coefficient of determination is defined as

$$R^2 = \frac{SS_{xy}^2}{SS_x \bullet SS_y} = 1 - \frac{SSE}{SS_y}$$

Example 16.5

Calculate the coefficient of determination for Example 16.1

Solution

$$R^2 = \frac{SS_{xy}^2}{SS_x \bullet SS_y} = \frac{(215.4)^2}{(57.6)(951.6)} = .846$$

The coefficient of determination tells us that 84.6% of the variation in y is explained by the variation in x. The remaining 15.4% is unexplained.

EXERCISES

16.3 Calculate SSE, s_ε^2 and s_ε for Exercise 16.1.

16.4 Calculate the standard error of estimate for Exercise 16.2. What does this value tell you about how well the model fits the data?

16.5 Refer to Exercise 16.1. Test to determine if there is sufficient evidence to conclude that x and y are linearly related. Use $\alpha = .10$.

H_0:

H_A:

Test statistic:

Rejection region:

Value of the test statistic:

Conclusion:

16.6 Is there enough evidence to indicate that the number of ads and the number of customers are positively linearly related in Exercise 16.2? Use $\alpha = .01$.

H_0:

H_A:

Test statistic:

Rejection region:

Value of the test statistic:

Conclusion:

16.7   The owner of the concession stands at a football stadium would like to be capable of predicting the number of cups of coffee sold during each game. He believes that the most important variable is the temperature at game time. To investigate the relationship, he recorded the number of cups of coffee sold and the temperature during nine randomly selected games. These data are shown below.

a)   Find the least squares regression line.

b)   Can we conclude at the 5% significance level that temperature and the number of cups of coffee sold are negatively linearly related?

H_0:
H_A:

Test statistic:

Rejection region:

Value of the test statistic:

Conclusion:

Game	Temperature, x (°F)	Number of Cups of Coffee Sold (100's), y
1	53	50
2	50	47
3	75	43
4	48	58
5	45	57
6	63	44
7	40	64
8	55	48
9	30	71

16.8   Calculate the coefficient of determination for Exercise 16.1.

16.9   Compute the coefficient of determination for Exercise 16.2.

16.10   Compute the coefficient of determination for Exercise 16.7. What does this value tell you about the strength of the linear relationship between temperature and the number of cups of coffee sold?

16.6   Using the Regression Equation

The confidence interval for predicting the particular value of y for a given x (commonly called the prediction interval) is

$$\hat{y} \pm t_{\alpha/2, n-2}\, s_\varepsilon \sqrt{1 + \frac{1}{n} + \frac{(x_g - \bar{x})^2}{SS_x}}$$

The confidence interval for estimating the expected value of y for a given x is

$$\hat{y} \pm t_{\alpha/2, n-2}\, s_\varepsilon \sqrt{\frac{1}{n} + \frac{(x_g - \bar{x})^2}{SS_x}}$$

Example 16.6

Refer to Example 16.1. Determine a 90% confidence interval for the income of an individual who has had 12 years of education.

Solution

$$\hat{y} = \hat{\beta}_0 + \hat{\beta}_1 x_g = -13.93 + 3.74(12) = 30.95$$

The 90% prediction interval is

$$\hat{y} \pm t_{\alpha/2, n-2} \, s_\varepsilon \sqrt{1 + \frac{1}{n} + \frac{(x_g - \bar{x})^2}{SS_x}}$$

$$= 30.95 \pm (1.860)(4.27) \sqrt{1 + \frac{1}{10} + \frac{(12 - 11.8)^2}{57.6}}$$

$$= 30.95 \pm 8.33$$

Thus, the prediction is that the income will fall between $22,620 and $39,280.

Example 16.7

Refer to Example 16.1. Determine a 90% confidence interval for the mean income of all individuals who have had 12 years of education.

Solution

The 90% confidence interval for the expected value of y is

$$\hat{y} \pm t_{\alpha/2, n-2} \, s_\varepsilon \sqrt{\frac{1}{n} + \frac{(x_g - \bar{x})^2}{SS_x}}$$

$$= 30.95 \pm (1.860)(4.27) \sqrt{\frac{1}{10} + \frac{(12 - 11.8)^2}{57.6}}$$

$$= 30.95 \pm 2.52$$

The mean income will fall between $28,430 and $33,470.

EXERCISES

16.11 Refer to Exercise 16.2. Find the 95% prediction interval for the number of customers entering the furniture store when the number of ads is 8.

16.12 Refer to Exercise 16.2. Find the 95% confidence interval estimate of the expected number of customers when the number of ads is 8.

16.13 Refer to Exercise 16.7. Find the 95% confidence interval estimate of the mean number of cups of coffee sold per game when the temperature is 50°F.

16.14 Refer to Exercise 16.7. Predict with 95% confidence the number of cups of coffee that will be sold during a game when the temperature is 50°F.

16.7 Coefficient of Correlation (Optional)

The sample coefficient of correlation is defined as

$$r = \frac{SS_{xy}}{\sqrt{SS_x \bullet SS_y}}$$

We can test for $\rho = 0$ as follows

$H_o: \rho = 0$

$H_A: \rho = 0$

Test statistic: $t = r\sqrt{\dfrac{n-2}{1-r^2}}$ d.f. $= n - 2$

The result is the same as testing $\beta_1 = 0$

Chapter 17: Multiple Regression

17.1   Introduction

In this chapter, we extended the concepts and techniques introduced in Chapter 16. Very few computations were required in this chapter, since the statistical technique requires the use of a computer. As a result, you are expected to know the following:

1. How to read and interpret computer output from various statistical application packages.
2. How to perform t-tests on the coefficients.
3. How to read and interpret the values of the standard error of estimate and the coefficient of determination.
4. How to perform the analysis of variance to test the model's utility.
5. How to detect violations of required conditions and multicollinearity.

17.2   Model and Required Conditions

In this section, we presented the multiple regression model and the conditions necessary to perform the statistical tests that follow. The conditions are the same as shown for the simple regression model discussed in Chapter 16.

17.3   Estimating the Coefficients and Assessing the Model

We assess the model by determining the value of the standard error of estimate and the coefficient of determination and by testing the model's utility. The latter is performed by the analysis of variance table, which is part of the computer output.

Example 17.1

A management consultant was hired to analyze the salary structure in a large multinational company.   As part of the analysis, he interviewed 50 employees and asked each to provide his or her annual income (in thousands of dollars), the number of years of education, the number of years of experience, and his or her age. The multiple regression model

$$y = \beta_0 + \beta_1 x_1 + \beta_2 x_2 + \beta_3 x_3 + \varepsilon$$

was estimated where y = Income, x_1 = Education, x_2 = Experience, and x_3 = Age. The Minitab computer output appears below.

The regression equation is

$$y = 6.111 + 1.261x1 + 0.836x2 + 0.373x3$$

Predictor	Coef	Stdev	t-ratio	p
Constant	6.111	4.883	1.251	0.2172
x1	1.261	0.351	3.593	0.0008
x2	0.836	0.390	2.144	0.0374
x3	0.373	0.214	1.743	0.0880

s=1.483   R-sq=59.8%   R-sq(adj)=57.2%

Analysis of Variance

SOURCE	DF	SS	MS	F	p
Regression	3	150.5	50.2	22.8	0.0000
Error	46	101.2	2.2		
Total	49	251.7			

a) Interpret each coefficient.

b) Test at the 5% significance level to determine if x_1, x_2 and X_3 are linearly related to y.

Solution

a) $\hat{\beta}_0 = 6.111$ cannot be interpreted, because the observed values of the independent variables do not include $x_1 = 0$, $x_2 = 0$, and $x_3 = 0$.

$\hat{\beta}_1 = 1.261$ implies that for each additional year of education the average income increases by $1.261 thousand.

$\hat{\beta}_2 = .836$ indicates that for each additional year of experience the average income increases by $.836 thousand.

$\hat{\beta}_3 = .373$ implies that for each additional year in age the average income increases by $.373 thousand.

b) To test each coefficient we proceed as follows:

H_0: $\beta_i = 0$

H_A: $\beta_i \neq 0$

Rejection region: $|t| > t_{\alpha/2, n-k-1} = t_{.025, 46} = 2.014$ (approximately)

Values of the test statistics:

For x_1: $t = 3.593$

For x_2: $t = 2.144$

For x_3: $t = 1.743$

Conclusions: There is sufficient evidence to indicate that x_1 and x_2 are linearly related to y. There is not enough evidence to indicate that x_3 and y are linearly related.

Example 17.2

In the output for Example 17.1, identify the coefficient of determination, interpret its value, and test the utility of the model (with $\alpha = .05$).

Solution

The coefficient of determination is $R^2 = 59.8\%$, which means that 59.8% of the variation in y is explained by the model. To test the model's utility, we proceed as follows:

H_0: $\beta_1 = \beta_2 = \beta_3 = 0$

H_A: At least one β is not equal to zero.

Rejection region: $F > F_{\alpha, k, n-k-1} = F_{.05, 3, 46} = 2.84$ (approximately)

Values of the test statistics: $F = 22.8$

Conclusion: Reject H_0.

There is sufficient evidence to indicate that the model is useful.

EXERCISES

17.1   As part of an effort to induce the public to conserve energy, an economist wanted to analyze the factors that determine home heating costs. In a city known for its long, cold winters the economist took a random sample of 35 houses and determined the following variables:

y = Cost of heating during the month of January

x_1 = House size in hundreds of square feet

x_2 = Number of windows

x_3 = Number of occupants

A multiple regression model was estimated with the Minitab computer output shown below. What do the values of the coefficients tell you?

```
The regression equation is

y = 11.088 + 5.632x1 + 3.179x2 + 15.431x3

Predictor      Coef      Stdev    t-ratio        p
Constant     11.088      4.532      2.45     0.0202
x1            5.632      1.489      3.78     0.0006
x2            3.179      1.966      1.62     0.1154
x3           15.431      6.850      2.25     0.0316

s = 34.898    R-sq = 55.4%    R-sq(adj) = 51.1%

Analysis of Variance

SOURCE          DF        SS         MS        F          p
Regression       3     46919    15639.7    12.84      0.000
Error           31     37754     1217.9
Total           34     84673
```

17.2   In Exercise 17.1, is there sufficient evidence at the 5% significance level to conclude that each
        independent variable is linearly related to the dependent variable?

H_0:

H_A:

Test statistic:

Rejection region:

Value of the test statistic:

Conclusions:

17.3   Refer to Exercise 17.1. Determine the standard error of estimate and interpret its value.

17.4   Refer to Exercise 17.1. Determine the coefficient of determination and interpret its value.

17.5   Test the utility of the model in Exercise 17.1. Use $\alpha = .05$.

H_0:

H_A:

Test statistic:

Rejection region:

Value of the test statistic:

Conclusion:

17.4   Qualitative Independent Variables

When we want to include a qualitative independent variable in the model, we must first convert it to one or more indicator variables. If the qualitative variable can take on p values (p categories), we must create $p - 1$ indicator variables. It is important that you be able to interpret the meaning of the values of the coefficients of these variables as well as the meaning of the t-tests.

Example 17.3

The manager of the beer concession at a major league baseball stadium wants to be able to predict the amount of beer sold during a baseball game. After some analysis, he decides that the most important variables are how many people attend the game and when the game occurs. The games are scheduled for weekday nights, Friday nights, Saturday afternoon, and Sunday afternoon. Create the regression model that the manager would use.

Solution

Let y = Number of beers sold

x_1 = Attendance

x_2 = 1 if game is played Friday night

= 0 otherwise

x_3 = 1 if game is played Saturday afternoon

= 0 otherwise

x_4 = 1 if game is played Sunday afternoon

= 0 otherwise

The model is

$$y = \beta_0 + \beta_1 x_1 + \beta_2 x_2 + \beta_3 x_3 + \beta_4 x_4 + \varepsilon$$

Example 17.4

To estimate the coefficients and test the model, the manager in Example 17.4 randomly selected 40 games and determined beer sales (in thousands), attendance (in thousands), and when the game was played. The data were then input into a computer, with the results shown below.

The regression equation is

$$y = -1.430 + 0.243X1 + 1.739X2 + 3.743X3 + 4.312X4$$

Predictor	Coef	Stdev	t-ratio	p
Constant	-1.430	1.258	-1.14	0.2610
X1	0.243	0.101	2.41	0.0214
X2	1.739	1.164	1.49	0.1452
X3	3.743	0.974	3.84	0.0004
X4	4.312	1.085	3.97	0.0004

Analysis of Variance

SOURCE	DF	SS	MS	F	P
Regression	4	794.4	198.6	19.19	0.0000
Error	35	362.1	10.35		
Total	39	1156.5			

a) Test the utility of the model with $\alpha = .05$.

b) What do the coefficients $\hat{\beta}_2$, $\hat{\beta}_3$, and $\hat{\beta}_4$ tell us?

c) What do the values of the t-statistics for $\hat{\beta}_2$, $\hat{\beta}_3$, and $\hat{\beta}_4$ tell us?

Solution

a) $H_0: \beta_1 = \beta_2 = \beta_3 = \beta_4 = 0$

H_A: At least one β_i is not equal to zero.

Rejection region: $F > 2.69$ (approximately)

Value of the test statistic: $F = 19.19$

Conclusion: Reject H_0.

There is sufficient evidence to support the model's utility.

b) Because of the way in which $x_2, x_3,$ and x_4 were defined, all comparisons are made with beer sales on weekday nights. It's important to realize that this definition was arbitrary. That is, had we defined $x_2, x_3,$ and x_4 differently, the comparison would be made with beer sales on some other day. For example, if we had let

x_2 = 1 if game is played on a weekday night
= 0 otherwise

x_3 = 1 if game is played on a Friday night

= 0 otherwise

x_4 = 1 if game is played on a Saturday afternoon

= 0 otherwise

then all comparisons would be made with beer sales on Sunday afternoon.

Therefore, we interpret the coefficients in the following way:

$\hat{\beta}_2$ = 1.739: On average, there are 1.739 thousand (1,739) more beers sold on Friday night than on a weekday night when the effect of attendance is removed. It should be noted that this difference is not due to higher attendance, since attendance is included in the model. As a result, even if a Wednesday night game and a Friday night game have the same attendance, we can expect to sell more beer on the Friday night. Another point to consider is that the value of β_2 (the population coefficient) may not be significantly different from zero, indicating that there may not be enough evidence to indicate that beer sales on weekday and Friday nights truly differ. This issue is resolved by the t-test.

$\hat{\beta}_3$ = 3.743: On average, 3.743 thousand more beers are sold on a Saturday afternoon than on a weekday night (when the effect of attendance is excluded).

$\hat{\beta}_4$ = 4.312: On average, 4.312 thousand more beers are sold on a Sunday afternoon than on a weekday night (with the effect of attendance removed).

c) The t-tests of the coefficients are used to determine if enough statistical evidence exists to conclude that each differs from zero. When the coefficient represents an indicator variable, the test can also test to determine if there is sufficient evidence to indicate a difference between the category referred to by the indicator variable and the common category. The t-test of β_2 tests for a significant difference between average beer sales on Friday nights and average beer sales on weekday nights. We would perform the test in the usual way:

H_0: $\beta_2 = 0$

H_A: $\beta_2 \neq 0$

Rejection region: $|t| > t_{\alpha/2, n-k-1}$

$$= t_{.025, 35} \text{ (with } \alpha = .05)$$

$$= 1.96$$

Value of the test statistic: $t = 1.49$

Conclusion: Do not reject H_0.

There is not enough evidence to conclude that beer sales on weekday and Friday nights differ.

We can perform similar tests on β_3 and β_4. We can also perform one-tail tests. For example, if we want to determine if the average beer sales on Saturday afternoons are greater than the average on weekday nights, we would test the following:

H_0: $\beta_3 = 0$

H_A: $\beta_3 > 0$

Rejection region: $|t| > t_{\alpha, n-k-1} = t_{.05, 35} = 1.690$

Value of the test statistic: $t = 3.84$

Conclusion: Reject H_0.

There is sufficient evidence to indicate that, on average, beer sales on Saturday afternoon exceed beer sales on weekday nights.

In a similar manner, we would conclude that beer sales on Sunday afternoon, on average, exceed beer sales on weekday nights.

Incidentally, had we wished to test to determine if beer sales on Sunday afternoon were less on average than weekday nights, we would have tested the following hypotheses:

H_0: $\beta_4 = 0$

H_A: $\beta_4 < 0$

EXERCISES

17.6   In one last effort to improve the model in Exercise 17.1, the economist decided to examine a model that includes house size (x_1) and the direction in which the front of the house faces. Since the second variable is qualitative, the following three dummy variables were created:

x_2 = 1 if house faces south
       = 0 otherwise

x_3 = 1 if house faces north
       = 0 otherwise

x_4 = 1 if house faces west
       = 0 otherwise

The Minitab computer output is shown below. Test the model's utility with $\alpha = .05$.

The regression equation:

$$Y = 53.193 + 8.477X1 - 6.849X2 + 4.607X3 - 1.252X4$$

Predictor	Coef	Stdev	t-ratio	p
Constant	53.193	29.548	1.80	0.0820
X1	8.477	2.906	2.92	0.0066
X2	-6.849	3.133	-2.19	0.0364
X3	4.607	3.759	1.23	0.2282
X4	-1.252	1.608	-.78	0.4416

s = 35.006   R-sq = 56.6%   R-sq(adj) = 50.8%

Analysis of Variance

SOURCE	DF	SS	MS	F	p
Regression	4	47911	11977.8	9.77	0.0000
Error	30	36762	1225.4		
Total	34	84673			

H_0:

H_A:

Test statistic:

Rejection region:

Value of the test statistic:

Conclusion:

17.7   Interpret the coefficients $\hat{\beta}_1$, $\hat{\beta}_2$, $\hat{\beta}_3$, and $\hat{\beta}_4$ in Exercise 17.6.

17.8   Refer to Exercise 17.6. Is there sufficient evidence at the 5% significance level to conclude that, on average, the January heating cost for a south-facing house is less than that of an east-facing house?

H_0:

H_A:

Test statistic:

Rejection region:

Value of the test statistic:

Conclusion:

17.9   Refer to Exercise 17.6. Do the results allow us to conclude with $\alpha = .05$ that, on average, the January heating cost for a north-facing house is greater than that of an east-facing house?

H_0:

H_A:

Test statistic:

Rejection region:

Value of the test statistic:

Conclusion:

Chapter 18: Statistical Process Control

18.1   Introduction

This chapter discussed how hypothesis testing can be used to help firms develop and maintain high-quality products. We introduced control charts and showed how they can be used to indicate when a production process goes out of control and begins to produce defective products.

At the completion of this chapter, you are expected to know the following:

1. Understand the logic of control charts.
2. How to draw an $\bar{x}$ chart.
3. How to draw an R chart.
4. How to draw a p chart.
5. How to apply pattern tests to determine whether a process is out of control.

18.2   Process Variation

In this section, we discussed the critical idea that no two products coming off an assembly line are exactly alike. That is, the process has built-in variation (chance variation) that is impossible to completely eliminate. All we can do is detect when the variation becomes a serious problem and take action to remedy the problem. The most commonly used method to detect changes in the process distribution is the control chart, which is simply an application of hypothesis testing.

18.3   Control Charts for Variables: $\bar{x}$ and S Charts

Control charts for variables can employ either the sample standard deviations or the sample ranges. To draw the $\bar{x}$ chart using sample standard deviations requires a computer and software. In the next section we discuss how to draw control charts for variables manually.

18.4   Control Charts for Variables: $\bar{x}$ and R Charts

When the process produces final products or subcomponents that we can measure quantitatively, we determine whether changes have taken place in the process distribution by computing sample means and sample ranges. We then construct the $\bar{x}$ chart and the R chart.

$\bar{x}$ Charts

The purpose of drawing an $\bar{x}$ chart is to determine if the mean of the process distribution has changed. Put simply, we draw an $\bar{x}$ chart to discover whether at some point the production process has started producing components that are larger or smaller than specified. The $\bar{x}$ chart is constructed by taking at least 25 samples, usually of between 3 and 10 units, off an assembly line at regular periods. For each sample, we compute the mean and the range. We then calculate the mean of the sample means and the mean of the sample ranges.

$$\bar{\bar{x}} = \frac{\sum\limits_{j=1}^{k} \bar{x}_j}{k}$$

$$\bar{R} = \frac{\sum\limits_{j=1}^{k} R_j}{k}$$

The centerline and the control limits of the $\bar{x}$ chart are defined as follows (values of A_2 are provided in Table 8 in Appendix B.):

Centerline $= \bar{\bar{x}}$

Upper control limit $= \bar{\bar{x}} + A_2\bar{R}$

Lower control limit $= \bar{\bar{x}} - A_2\bar{R}$

Question: Why do we use the sample ranges to estimate the process distribution dispersion?

Answer: The range is easier to compute than the standard deviation. In most factories, the calculations for control charts are done by machine operators on the spot. As a result, ease of calculation is an important consideration. That's why in actual practice the $\bar{x}$ chart is frequently constructed by computing sample means and ranges.

R Charts

The R chart is designed to determine whether the dispersion of the process distribution has changed. A certain amount of variability is normal and inevitable. However, when the variability appears to increase, we need to be concerned, because the process will then produce products that are outside the specifications. The centerline and control limits of the R chart are determined in the following way (values of D_3 and D_4 are listed in Table 8.):

Centerline $= \bar{R}$

Upper control limit $= D_4\bar{R}$

Lower control limit $= D_3\bar{R}$

Example 18.1

Catsup bottles are filled on an assembly line using a device that controls the amount of catsup. To determine if the device is operating effectively, statistical process control is employed. Every hour, four 16-ounce bottles of catsup are sampled. The exact amount of catsup is measured. The data in the accompanying table represent the last 25 samples.

a) Draw the R chart.
b) Draw the $\bar{x}$ chart.
c) What conclusion can be drawn from the two control charts?

Sample				
1	16.00	16.04	16.09	16.00
2	15.99	16.04	16.02	16.12
3	16.00	15.94	15.96	15.92
4	16.04	16.03	16.00	16.00
5	15.96	15.96	16.04	15.94
6	16.08	16.02	15.97	15.97
7	15.99	15.92	16.03	16.04
8	16.03	16.09	15.99	15.95
9	16.06	15.94	15.96	15.99
10	15.92	16.02	16.12	15.93
11	16.07	16.02	16.01	15.99
12	15.94	16.09	15.96	15.94
13	16.00	15.99	16.06	15.99
14	16.00	16.06	16.06	15.98
15	16.01	16.01	15.93	16.02
16	16.02	15.91	16.11	16.01
17	16.05	16.08	16.05	15.99
18	15.95	16.09	16.02	16.04
19	15.94	15.93	15.92	16.08
20	16.03	16.00	16.04	16.06
21	15.94	16.00	16.05	15.99
22	16.06	15.93	16.06	16.00
23	16.00	16.02	16.08	16.01
24	15.90	15.94	16.10	15.98
25	15.98	16.00	16.06	16.02

Solution

We begin by calculating the means and ranges of the samples (shown below). The centerline and control limits for the R chart are computed using $\bar{R}$ and Table 8 in Appendix B in the textbook.

Sample	$\bar{x}_j$	R_j
1	16.03	.09
2	16.04	.13
3	15.96	.08
4	16.02	.04
5	15.98	.10
6	16.01	.11
7	16.00	.12
8	16.02	.14
9	15.99	.12
10	16.00	.20
11	16.02	.08
12	15.98	.15
13	16.01	.07
14	16.03	.08
15	15.99	.09
16	16.01	.20
17	16.04	.09
18	16.03	.14
19	15.97	.16
20	16.03	.06
21	16.00	.11
22	16.01	.13
23	16.03	.08
24	15.98	.20
25	16.02	.08
	$\bar{\bar{x}} = 16.01$	$\bar{R} = .114$

a) R chart:

Centerline $= \overline{R} = .114$

Upper control limit $= D_4\overline{R} = 2.282(.114) = .260$

Lower control limit $= D_3\overline{R} = 0$

We construct the R chart by plotting the 25 sample ranges and drawing the centerline, lower, and upper cont rol limits.

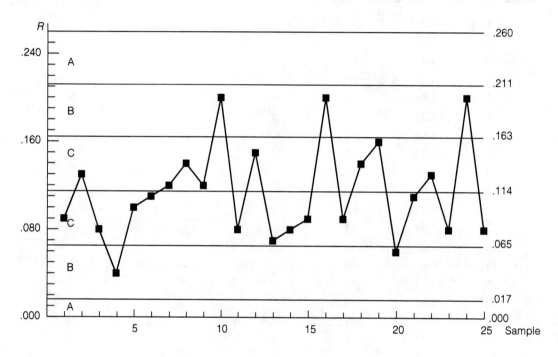

b) $\bar{x}$ chart:

Centerline $= \overline{\overline{x}} = 16.01$.

Upper control limit $= \bar{x} + A_2\overline{R} = 16.01 + .729(.114) = 16.09$

Lower control limit $= \bar{x} - A_2\overline{R} = 16.01 - .729(.114) = 15.93$

The boundaries of the zones are as shown below:

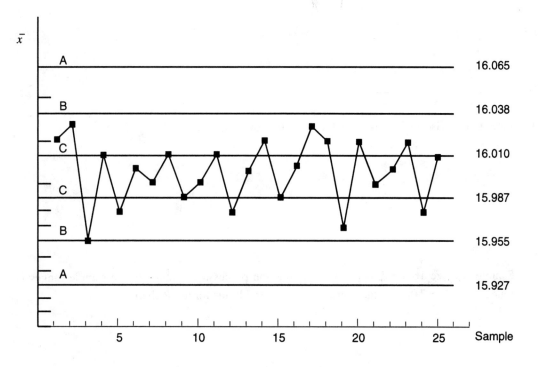

$$\bar{\bar{x}} + A_2\bar{R} = 16.093$$

$$\bar{\bar{x}} + 2/3\,A_2\bar{R} = 16.01 + 2/3(.729)(.114) = 16.065$$

$$\bar{\bar{x}} + 1/3\,A_2\bar{R} = 16.01 + 1/3(.729)(.114) = 16.038$$

$$\bar{\bar{x}} = 16.010$$

$$\bar{\bar{x}} - 1/3\,A_2\bar{R} = 16.01 - 1/3(.729)(.114) = 15.982$$

$$\bar{\bar{x}} - 2/3\,A_2\bar{R} = 16.01 - 2/3(.729)(.114) = 15.955$$

$$\bar{\bar{x}} - A_2\bar{R} = 15.927$$

c)   There appears to be no evidence that the process is out of control.

EXERCISES

18.1   Suppose samples of size 10 are taken from an assembly line. The mean of the sample means and the mean of the sample ranges are calculated and are exhibited below. Determine the centerline and control limits for the $\bar{x}$ chart.

$$\bar{\bar{x}} = 405 \qquad \bar{R} = 30$$

18.2   Refer to Exercise 18.1. Calculate the boundaries of the zones for the $\bar{x}$ chart.

18.3   Refer to Exercise 18.1. Determine the centerline and control limits for the R chart.

18.4   Samples of size 16 are drawn from a production process. The mean of the sample ranges is found to be $\bar{R} = 7.0$. Find the centerline and control limits for the R chart.

18.5 Statistical process control is used by a hardware manufacturer to ensure the quality of its products. One such product is a 3-inch door hinge. In this hinge, there are six interlocking parts through which the pin must pass. Each part must be 1/2 inch long. If they are any longer, the parts won't fit; if they are any shorter, the door will wobble. Random samples of three hinges are taken every 2 hours. The data from the last 25 samples are shown in the accompanying table.

a) Draw the R chart.

b) Draw the $\bar{x}$ chart.

c) What do the control charts tell you about the production process?

Sample			
1	.512	.499	.500
2	.483	.509	.503
3	.506	.520	.497
4	.507	.488	.513
5	.513	.491	.514
6	.503	.499	.515
7	.484	.510	.502
8	.509	.506	.513
9	.511	.511	.487
10	.499	.507	.521
11	.491	.499	.501
12	.500	.490	.493
13	.498	.499	.486
14	.513	.496	.517

Sample			
15	.518	.491	.515
16	.504	.507	.524
17	.513	.494	.503
18	.507	.500	.487
19	.511	.509	.494
20	.504	.507	.518
21	.517	.511	.504
22	.504	.518	.509
23	.514	.510	.522
24	.510	.514	.506
25	.514	.508	.503
26	.515	.505	.507
27	.498	.518	.509
28	.511	.523	.503
29	.494	.508	.505
30	.511	.502	.507

18.5   Control Charts for Attributes: *p* Chart

With many products or subcomponents, we're interested only in determining whether they work properly. Thus, rather than measuring some dimension of the unit, we classify it as either defective or nondefective. We acknowledge that even when the process is operating properly some defectives will be produced. However, when the proportion of defectives becomes large, we conclude that the process is out of control and requires corrective action. We use a *p* chart to tell us when the proportion of defectives is too large to be caused by simple random variation. To construct a *p* chart, we take at least 25 samples and count the number of defectives in each sample. The sample proportions $\hat{p}_j$ and the mean of the sample proportions $\bar{p}$ are calculated where

$$\bar{p} = \frac{\sum\limits_{j=1}^{k} \hat{p}_j}{k}$$

The centerline and control limits are determined as follows:

Centerline $= \bar{p}$

Upper control limit $= \bar{p} + 3\sqrt{\dfrac{\bar{p}(1-\bar{p})}{n}}$

$$\text{Lower control limit} = \bar{p} - 3\sqrt{\frac{\bar{p}(1 - \bar{p})}{n}}$$

In order to apply the pattern tests, we need the zones. These are calculated as shown below.

Example 18.2

A company that produces light bulbs wants to reduce the number of defective bulbs that it produces. Consequently, the company has adopted statistical process control methods. Random samples of 500 bulbs are taken off the 60-watt light bulb production line every hour. The number of defectives in the last 30 samples is shown in the accompanying table. Construct the p chart to determine if the process is under control.

Sample	Number of Defectives		Sample	Number of Defectives
1	7		16	7
2	12		17	8
3	15		18	6
4	9		19	7
5	4		20	9
6	9		21	9
7	11		22	5
8	11		23	11
9	7		24	29
10	4		25	21
11	10		26	32
12	7		27	25
13	12		28	29
14	15		29	30
15	10		30	27

Solution

The sample proportions are computed (as shown below), and from these figures we calculate their mean:

$$\bar{p} = \frac{\sum\limits_{j=1}^{k} \hat{p}_j}{k} = .0265$$

Sample	Number of Defectives	Sample Proportions $\hat{p}_j$
1	7	.014
2	12	.024
3	15	.030
4	9	.018
5	4	.008
6	9	.018
7	11	.022
8	11	.022
9	7	.014
10	4	.008
11	10	.020
12	7	.014
13	12	.024
14	15	.030
15	10	.020
16	7	.014
17	8	.016
18	6	.012
19	7	.014
20	9	.018
21	9	.018
22	5	.010
23	11	.022
24	29	.058
25	21	.042
26	32	.064
27	25	.050
28	29	.058
29	30	.060
30	27	.054

$$\bar{p} = .0265$$

The centerline, control limits, and zone boundaries can now be calculated.

$\hat{p}$

$$\bar{p} + 3\sqrt{\frac{\bar{p}(1-\bar{p})}{n}} = .0265 + 3\sqrt{\frac{(.0265)(.9735)}{500}} = .0481$$

A

$$\bar{p} + 2\sqrt{\frac{\bar{p}(1-\bar{p})}{n}} = .0265 + 2\sqrt{\frac{(.0265)(.9735)}{500}} = .0409$$

B

$$\bar{p} + \sqrt{\frac{\bar{p}(1-\bar{p})}{n}} = .0265 + \sqrt{\frac{(.0265)(.9735)}{500}} = .0337$$

C

$$\bar{p} = .0265$$

C

$$\bar{p} - \sqrt{\frac{\bar{p}(1-\bar{p})}{n}} = .0265 - \sqrt{\frac{(.0265)(.9735)}{500}} = .0193$$

B

$$\bar{p} - 2\sqrt{\frac{\bar{p}(1-\bar{p})}{n}} = .0265 - 2\sqrt{\frac{(.0265)(.9735)}{500}} = .0121$$

A

$$\bar{p} - 3\sqrt{\frac{\bar{p}(1-\bar{p})}{n}} = .0265 - 3\sqrt{\frac{(.0265)(.9735)}{500}} = .0050$$

Finally, we plot the sample proportions to complete the *p* chart.

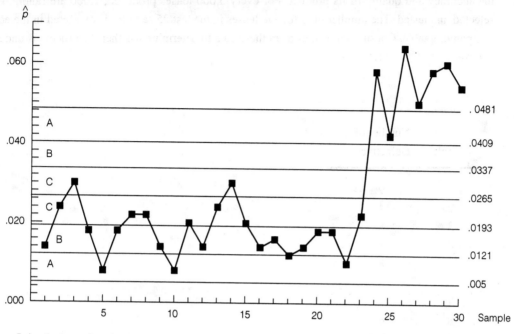

It is obvious that the process went out of control before sample number 24 was drawn.

EXERCISES

18.6   Random samples of 100 units are taken from a production process and the number of defectives counted. The mean of the sample proportions was found to be $\bar{p} = .11$. Find the centerline and control limits for the *p* chart.

18.7   Refer to Exercise 18.6. Find the boundaries of the zones for the *p* chart.

18.8   A company that manufactures lenses for cameras employs statistical process control to maintain the accuracy and quality of its product. For every 5,000 lenses produced, 1,000 are randomly selected and tested. The number of defective lenses in the last 25 samples is exhibited in the accompanying table. Construct a p chart from these data to determine whether the process is under control.

Sample	Number of Defectives
1	9
2	4
3	8
4	8
5	8
6	6
7	4
8	6
9	7
10	10
11	3
12	5
13	8
14	6
15	4
16	7
17	5
18	6
19	5
20	6
21	12
22	7
23	4
24	5
25	7

Chapter 19: Statistical Inference: Conclusion

This chapter of the Study Guide gives you an opportunity to practice identifying and using the correct statistical technique by providing 18 more exercises. These exercises require the use of most of the statistical methods introduced in the 10 chapters on statistical inference. Notice that in each exercise we encourage you to write down the answers to the questions that appear in the flowchart provided in Chapter 19 of the textbook. The first two questions ask you to identify the problem objective and the type of data. Depending on this combination, you may need to recognize additional factors. After determining the correct method to use in each exercise, specify the hypotheses, the test statistic, and the rejection region and/or the confidence interval estimator. You may, if you wish, complete the problem by performing the computations. However, we don't think that it's terribly important to do so—it involves only arithmetic. Concentrate on the critical aspects of the problem, that is, recognizing the technique to use and preparing for the solution.

EXERCISES

19.1   Have North American automobile manufacturers improved the quality of their products? Fifteen years ago a sample of 500 people who had purchased a new General Motors, Ford, or Chrysler car were asked if they had found any major defects in their newly purchased automobiles. A total of 48 people responded affirmatively. This year in a sample of 800 purchasers of new General Motors, Ford, or Chrysler cars, 50 complained of major defects.

   a)   Can we conclude at the 5% significance level that North American car manufacturers improved the quality of their automobiles in the last 15 years?

   Problem objective:

   Data type:

   Other factors:

   Statistical technique:

   H_0:

   H_A:

Test statistic:

Rejection region:

Value of the test statistic:

Conclusion:

b) Estimate the parameter tested above with 95% confidence.

Confidence interval estimator:

Statistics:

Confidence interval estimate:

LCL =

UCL =

19.2 A car dealership wanted to get some information about new car buyers who arranged for a car loan. In particular, dealers wanted to know what proportion of the total price was the buyer's down payment. As a preliminary study, they randomly sampled 15 new car buyers who arranged for loans and found the proportion representing the down payment. These values are shown below. Find the 95% confidence interval estimate of the relevant parameter.

25, 20, 32, 10, 12, 27, 16, 28, 30, 50, 23, 28, 17, 20, 22

Problem objective:

Data type:

Other factors:

Confidence interval estimator:

Statistics:

Confidence interval estimate:

LCL =

UCL =

19.3   It's important for real estate agents to know if certain areas of a city have more costly houses. In order to examine the issue, a real estate agent found the selling price of five randomly selected two-storied four-bedroom houses in each of five geographical areas of the city. The prices (in tens of thousands of dollars) are shown below. Do these data allow us to conclude at the 10% significance level that there are differences in house prices among the five areas? (Assume that the prices are normally distributed.)

Selling Prices of Homes (in $10,000s)

		Area		
1	2	3	4	5
5	10	12	14	11
6	12	17	18	12
10	13	19	20	12
18	21	27	25	18
20	23	30	31	18

Problem objective:

Data type:

Other factors:

Statistical technique:

H_0:

H_A:

Test statistic:

Rejection region:

Value of the test statistic:

Conclusion:

19.4   An urban planner is in the process of examining the residential makeup of homes that are owned by the city's residents. In particular, she would like to know if there are differences among five geographic areas of a city in terms of the number of condominium apartments, condominium townhouses, one-storied bungalows, two-storied three-bedroom houses, and two-storied four-bedroom houses. As an experiment, 422 residential telephone numbers are randomly selected, and the area and the type of home for each number is determined. The results are shown below. Do these data allow us to conclude at the 10% significance level that there are differences among the five geographic areas in terms of the types of homes?

Number of Homes

Type of Home	Area				
	1	2	3	4	5
Condo apartment	5	10	12	14	11
Condo townhouse	6	12	17	18	12
Bungalow	10	13	19	20	12
Two-storied (3-bedroom)	18	21	27	25	18
Two-storied (4-bedroom)	20	23	30	31	18

Problem objective:

Data type:

Other factors:

Statistical technique:

H_0:

H_A:

Test statistic:

Rejection region:

Value of the test statistic:

Conclusion:

19.5   Portable small-screen (4.5 inch) television sets have become quite popular in the last few years. Most use 8 D-cells to provide power. However, the power requirements are so great that the batteries are usually drained after only 1 1/2 hours of use. In an attempt to improve on this feature, a new type of television receiver was invented. To determine if the new receiver operates for longer periods of time, an experiment was undertaken. Six portable televisions using the current technology and six using the new technology were operated until the batteries wore out. The times were recorded and are shown below.

Battery Lives (Hours)	
Old Technology	New Technology
1.6	1.5
1.4	1.6
1.6	1.7
1.5	1.8
1.3	1.6
1.4	1.7

a)   Can we conclude at the 5% significance level that the new technology prolongs battery lives when compared to the current technology? (Assume that the times are normally distributed.)

Problem objective:

Data type:

Other factors:

Statistical technique:

H_0:

H_A:

Test statistic:

Rejection region:

Value of the test statistic:

Conclusion:

b)   Estimate the parameter tested above with 99% confidence.

Confidence interval estimator:

Statistics:

Confidence interval estimate:

LCL =

UCL =

19.6   A television repairman believes that there is a relationship between the make of the television and the type of repair required. In order to investigate this issue, he kept track of the makes and repairs of all five-year-old television sets brought in during the past month. He decided to restrict the study to televisions made by Sony, Toshiba, and Zenith. He categorized each repair in the following way:

Category 1: Picture problem

Category 2: Reception problem

Category 3: Sound problem

For each of the three television makes, he has observed the following:

Sony: 1, 1, 2, 3, 1, 1, 3, 1, 1, 2, 3, 2, 1, 2, 1, 3, 1, 2, 3, 2

Toshiba: 1, 2, 3, 1, 1, 2, 1, 2, 2, 1, 3, 1, 2, 2, 1, 3, 1, 2, 3

Zenith: 1, 3, 2, 2, 3, 2, 1, 2, 2, 3, 2, 1, 2, 2, 2, 3, 2, 3, 3, 2, 2, 1, 2

Do these data provide sufficient evidence at the 1% significance level to support the repairman's belief?

Problem objective:

Data type:

Other factors:

Statistical technique:

H_0:

H_A:

Test statistic:

Rejection region:

Value of the test statistic:

Conclusion:

19.7 A school board in a large metropolitan area has been concerned about the truancy rate. Ten years ago, an extensive study revealed that 1 student in 10 was absent on any given day. An official of the school board believes that the absenteeism rate is even higher today. A random sample of 200 pupils indicates that 28 of them are absent today. Do these data provide sufficient evidence at the 5% significance level to support the official's belief?

Problem objective:

Data type:

274

Other factors:

Statistical technique:

H_0:

H_A:

Test statistic:

Rejection region:

Value of the test statistic:

Conclusion:

19.8   A restaurateur who owns and operates a restaurant located in a large office building believes that gross sales vary according to the day of the week. To examine his belief, he takes a random sample of 22 days' gross sales. He records the sales amounts and the days of the week. These data are shown below. Can we conclude with $\alpha = .01$ that there are differences in gross sales among the days of the week? (Assume that sales are normally distributed.)

Day of the Week	Gross Sales (in $100s)	Day of the Week	Gross Sales (in $100s)
Th	18	F	23
T	10	T	12
M	23	F	19
T	17	W	17
Th	15	F	19
F	20	Th	16
W	14	T	15
W	22	M	22
W	15	W	19
M	18	Th	20
Th	15	W	22

Problem objective:

Data type:

Other factors:

Statistical technique:

H_0:

H_A:

Test statistic:

Rejection region:

Value of the test statistic:

Conclusion:

19.9   A statistics professor gives several quizzes each semester. Students are given 30 minutes to complete the quiz but may hand in their quiz papers at any time prior to the deadline. The professor believes that the longer the student takes to complete the quiz, the lower the mark will be. To test his belief, he keeps track of how long each student took to complete the quiz and their mark for a class of 20 students. The results are shown below. At the 1% significance level, can the professor conclude that his belief is correct?

Time in Minutes	Marks
25	87, 93, 84
26	79, 71, 69
27	72
28	85, 79, 75
29	61, 65, 75, 69
30	73, 71, 62, 65, 58, 60

Problem objective:

Data type:

Other factors:

Statistical technique:

H_0:

H_A:

Test statistic:

Rejection region:

Value of the test statistic:

Conclusion:

Exercises 19.10 to 19.16 are based on the following problem and data: The medical profession in North America has been subject to both praise and criticism in recent years. Some medical advances in the fields of cancer and heart disease have been extraordinary. However, the high cost of health insurance and the perception that physicians are motivated by money alone have drawn the concern of large numbers of people. In order to examine this issue, a survey was undertaken. Among other things, individuals were categorized by sex and age (young adult, middle age, and senior citizen) and were asked the following questions.

a)   How frequently in the last 12 months did you visit your physician?

b)   What was the purpose of your last visit?

  1.   Routine checkup

  2.   Treatment for a previously diagnosed condition

  3.   New problem

The data for 60 respondents are shown in the accompanying table.

Exercises 19.10 to 19.16 each describe a belief of the researchers who undertook the survey. Test each belief at the 5% significance level. (Assume that the frequencies in question (a) are normally distributed.)

Sex	Age Category	a	b
F	Y	0	2
F	Y	1	3
F	Y	1	2
F	Y	2	1
F	Y	2	3
F	Y	1	2
F	Y	0	3
F	Y	0	3
F	Y	1	3
F	Y	2	2
F	M	2	3
F	M	1	1
F	M	1	2
F	M	2	1
F	M	3	1
F	M	2	2
F	M	4	3
F	M	3	1
F	M	4	2
F	M	3	2
F	S	3	2
F	S	5	2
F	S	2	2

Sex	Age Category	a	b
F	S	1	3
F	S	2	1
F	S	3	2
F	S	5	3
F	S	6	1
F	S	2	2
F	S	5	3
M	Y	0	3
M	Y	0	1
M	Y	1	3
M	Y	2	2
M	Y	1	3
M	Y	1	2
M	Y	0	3
M	Y	0	3
M	Y	0	1
M	Y	1	2
M	M	0	1
M	M	2	1
M	M	1	2
M	M	2	3
M	M	1	1
M	M	3	3
M	M	2	1
M	M	0	1
M	M	2	1
M	M	3	2
M	S	4	3
M	S	1	2
M	S	0	1
M	S	5	2
M	S	2	1
M	S	4	2
M	S	1	2
M	S	1	2
M	S	4	3
M	S	2	1

19.10   Belief: There are differences in the frequency of visits among the age categories.

Problem objective:

Data type:

Other factors:

Statistical technique:

H_0:

H_A:

Test statistic:

Rejection region:

Value of the test statistic:

Conclusion:

19.11   Belief: Females visit their doctors more frequently than males.

Problem objective:

Data type:

Other factors:

Statistical technique:

H_0:

H_A:

Test statistic:

Rejection region:

Value of the test statistic:

Conclusion:

19.12 Belief: Males are more likely to visit their physicians for a routine checkup than are females.

Problem objective:

Data type:

Other factors:

Statistical technique:

H_0:

H_A:

Test statistic:

Rejection region:

Value of the test statistic:

Conclusion:

19.13 Belief: There are differences in the reasons for physician visits among the age categories.

Problem objective:

Data type:

Other factors:

Statistical technique:

H_0:

H_A:

Test statistic:

Rejection region:

Value of the test statistic:

Conclusion:

19.14 Belief: Less than half of all visits are for routine checkups.

Problem objective:

Data type:

Other factors:

Statistical technique:

H_0:

H_A:

Test statistic:

Rejection region:

Value of the test statistic:

Conclusion:

19.15   Belief: The average patient visits his or her physician at least one and a half times per year.

Problem objective:

Data type:

Other factors:

Statistical technique:

H_0:

H_A:

Test statistic:

Rejection region:

Value of the test statistic:

Conclusion:

19.16 Belief: The purpose of the visit is equally divided among the three responses.

Problem objective:

Data type:

Other factors:

Statistical technique:

H_0:

H_A:

Test statistic:

Rejection region:

Value of the test statistic:

Conclusion:

19.17 During the 1996 baseball season, the large number of home runs caused sports announcers to speculate that the baseball was livelier than in previous years. To investigate this issue, 10 baseball players were asked to participate in an experiment. Each player had two balls pitched to him. One ball was produced from the usual source in 1996, and the other was produced in 1995. The distances the balls traveled were recorded and are presented below. Can we conclude from these data that the 1996 ball is livelier? Use $\alpha = .05$. (Assume that distances are normally distributed.)

	Distance in Feet	
Player	1996 Ball	1995 Ball
Albert Belle	417	428
Ellis Burke	425	395
Joe Carter	363	350
Ryon Klesko	395	371
Fred McGriff	408	382
Mark McGwire	415	414
Paul O'Neill	360	350
Ed Sprague	410	383
Ruben Sierra	380	369
Bernie Williams	421	402

Problem objective:

Data type:

Other factors:

Statistical technique:

H_0:

H_A:

Test statistic:

Rejection region:

Value of the test statistic:

Conclusion:

19.18   A number of companies have adopted a flex-time policy wherein employees set their own starting time for their shifts. One such company wanted to determine if productivity is affected by the choice of a starting time. Three employees who chose different starting times were randomly selected. Their productivity was measured on a 100-point scale for each day of a week. The results are shown below. Is there sufficient evidence at the 5% significance level to infer that productivity is affected by the shift starting time? (Assume that the productivity measures are normally distributed.)

	Shift Starting Time		
Weekday	7:00 A.M.	8:00 A.M.	9:00 A.M.
Monday	87	85	83
Tuesday	93	95	90
Wednesday	91	96	93
Thursday	88	91	90
Friday	86	89	91

Problem objective:

Data type:

Other factors:

Statistical technique:

H_0:

H_A:

Test statistic:

Rejection region:

Value of the test statistic:

Conclusion:

Appendix:
Answers to Exercises

Chapter 1

1.1 a) The population is the collection of all unpaid account balances at the store. Its parameter is the average of the population of balances.

     b) The sample is the unpaid balances for the 50 accounts.

     c) The figure $75 is the average of the sample of 50 unpaid balances. Thus, $75 is a statistic.

1.2 a) The population parameter is the percentage of school children in New York State who spend at least 25 hours a week watching television.

        The sample statistic is the percentage of the 250 school children interviewed who spend at least 25 hours a week watching television.

     b) The inference should be restricted to the population from which the sample was taken: the school children in New York State.

Chapter 2

2.1 Quantitative data are numerical observations. Qualitative data are categorical observations; i.e., observations that can be sorted into categories on the basis of qualitative attributes such as marital status and occupation.

2.2 a) qualitative; b) qualitative; c) quantitative; d) ranked; e) quantitative

2.3 a) quantitative; b) ranked; c) qualitative; d) qualitative; e) quantitative

2.4 a)

Stem	Leaf
1	73, 60, 75, 91, 65, 80, 58, 79
2	08, 65, 25, 56, 15, 63, 81, 26, 90, 30, 39, 75, 28, 98, 52, 11, 26, 00, 24, 20, 84, 45, 60, 32, 04, 17
3	48, 34, 00, 15, 54
4	22

b)

Class Limits	Frequency
150 up to 200	8
200 up to 250	16
250 up to 300	10
300 up to 350	4
350 up to 400	1
400 up to 450	1

2.5

Class Limits	Relative Frequency	Cumulative Relative Frequency
150 up to 200	.200	.200
200 up to 250	.400	.600
250 up to 300	.250	.850
300 up to 350	.100	.950
350 up to 400	.025	.975
400 up to 450	.025	1.000

a)

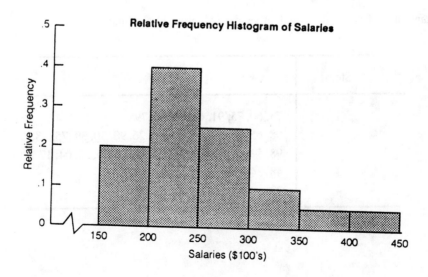

Relative Frequency Histogram of Salaries

b)

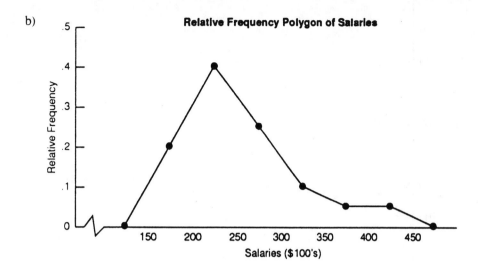

c)

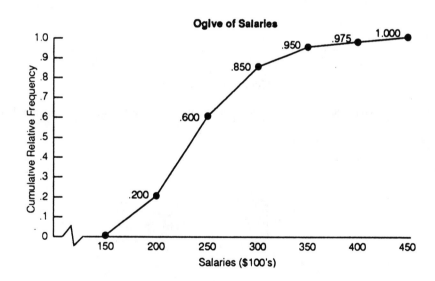

2.6

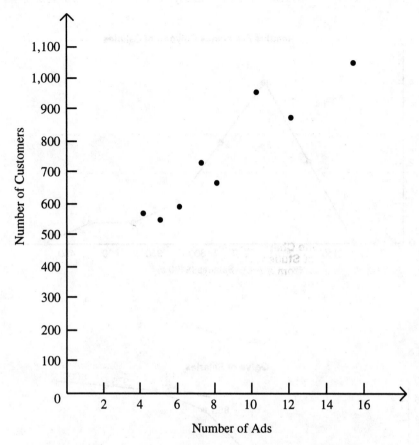

There is a positive linear relationship between the number of ads placed and the number of customers.

2.7	Age	Frequency	Proportion	Degrees
	16 up to 20	1,560,000	.26	93.6
	20 up to 25	960,000	.16	57.6
	25 up to 60	3,000,000	.50	180.0
	60 and over	480,000	.08	28.8
	Total	6,000,000	1.00	360.0

b)

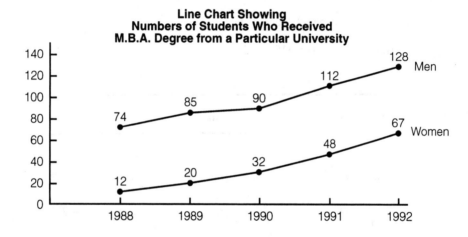

Line Chart Showing
Numbers of Students Who Received
M.B.A. Degree from a Particular University

Chapter 4

4.1 a) 30.3
    b) 30
    c) 32

4.2 a) 243.2
    b) 229
    c) 200 up to 250

4.3 a) mean, median, mode
    b) mode
    c) median, mode

4.4 a) 20.5

b) 14

c) 27.5

d) 5.24

4.5 a) 20.5

b) 22.92

c) 4.79

4.6 a) .68

b) .025

4.7 $s \cong 10.75$; the distribution is asymmetrical.

4.8 a) 206 (midpoint between 204 and 208)

b) 229 (midpoint between 228 and 230)

c) 278 (midpoint between 275 and 281)

d) 324.5 (midpoint between 315 and 334)

4.9 a)

Descriptive Statistic	Rank	Numerical Value
S	1	160
Q_1	10.5	$206 = \dfrac{204 + 208}{2}$
Q_2	20.5	$229 = \dfrac{228 + 230}{2}$
Q_3	30.5	$278 = \dfrac{275 + 281}{2}$
L	40	422

4.9 b) $IQR = Q_3 - Q_1 = 278 - 206 = 72$

$1.5(IQR) = 1.5(7.2) = 108$

The value 422 is an outlier, because it is outside the interval $(206 - 108, 278 + 108) = (98, 386)$

Box Plot of 40 Salaries

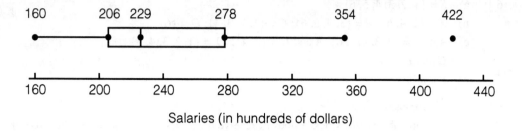

Salaries (in hundreds of dollars)

c) The data are skewed to the right, because the right whisker is longer than the left whisker.

4.10 $\bar{x} = 8.375$

$s_x = 3.74$

$\bar{y} = 740.5$

$s_y = 201.68$

x	y	$(x - \bar{x})$	$(y - \bar{y})$	$(x - \bar{x})(y - \bar{y})$
5	528	−3.375	−212.5	717.1875
12	876	3.625	135.5	491.1875
8	653	−0.375	−87.5	32.8125
6	571	−2.375	−169.5	402.5625
4	556	−4.375	−184.5	807.1875
15	1058	6.625	317.5	2103.438
10	963	1.625	222.5	361.5625
7	719	−1.375	−21.5	<u>29.5625</u>
				4945.5

$$\text{cov}(X,Y) = \frac{\sum(x_i - \bar{x})(y_i - \bar{y})}{n-1} = \frac{4945.5}{7} = 706.5$$

$$r = \frac{\text{cov}(X,Y)}{s_x s_y} = \frac{706.5}{(3.74)(201.68)} = 0.937$$

There is a reasonably strong linear relationship between X and Y.

Chapter 6

6.1 a) $S = \{1, 2, 3, 4, 5, 6\}$
    b) $A = \{2, 4, 6\}$; $B = \{3, 4, 5, 6\}$; $C = \{1, 2, 3, 4\}$; $D = \{6\}$
    c) A or $B = \{2, 3, 4, 5, 6\}$; A and $C = \{2, 4\}$; $\overline{D} = \{1, 2, 3, 4, 5\}$
    d) C and D
    e) B and C

6.2 a) 1/6 for each
    b) The probability that stock A doesn't receive the lowest rating, or stock C receives the highest rating, or both, is 5/6.
       The probability that neither stock A nor stock B receives the lowest rating is 2/6.
       The probability that stock B receives the lowest rating is 2/6.

6.3 a) The employee has worked for the company for less than two years.
    b) The employee is male, or the employee has worked for the company for two years or more, or both.
    c) The employee is female and has worked for the company for two years or more.
    d) The employee is female, or has worked for the company for less than two years, or both.

6.4 a) .27
    b) .87
    c) .41
    d) .59

6.5 a) The probability that the caller is primarily interested in corporate tax, given that he or she became aware of the report through the newspaper, is 7/9.
    b) The probability that the caller became aware of the report through the newspaper, given that he or she is primarily interested in corporate tax, is 7/12.
    c) The probability that the caller is primarily interested in personal tax, given that he or she became aware of the report through the newspaper, is 2/9.
    d) The probability that the caller is primarily interested in personal tax, given that he or she did not become aware of the report through the newspaper, is 6/11.

6.6 a) 106/120
    b) no

6.7 a) 24.3%
    b) 91.7%

6.8 a) .12
    b) yes
    c) no

6.9 0.96

6.10 16/30

6.11 36/43

6.12 3/7

6.13 a) discrete; $x = 0, 1, 2, \ldots$
    b) continuous; $x > 0$
    c) discrete; $x = 0, 1, 2, \ldots$
    d) discrete; $x = 0, 1, 2, \ldots, 14, 15$
    e) continuous; $x > 0$

6.14 a) .021
    b) .433
    c) .284
    d) .883

6.15

x	1	2	3
$p(x)$	.04	.32	.64

6.16 a) .291
    b) .92; 1.1576
    c) .979

6.17 $1,300; $640.31

6.18 a) $300; $640.31
    b) $900; $5,762.79

6.19 a)

x	$p(x)$	y	$p(y)$
2	.6	4	.7
4	.4	8	.3

    b) $\mu_x = 2.8$

        $\mu_y = 5.2$

        $V(X) = .960$

        $V(Y) = 3.36$

        $\sigma_x = .98$

$\sigma_x = 1.83$

c) $COV(X,Y) = -.16$

d) $\rho = -.089$

6.20

x	0	1	2	3
$p(x)$	.389	.432	.160	.020

6.21 a) .902
b) .000
c) .002
d) .510

6.22 a) 9; 1.897
b) .403
c) .783

6.23 a) .0655
b) .065
c) .215

6.24 a) .182   b) .181

Chapter 7

7.1 a)

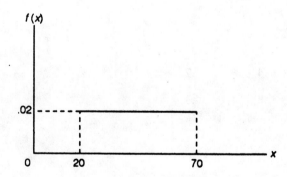

b) (1) $f(x) \geq 0$ for all values of x
   (2) Area under graph of $f(x) = (70 - 20)(.02) = 1$
c) .6
d) .38

7.2 a)

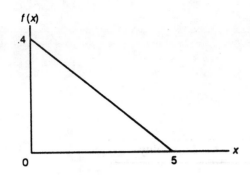

b) (1) $f(x) \geq 0$ for $0 \leq x \leq 5$

(2) Area under graph of $f(x) = \dfrac{1}{2}\,bh = \dfrac{1}{2}(5)(.4) = 1$

c) .16   d) .64   e) 0

7.3 a) .0322
    b) .9678
    c) .7214
    d) .1009

7.4 a) 1.645   b) 2.33

7.5 a) .2389   b) .6165   c) .0262

7.6 a) .0018   b) .8944   c) 55.36 mm

7.7 .5646

7.8 a) .135   b) .406

7.9 a) .181   b) .247   c) .468

Chapter 8

8.1 $p(102 < \bar{x} < 112)$

$$= p\left(\frac{102-100}{40/\sqrt{64}} < \frac{\bar{x}-\mu}{\sigma/\sqrt{n}} < \frac{112-100}{40/\sqrt{64}} \right)$$

$$= p(.4 < z < 2.4) = .3364$$

8.2

$$P(\bar{x} > 23)$$

$$= P\left(\frac{\bar{x} - \mu}{\sigma / \sqrt{n}} > \frac{23 - 20}{10 / \sqrt{25}}\right)$$

$$= P(z > 1.5) = .0668$$

8.3

Sample	$\bar{x}$	Probability
0,0,0	0	.343
0,0,1	1/3	.147
0,1,0	1/3	.147
1,0,0	1/3	.147
0,1,1	2/3	.063
1,0,1	2/3	.063
1,1,0	2/3	.063
1,1,1	1	.027

$\bar{x}$	$P(\bar{x})$
0	.343
1/3	.441
2/3	.189
1	.027

$$\mu_{\bar{x}} = .3$$

$$\sigma_{\bar{x}}^2 = .07$$

Chapter 9

9.1 An estimator is a random variable that is a function of the sample data. An estimate is the calculation of a specific value of this random variable.

9.2 a) An estimator of a parameter is unbiased if the expected value of the estimator is equal to the parameter.

b) An unbiased estimator is consistent if the difference between the estimator and the parameter grows smaller as the sample size grows larger.

9.3 We've already shown that $E(\bar{x}) = \mu$.

9.4 $E(s^2) = \sigma^2$

9.5 $\bar{x}$ is a consistent estimator of μ since $\sigma_{\bar{x}}^2 = \sigma^2/n$.

9.6   a) $\bar{x} \pm z_{\alpha/2} \dfrac{\sigma}{\sqrt{n}} = 1{,}275 \pm 1.96 \dfrac{250}{\sqrt{50}} = 1{,}275 \pm 69.30$

        b) $\bar{x} \pm z_{\alpha/2} \dfrac{\sigma}{\sqrt{n}} = 1{,}275 \pm 1.78 \dfrac{250}{\sqrt{50}} = 1{,}275 \pm 62.93$

9.7 $\bar{x} \pm z_{\alpha/2} \dfrac{\sigma}{\sqrt{n}} = 10.75 \pm 2.575 \dfrac{5}{\sqrt{8}} = 10.75 \pm 4.55$

9.8 $\bar{x} \pm z_{\alpha/2} \dfrac{\sigma}{\sqrt{n}} = 73 \pm 1.96 \dfrac{8}{\sqrt{15}} = 73 \pm 4.05$

9.9 $n = 2{,}663$

9.10 $n = 266{,}256$

9.11 $n = 1{,}537$

Chapter 10

10.1   a)   Reject H_0 when it is true.
        b)   Do not reject H_0 when it is false.
        c)   Region of values of the test statistic where H_0 is rejected

10.2 α (the significance level)

10.3 β

10.4   the specified value of α

10.5   the sample mean, $\bar{x}$

10.6   a) $|z| > 1.96$
        b) $z > 2.33$
        c) $z < -1.28$

10.7   a)   Rejection region: $z > 1.645$

            Test statistic: $z = 6.93$

            Conclusion: Reject H_0.

        b)   Rejection region: $|z| > 2.575$

Test statistic: $z = 2.5$

Conclusion: Do not reject H_0.

10.8 H_0: $\mu = 25$
H_A: $\mu > 25$

Rejection region: $z > 1.645$

10.9 H_0: $\mu = 25$
H_A: $\mu < 25$

Rejection region: $z < -1.645$

10.10 H_0: $\mu = 25$
H_A: $\mu < 25$

Test statistic: $z = \dfrac{\bar{x} - \mu}{\sigma/\sqrt{n}}$

Rejection region: $z < -1.645$

Value of the test statistic: $z = -1.63$

Conclusion: Do not reject H_0.

There is not enough evidence to indicate that the students have not accepted her advice.

10.11 H_0: $\mu = 33$
H_A: $\mu < 33$

Test statistic: $z = \dfrac{\bar{x} - \mu}{\sigma/\sqrt{n}}$

Rejection region: $z < -1.28$

Value of the test statistic: $z = -2.25$

Conclusion: Reject H_0.

There is enough evidence to show that the pizza parlor is correct.

10.12 a) Reject H_0.
      b) Do not reject H_0.
      c) Do not reject H_0.

10.13 .1587

10.14 .5

10.15 .9938

10.16 a) $P(z > 1.0) = .1587$

      b) $P(z > 2.0) = .0228$

      c) $P(z > 3.0) = .0013$

      d) $P(z > 4.0) = 0$

10.17 Rejection region: $\bar{x} < 190.68$

10.18 .8599

10.19 .2514

10.20 $H_0: \mu = 10$

      $H_A: \mu > 10$

      Rejection region: $\bar{x} > 10.82$

      $\beta = P(\bar{x} < 10.82 \,|\, \mu = 11.5) = .0119$

Chapter 11

11.1 a) 1.740

     b) −2.467

     c) 1.303

11.2 $t < -1.746$

11.3 $t < -1.684$

11.4 $\bar{x} \pm t_{\alpha/2} \dfrac{s}{\sqrt{n}} = 4.0 \pm 3.707 \dfrac{4.0}{\sqrt{7}} = 4.0 \pm 5.60$

11.5 $\bar{x} \pm t_{\alpha/2} \dfrac{s}{\sqrt{n}} = 57.3 \pm 2.681 \dfrac{6.8}{\sqrt{13}} = 57.3 \pm 5.06$

11.6 $\bar{x} \pm z_{\alpha/2} \dfrac{\sigma}{\sqrt{n}} = 57.3 \pm 2.33 \dfrac{6.8}{\sqrt{13}} = 57.3 \pm 4.39$

11.7 a) $\bar{x} \pm t_{\alpha/2} \dfrac{s}{\sqrt{n}} = 1{,}550 \pm 1.660 \dfrac{125}{\sqrt{100}} = 1{,}550 \pm 20.75$

     b) $H_0: \mu = 1{,}500$

       $H_A: \mu \neq 1{,}500$

     Test statistic: $t = \dfrac{\bar{x} - \mu}{s/\sqrt{n}}$

     Rejection region: $|t| > 2.626$ (approximately)

     Value of the test statistic: $t = 4.0$

Conclusion: Reject H_0.

There is enough evidence to conclude that μ is not equal to 1,500.

11.8 $H_0: \mu = 24$
        $H_A: \mu > 24$

Test statistic: $t = \dfrac{\bar{x} - \mu}{s/\sqrt{n}}$

Rejection region: $|t| > 1.676$ (approximately)

Value of the test statistic: $t = 2.14$

Conclusion: Reject H_0.

There is enough evidence to conclude that the new type of oil is effective in increasing gas mileage.

11.9 $\bar{x} \pm t_{\alpha/2} \dfrac{s}{\sqrt{n}} = 26.3 \pm 2.678 \dfrac{7.6}{\sqrt{50}} = 26.3 \pm 2.88$

11.10 $\bar{x} \pm t_{\alpha/2} \dfrac{s}{\sqrt{n}} = 54.55 \pm 2.201 \dfrac{2.68}{\sqrt{12}} = 54.55 \pm 1.70$

11.11   a) $\chi^2 > 42.5569$ or $\chi^2 < 17.7083$
        b) $\chi^2 > 124.116$
        c) $\chi^2 < 13.8484$

11.12 $H_0: \sigma^2 = 200$
        $H_A: \sigma^2 \neq 200$

Test statistic: $\chi^2 = \dfrac{(n-1)s^2}{\sigma^2}$

Rejection region: $\chi^2 > 14.4494$ or $\chi^2 < 1.237347$

Value of the test statistic: $\chi^2 = 9.29$

Conclusion: Do not reject H_0.

There is not enough evidence to conclude that σ^2 is not equal to 200.

11.13 $H_0: \sigma^2 = 75$
        $H_A: \sigma^2 < 75$

Test statistic: $\chi^2 = \dfrac{(n-1)s^2}{\sigma^2}$

Rejection region: $\chi^2 < 6.40776$

Value of the test statistic: $\chi^2 = 12.988$

Conclusion: Do not reject H_0.

There is not enough evidence to conclude that σ^2 is less than 75.

11.14 H_0: $\sigma^2 = .012$
H_A: $\sigma^2 > .012$

Test statistic: $\chi^2 = \dfrac{(n-1)s^2}{\sigma^2}$

Rejection region: $\chi^2 > 39.0875$

Value of the test statistic: $\chi^2 = 43.5$

Conclusion: Reject H_0.

There is enough evidence to indicate that the contract has been violated.

11.15 $\mathrm{LCL} = \dfrac{(n-1)s^2}{\chi_{\alpha/2}} = \dfrac{29(.018)}{45.7222} = .011$

$\mathrm{UCL} = \dfrac{(n-1)s^2}{\chi_{1-\alpha/2}} = \dfrac{29(.018)}{16.0471} = .033$

11.16 $\hat{p}$ is an unbiased estimator of p because $E(\hat{p}) = p$.

11.17 $\hat{p}$ is a consistent estimator of p because $\sigma_{\hat{p}} = \sqrt{pq/n}$.

11.18 H_0: $p = .03$
H_A: $p > .03$

Test statistic: $z = \dfrac{\hat{p} - p}{\sqrt{pq/n}}$

Rejection region: $z > 1.645$

Value of the test statistic: $z = 1.67$

Conclusion: Reject H_0.

There is sufficient evidence to conclude that p is more than 3%.

11.19 .0475

11.20 $\hat{p} \pm z_{\alpha/2} \sqrt{\dfrac{\hat{p}\hat{q}}{n}} = .048 \pm 1.96 \sqrt{\dfrac{(.048)(.952)}{250}} = .048 \pm .026$

11.21 H_0: $p = .04$

$H_A: p < .04$

Test statistic: $z = \dfrac{\hat{p} - p}{\sqrt{pq/n}}$

Rejection region: $z < -1.28$

Value of the test statistic: $z = -1.66$

Conclusion: Reject H_0.

There is enough evidence to conclude that the RIDE Program is successful.

11.22 .0485

11.23 $\hat{p} \pm z_{\alpha/2} \sqrt{\dfrac{\hat{p}\hat{q}}{n}} = .12 \pm 1.96 \sqrt{\dfrac{(.12)(.88)}{100}} = .12 \pm .064$

11.24 $n = 385$

11.25 $n = 246$

11.26 $n = 139$

Chapter 12

12.1 $H_0: (\mu_1 - \mu_2) = 0$
$H_A: (\mu_1 - \mu_2) > 0$

Test statistic: $t = \dfrac{(\bar{x}_1 - \bar{x}_2) - (\mu_1 - \mu_2)}{\sqrt{s_p^2(1/n_1 + 1/n_2)}}$

Rejection region: $t > 1.622$

Value of the test statistic: $t = 3.45$

Conclusion: Reject H_0.

There is enough evidence to indicate that μ_1 exceeds μ_2.

12.2 $(\bar{x}_1 - \bar{x}_2) \pm t_{\alpha/2} \sqrt{s_p^2 \left(\dfrac{1}{n_1} + \dfrac{1}{n_2} \right)} = (28 - 20) \pm 1.987 \sqrt{119.5 \left(\dfrac{1}{50} + \dfrac{1}{40} \right)}$

$= 8 \pm 4.61$

12.3 $H_0: (\mu_1 - \mu_2) = 0$
$H_A: (\mu_1 - \mu_2) \neq 0$

Test statistic: $t = \dfrac{(\bar{x}_1 - \bar{x}_2) - (\mu_1 - \mu_2)}{\sqrt{s_1^2/n_1 + s_2^2/n_2}}$

d.f. $= \dfrac{\left(s_1^2/n_1 + s_2^2/n_2\right)^2}{\dfrac{\left(s_1^2/n_1\right)^2}{n_1 - 1} + \dfrac{\left(s_2^2/n_2\right)^2}{n_2 - 1}}$

Rejection region: (d.f. = 47.5 $\approx$ 50) $|t| > 1.676$

Value of the test statistic: $t = -1.69$

Conclusion: Reject H_0.

There is enough evidence to conclude that the mean drying times differ.

12.4 $(\bar{x}_1 - \bar{x}_2) \pm t_{\alpha/2}\sqrt{s_1^2/n_1 + s_2^2/n_2}$ $= (185 - 201) \pm 2.678\sqrt{20^2/45 + 57^2/40}$

$$= -16 \pm 25$$

12.5 $(\bar{x}_1 - \bar{x}_2) \pm t_{\alpha/2}\sqrt{s_p^2(1/n_1 + 1/n_2)}$ $= (80.23 - 70.10) \pm 2.306\sqrt{92.05(1/5 + 1/5)}$

$$= 10.22 \pm 13.99$$

12.6 H_0: $(\mu_1 - \mu_2) = 0$
H_A: $(\mu_1 - \mu_2) > 0$

Test statistic: $t = \dfrac{(\bar{x}_1 - \bar{x}_2) - (\mu_1 - \mu_2)}{\sqrt{s_p^2(1/n_1 + 1/n_2)}}$

Rejection region: $t > 1.943$

Value of the test statistic: $t = .79$

Conclusion: Do not reject H_0.

There is not enough evidence to conclude that the experimental spark plug is effective in increasing gas mileage.

12.7 $(\bar{x}_1 - \bar{x}_2) \pm t_{\alpha/2}\sqrt{s_p^2(1/n_1 + 1/n_2)}$ $= (27.75 - 25) \pm 3.707\sqrt{24.46(1/4 + 1/4)}$

$$= 2.75 \pm 12.96$$

12.8 H_0: $\mu_D = 0$
H_A: $\mu_D > 0$

Test statistic: $t = \dfrac{\bar{x}_D - \mu_D}{s_D/\sqrt{n_D}}$

Rejection region: $t > 2.015$

Value of the test statistic: $t = 2.53$

Conclusion: Reject H_0.

There is enough evidence to indicate that the adoption of method 2 results in a lower after-tax profit.

12.9 $\quad \bar{x}_D \pm t_{\alpha/2} \dfrac{s_D}{\sqrt{n_D}} = 2.67 \pm 4.032 \dfrac{2.58}{\sqrt{6}} = 2.67 \pm 4.25$

12.10 $\quad \bar{x}_D \pm t_{\alpha/2} \dfrac{s_D}{\sqrt{n_D}} = 7.80 \pm 4.604 \dfrac{5.89}{\sqrt{5}} = 7.80 \pm 12.13$

12.11 $\quad H_0: \mu_D = 0$
$\quad\quad H_A: \mu_D > 0$

Test statistic: $t = \dfrac{\bar{x}_D - \mu_D}{s_D/\sqrt{n_D}}$

Rejection region: $t > 2.353$

Value of the test statistic: $t = 3.65$

Conclusion: Reject H_0.

There is enough evidence to conclude that the experimental spark plug is effective in increasing gas mileage.

12.13 $\quad \bar{x}_D \pm t_{\alpha/2} \dfrac{s_D}{\sqrt{n_D}} = 1.75 \pm 3.182 \dfrac{.96}{\sqrt{4}} = 1.75 \pm 1.53$

12.14 $\quad H_0: \sigma_1^2/\sigma_2^2 = 1$
$\quad\quad H_A: \sigma_1^2/\sigma_2^2 > 1$

Test statistic: $F = s_1^2/s_2^2$

Rejection region: $F > 3.29$

Value of the test statistic: $F = 2.84$

Conclusion: Do not reject H_0.

There is not enough evidence to conclude that σ_1^2 exceeds σ_2^2.

12.15 $\quad \text{LCL} = \dfrac{s_1^2}{s_2^2} \dfrac{1}{F_{\alpha/2, v_1, v_2}} = (2.84) \dfrac{1}{5.61} = .51$

$$\text{UCL} = \frac{s_1^2}{s_2^2} F_{\alpha/2, v_2, v_1} = (2.84)(6.72) = 19.08$$

12.16 H_0: $\sigma_1^2/\sigma_2^2 = 1$
H_A: $\sigma_1^2/\sigma_2^2 < 1$

Test statistic: $F = s_1^2/s_2^2$

Rejection region: $F < .51$

Value of the test statistic: $F = .84$

Conclusion: Do not reject H_0.

There is not enough evidence to conclude that σ_1^2 is less than σ_2^2.

12.17 $\text{LCL} = \frac{s_1^2}{s_2^2} \frac{1}{F_{\alpha/2, v_1, v_2}} = (.84)\frac{1}{2.27} = .37$

$\text{UCL} = \frac{s_1^2}{s_2^2} F_{\alpha/2, v_2, v_1} = (.84)(2.27) = 1.91$

12.18 H_0: $(p_1 - p_2) = 0$
H_A: $(p_1 - p_2) < 0$

Test statistic: $z = \dfrac{(\hat{p}_1 - \hat{p}_2)}{\sqrt{\hat{p}\hat{q}\ (1/n_1 + 1/n_2)}}$

Rejection region: $z < -1.645$

Value of the test statistic: $z = -2.79$

Conclusion: Reject H_0.

There is sufficient evidence to conclude that p_1 is less than p_2.

12.19 H_0: $(p_1 - p_2) = -.05$
H_A: $(p_1 - p_2) < -.05$

Test statistic: $z = \dfrac{(\hat{p}_1 - \hat{p}_2) - (p_1 - p_2)}{\sqrt{\hat{p}_1\hat{q}_1/n_1 + \hat{p}_2\hat{q}_2/n_2}}$

Rejection region: $z < -2.33$

Value of the test statistic: $z = -1.81$

Conclusion: Do not reject H_0.

There is not enough evidence to conclude that p_2 exceeds p_1 by more than 5%.

12.20 $(\hat{p}_1 - \hat{p}_2) \pm z_{\alpha/2}\sqrt{\hat{p}_1\hat{q}_1/n_1 + \hat{p}_2\hat{q}_2/n_2}$

$= (.10 - .20) \pm 1.645\sqrt{(.10)(.90)/250 + (.20)(.80)/400}$

$= -.10 \pm .045$

12.21 $H_0: (p_1 - p_2) = 0$
$H_A: (p_1 - p_2) > 0$

Test statistic: $z = \dfrac{(\hat{p}_1 - \hat{p}_2)}{\sqrt{\hat{p}\hat{q}\,(1/n_1 + 1/n_2)}}$

Rejection region: $z > 2.33$

Value of the test statistic: $z = 5.18$

Conclusion: Reject H_0.

There is sufficient evidence to conclude that support has fallen between 1982 and 1987.

12.22 $H_0: (p_1 - p_2) = .05$
$H_A: (p_1 - p_2) > .05$

Test statistic: $z = \dfrac{(\hat{p}_1 - \hat{p}_2) - (p_1 - p_2)}{\sqrt{\hat{p}_1\hat{q}_1/n_1 + \hat{p}_2\hat{q}_2/n_2}}$

Rejection region: $z > 2.33$

Value of the test statistic: $z = 2.31$

Conclusion: Do not reject H_0.

There is not enough evidence to conclude that support has fallen by more than 5 percentage points.

12.23 $(\hat{p}_1 - \hat{p}_2) \pm z_{\alpha/2}\sqrt{\hat{p}_1\hat{q}_1/n_1 + \hat{p}_2\hat{q}_2/n_2}$

$= (.70 - .61) \pm 1.96\sqrt{(.70)(.30)/1{,}500 + (.61)(.39)/1{,}500} = .09 \pm .034$

12.24 $H_0: (p_1 - p_2) = 0$
$H_A: (p_1 - p_2) > 0$

Test statistic: $z = \dfrac{(\hat{p}_1 - \hat{p}_2)}{\sqrt{\hat{p}\hat{q}\,(1/n_1 + 1/n_2)}}$

Rejection region: $z > 1.645$

Value of the test statistic: $z = 1.93$

Conclusion: Reject H_0.

There is enough evidence to indicate that the new product is better than the existing product.

12.25 $(\hat{p}_1 - \hat{p}_2) \pm z_{\alpha/2}\sqrt{\hat{p}_1\hat{q}_1/n_1 + \hat{p}_2\hat{q}_2/n_2}$

$= (.090 - .058) \pm 1.645\sqrt{(.09)(.91)/500 + (.058)(.942)/500} = .032 \pm .027$

Chapter 13

13.1 H_0: $(\mu_1 - \mu_2) = 0$
H_A: $(\mu_1 - \mu_2) < 0$

Test statistic: $t = \dfrac{(\bar{x}_1 - \bar{x}_2) - (\mu_1 - \mu_2)}{\sqrt{s_1^2/n_1 + s_2^2/n_2}}$

Rejection region: (d.f. $= 68.9 \approx 70$) $t < -1.667$

Value of the test statistic: $t = -2.28$

Conclusion: Reject H_0.

There is enough evidence to conclude that the experimental squash ball is superior.

13.2 H_0: $p = .15$
H_A: $p > .15$

Test statistic: $z = \dfrac{\hat{p} - p}{\sqrt{pq/n}}$

Rejection region: $z > 1.28$

Value of the test statistic: $z = 2.98$

Conclusion: Reject H_0.

There is sufficient evidence to indicate that the distributor is in financial trouble.

13.3 H_0: $(p_1 - p_2) = 0$
H_A: $(p_1 - p_2) < 0$

Test statistic: $z = \dfrac{(\hat{p}_1 - \hat{p}_2)}{\sqrt{\hat{p}\hat{q}\,(1/n_1 + 1/n_2)}}$

Rejection region: $z < -1.28$

Value of the test statistic: $z = -.64$

Conclusion: Do not reject H_0.

The company should drill in region 1.

13.4 H_0: $\sigma_1^2 / \sigma_2^2 = 1$
H_A: $\sigma_1^2 / \sigma_2^2 < 1$

Test statistic: $F = s_1^2 / s_2^2$

Rejection region: $F < .426$

Value of the test statistic: $F = .391$

Conclusion: Reject H_0.

There is enough evidence to support the spokesman's claim.

13.5 H_0: $(\mu_1 - \mu_2) = 0$
H_A: $(\mu_1 - \mu_2) < 0$

Test statistic: $t = \dfrac{(\bar{x}_1 - \bar{x}_2) - (\mu_1 - \mu_2)}{\sqrt{s_p^2 (1/n_1 + 1/n_2)}}$

Rejection region: $t < -1.812$

Value of the test statistic: $t = -2.05$

Conclusion: Reject H_0.

There is sufficient evidence to conclude that the doctor is correct.

13.6 H_0: $\mu_D = 0$
H_A: $\mu_D > 0$

Test statistic: $t = \dfrac{\bar{x}_D - \mu_D}{s_D / \sqrt{n_D}}$

Rejection region: $t > 2.015$

Value of the test statistic: $t = 3.41$

Conclusion: Reject H_0.

There is sufficient evidence to to infer that the chemical solution is effective.

13.7 $H_0: (p_1 - p_2) = 0$
$H_A: (p_1 - p_2) \neq 0$

Test statistic: $z = \dfrac{(\hat{p}_1 - \hat{p}_2)}{\sqrt{\hat{p}\hat{q}\,(1/n_1 + 1/n_2)}}$

Rejection region: $|z| > 1.96$

Value of the test statistic: $z = -1.22$

Conclusion: Do not reject H_0.

We cannot conclude that a difference exists between men and women in their soft drink preference.

13.8 $H_0: \mu_D = 0$
$H_A: \mu_D > 0$

Test statistic: $t = \dfrac{\bar{x}_D - \mu_D}{s_D/\sqrt{n_D}}$

Rejection region: $t > 1.895$

Value of the test statistic: $t = 1.17$

Conclusion: Do not reject H_0.

There is not enough evidence to conclude that the campus bookstore is more expensive than the off-campus bookstore.

13.9 $H_0: \mu = 3{,}600$
$H_A: \mu > 3{,}600$

Test statistic: $t = \dfrac{\bar{x} - \mu}{s/\sqrt{n}}$

Rejection region: $t > 1.729$

Value of the test statistic: $t = 2.81$

Conclusion: Reject H_0.

There is sufficient evidence to conclude that the loan manager is correct.

13.10 $H_0: p = .001$
$H_A: p > .001$

Test statistic: $z = \dfrac{\hat{p} - p}{\sqrt{pq/n}}$

Rejection region: $z > 1.645$

Value of the test statistic: $z = 2.82$

Conclusion: Reject H_0.

There is enough evidence to indicate that the post office's claim is correct.

Chapter 14

14.1   Rejection region: $F > 2.90$

Source	d.f.	Sums of Squares	Mean Squares	F-ratio
Treatments	5	500	100	.5
Error	15	3,000	200	
Total	20	3,500		

Conclusion: Do not reject H_0.

14.2   Rejection region: $F > 4.07$

Source	d.f.	Sums of Squares	Mean Squares	F-ratio
Treatments	4	90	22.50	10.51
Error	28	60	2.14	
Total	32	150		

Conclusion: Reject H_0.

14.3   Rejection region: $F > 2.59$

Source	d.f.	Sums of Squares	Mean Squares	F-ratio
Treatments	2	375.65	187.83	2.18
Error	20	1,720.00	86.00	
Total	22	2,095.65		

Conclusion: Do not reject H_0.

14.4 $H_0: \mu_1 = \mu_2 = \mu_3 = \mu_4$
H_A: At least two means differ.

Rejection region: $F > 2.84$ (approximately)

Value of the test statistic:

Source	d.f.	Sums of Squares	Mean Squares	F-ratio
Treatments	3	166.11	55.37	1.45
Error	41	1,561.67	38.09	
Total	44	1,727.78		

Conclusion: Do not reject H_0.

14.5 $H_0: \mu_1 = \mu_2 = \mu_3 = \mu_4$
H_A: At least two means differ.

Rejection region: $F > 3.10$

Value of the test statistic:

Source	d.f.	Sums of Squares	Mean Squares	F-ratio
Treatments	3	15,552	5,184	3.30
Error	20	31,383	1,569	
Total	23	46,936		

Conclusion: Reject H_0.

There is enough evidence to conclude that the selling prices differ among the four cities.

	Source	d.f.	Sums of Squares	Mean Squares	F-ratio
14.6	Treatments	5	300	60	6.0
	Blocks	8	300	37.5	3.75
	Error	40	400	10	
	Total	53	1,000		

14.7 Rejection region: $F > 3.51$

Value of the test statistic: $F = 6.0$

Conclusion: Reject H_0.

There are differences among the treatment means.

14.8 Rejection region: $F > 2.99$

Value of the test statistic: $F = 3.75$

Conclusion: Reject H_0.

There are differences among the block means.

14.9 $H_0: \mu_1 = \mu_2 = \mu_3$
H_A: At least two means differ.

Rejection region: $F > 2.73$

318

Value of the test statistic:

Source	d.f.	Sums of Squares	Mean Squares	F-ratio
Treatments	2	523	262	.44
Blocks	7	205,135	29,305	49.09
Error	14	8,360	597	
Total	23	214,018		

Conclusion: Do not reject H_0.

There is not enough evidence to conclude that there are differences in bicycle sales among the stores using the three catalogues.

Chapter 15

15.1 The observed values are consistent with the hypothesized proportions. Therefore, the data support the null hypothesis.

15.2 The data support the alternative hypothesis.

15.3

Value of χ^2 for Exercise 15.1

Cell	Observed Frequency o_i	Expected Frequency e_i	$(o_i - e_i)^2$	$\dfrac{(o_i - e_i)^2}{e_i}$
1	20	20	0	0
2	30	30	0	0
3	50	50	0	0
Total	100	100		$0 = \chi^2$

Value of χ^2 for Exercise 15.2

Cell	Observed Frequency o_i	Expected Frequency e_i	$(o_i - e_i)^2$	$\dfrac{(o_i - e_i)^2}{e_i}$
1	60	20	1,600	80.00
2	10	30	400	13.33
3	30	50	400	8.00
Total	100			$101.33 = \chi^2$

15.4 H_0: $p = .40$
H_A: $p \neq .40$

Test statistic: $z = \dfrac{\hat{p} - p}{\sqrt{pq/n}}$

Rejection region: $|z| > 1.645$

Value of the test statistic: Since $\hat{p} = \dfrac{34}{100} = .34$

$\quad$ $z = -1.225$

Conclusion: Do not reject H_0.

15.5 H_0: $p_1 = 1/3$, $p_2 = 1/3$, $p_3 = 1/3$
H_A: At least one p_i is not equal to its specified value.

Test statistic: $\chi^2 = \sum (o_i - e_i)^2 / e_i$

Rejection region: $\chi^2 > 5.99147$

Value of the test statistic: $\chi^2 = 6.54$

Conclusion: Reject H_0.

There is reason to believe that the stations' market shares have changed.

15.6 H_0: $p_1 = 1/3$, $p_2 = 1/3$, $p_3 = 1/3$
H_A: At least one p_i is not equal to its specified value.

Test statistic: $\chi^2 = \sum (o_i - e_i)^2 / e_i$

Rejection region: $\chi^2 > 5.99147$

Value of the test statistic: $\chi^2 = 3.26$

Conclusion: Do not reject H_0.

There is not enough evidence to conclude that the stations' market shares have changed.

15.7   The data support the null hypothesis.

15.8   The data support the alternative hypothesis.

15.9

Value of χ^2 for Exercise 15.7
_____

$$\chi^2 = \sum \frac{(o_i - e_i)^2}{e_i} = 0$$

Value of χ^2 for Exercise 15.8
_____

$$\chi^2 = \sum \frac{(o_i - e_i)^2}{e_i} = 25.0$$

15.10 H_0: The two classifications are independent.
H_A: The two classifications are dependent.

Test statistic: $\chi^2 = \sum \frac{(o_i - e_i)^2}{e_i}$

Rejection region: $\chi^2 > 2.70554$

Value of the test statistic: $\chi^2 = 1.77$

Conclusion: Do not reject H_0.

There is not enough evidence to conclude that differences exist between the new drug and the placebo.

15.11 p_1 = proportion taking new drug who suffer serious side effect
p_2 = proportion taking placebo who suffer serious side effect

H_0: $(p_1 - p_2) = 0$
H_A: $(p_1 - p_2) \neq 0$

Test statistic: $z = \dfrac{(\hat{p}_1 - \hat{p}_2)}{\sqrt{\hat{p}\hat{q}(1/n_1 + 1/n_2)}}$

Rejection region: $|z| > 1.645$

Value of the test statistic: $z = 1.33$

Conclusion: Do not reject H_0.

15.12 H_0: The two classifications are independent.

        H_A: The two classifications are dependent.

Test statistic: $\chi^2 = \sum \dfrac{(o_i - e_i)^2}{e_i}$

Rejection region: $\chi^2 > 4.60517$

Value of the test statistic: $\chi^2 = 17.92$

Conclusion: Reject H_0.

There is enough evidence to infer that differences exist between the new drug and the placebo.

15.13 H_0: The two classifications are independent (no differences between American and Canadian firms).

        H_A: The two classifications are dependent (some difference between American and Canadian firms).

Test statistic: $\chi^2 = \sum (o_i - e_i)^2 / e_i$

Rejection region: $\chi^2 > 10.5966$

Value of the test statistic: $\chi^2 = 16.83$

Conclusion: Reject H_0.

There is sufficient evidence to conclude that there are differences between American and Canadian firms in terms of their preferences for organizational structures.

15.14 H_0: The two classifications are independent (no differences among the four regions).

        H_A: The two classifications are dependent (some difference among the four regions).

Test statistic: $\chi^2 = \sum (o_i - e_i)^2 / e_i$

Rejection region: $\chi^2 > 16.8119$

Value of the test statistic: $\chi^2 = 38.47$

Conclusion: Reject H_0.

There is sufficient evidence to conclude that there are differences in attitudes among the four regions.

Chapter 16

16.1 $\hat{y} = 2x$

16.2 $\hat{y} = 316.32 + 50.53x$

16.3 $\text{SSE} = 100$

$s_\varepsilon^2 = 7.69$

$s_\varepsilon = 2.77$

16.4 $s_\varepsilon = 76.19$; the fit appears to be reasonably good.

16.5 $H_0: \beta_1 = 0$
$H_A: \beta_1 \neq 0$

Test statistic: $t = \dfrac{\hat{\beta}_1 - \beta_1}{s_{\hat{\beta}_1}}$

Rejection region: $|t| > 1.771$

Value of the test statistic: $t = 6.59$

Conclusion: Reject H_0.

There is enough evidence to conclude that x and y are linearly related.

16.6 $H_0: \beta_1 = 0$
$H_A: \beta_1 > 0$

Test statistic: $t = \dfrac{\hat{\beta}_1 - \beta_1}{s_{\hat{\beta}_1}}$

Rejection region: $t > 3.143$

Value of the test statistic: $t = 6.56$

Conclusion: Reject H_0.

There is enough evidence to infer that the number of ads and the number of customers are positively linearly related.

16.7 a) $\hat{y} = 87.83 - .67x$

b) $H_0: \beta_1 = 0$
$H_A: \beta_1 < 0$

Test statistic: $t = \dfrac{\hat{\beta}_1 - \beta_1}{s_{\hat{\beta}_1}}$

Rejection region: $t < -1.895$

Value of the test statistic: $t = -5.83$

Conclusion: Reject H_0.

We can conclude that temperature and the number of cups of coffee sold are negatively linearly related.

16.8 $R^2 = .769$

16.9 $R^2 = .878$

16.10 $R^2 = .829$; this tells us that 82.9% of the variation in y is explained by the variation in x.

16.11 721.6 ± 197.9

16.12 721.6 ± 66.3

16.13 54.23 ± 3.34

16.14 54.23 ± 10.55

Chapter 17

17.1 $\hat{\beta}_0 = 11.088$; we cannot interpret this value.

$\hat{\beta}_1 = 5.632$; for each additional 100 square feet, the heating cost increases on the average by $5.63.

$\hat{\beta}_2 = 3.179$; for each additional window, the heating cost increases on the average by $3.18.

$\hat{\beta}_3 = 15.431$; for each additional household occupant, the heating cost increases on the average by $15.43.

17.2 $H_0: \beta_i = 0$
$H_A: \beta_i \neq 0$

Test statistic: $t = \dfrac{\hat{\beta}_i - \beta_i}{s_{\hat{\beta}_i}}$

Rejection region: $|t| > 2.042$ (approximately)

Values of the test statistics:

For x_1: $t = 3.78$

For x_2: $t = 1.62$

For x_3: $t = 2.25$

Conclusions: There is sufficient evidence to indicate that x_1 and x_3 are linearly related to y.

17.3 $s_\varepsilon = 34.898$; this indicates that the model's fit is good but not excellent.

17.4 $R^2 = 55.4\%$; this indicates that 55.4% of the variation in y is explained by the model. The remainder, 44.6%, is unexplained.

17.5 H_0: $\beta_1 = \beta_2 = \beta_3 = 0$
H_A: At least one β_i is not equal to zero.

Test statistic: $F = $ MSR/MSE

Rejection region: $F > 2.92$ (approximately)

Value of the test statistic: $F = 12.84$

Conclusion: Reject H_0.

We conclude that the model is useful in predicting the dependent variable.

17.6 H_0: $\beta_1 = \beta_2 = \beta_3 = \beta_4 = 0$
H_A: At least one β_i is not equal to zero.

Test statistic: $F = $ MSR/MSE

Rejection region: $F > 2.69$

Value of the test statistic: $F = 9.77$

Conclusion: Reject H_0.

The model is useful.

17.7 $\hat{\beta}_1 = 8.477$; for each additional 100 square feet, the heating cost increases on average by $8.48.

$\hat{\beta}_2 = -6.849$; a south-facing house costs on average $6.85 less to heat in January than an east-facing house.

$\hat{\beta}_3 = 4.607$; a north-facing house costs an average $4.61 more to heat in January than an east-facing house.

$\hat{\beta}_4 = -1.252$; a west-facing house costs an average $1.25 less to heat in January than an east-facing house.

17.8 $H_0: \beta_2 = 0$
$H_A: \beta_2 < 0$

Test statistic: $t = \dfrac{\hat{\beta}_2 - \beta_2}{s_{\hat{\beta}_2}}$

Rejection region: $t < -1.697$

Value of the test statistic: $t = -2.19$

Conclusion: Reject H_0.

There is enough evidence to show that, on average, a south-facing house costs less to heat in January than an east-facing house.

17.9 $H_0: \beta_3 = 0$
$H_A: \beta_3 > 0$

Test statistic: $t = \dfrac{\hat{\beta}_3 - \beta_3}{s_{\hat{\beta}_3}}$

Rejection region: $t > 1.697$

Value of the test statistic: $t = 1.23$

Conclusion: Do not reject H_0.

There is not enough evidence to infer that, on average, a north-facing house costs more to heat in January than an east-facing house.

Chapter 18

18.1   Centerline = $\bar{\bar{x}} = 405$

Upper control limit = $\bar{\bar{x}} + A_2\bar{R} = 405 + .308(30) = 414.24$

Lower control limit = $\bar{\bar{x}} - A_2\bar{R} = 405 - .308(30) = 395.76$

18.2 $\bar{x}$

$\bar{\bar{x}} + A_2\bar{R} = 414.24$

A

$\bar{\bar{x}} + 2/3A_2\bar{R} = 411.16$

B

$\bar{\bar{x}} + 1/3A_2\bar{R} = 408.08$

C

$\bar{\bar{x}} = 405$

C

$\bar{\bar{x}} - 1/3A_2\bar{R} = 401.92$

B

$\bar{\bar{x}} - 2/3A_2\bar{R} = 398.84$

A

$\bar{\bar{x}} - A_2\bar{R} = 395.76$

18.3 Centerline $= \bar{R} = 30$

Upper control limit $= D_4\bar{R} = 1.777(30) = 53.31$

Lower control limit $= D_3\bar{R} = .223(30) = 6.9$

18.4 Centerline $= \bar{R} = 7.0$

Upper control limit $= D_4\bar{R} = 1.636(7.0) = 11.452$

Lower control limit $= D_3\bar{R} = .364(7.0) = 2.548$

18.5 The sample means and ranges and their means are computed as shown in the table below.

Sample	$\bar{x}_j$	R_j
1	.504	.013
2	.498	.026
3	.508	.023
4	.503	.025
5	.506	.023
6	.506	.016
7	.499	.026
8	.509	.007
9	.503	.024
10	.509	.022
11	.497	.010
12	.494	.010
13	.494	.013
14	.509	.021
15	.508	.027
16	.512	.020
17	.503	.019
18	.498	.020
19	.505	.017
20	.510	.014
21	.511	.013
22	.510	.014
23	.515	.012
24	.510	.008
25	.508	.011
26	.509	.010
27	.508	.020
28	.512	.020
29	.502	.014
30	.507	.009
	$\bar{\bar{x}} = .5056$	$\bar{R} = .0169$

a) *R* chart:

Centerline $= \overline{R} = .0169$

Upper control limit $= D_4\overline{R} = 2.575(.0169) = .0435$

Lower control limit $= D_3\overline{R} = 0$

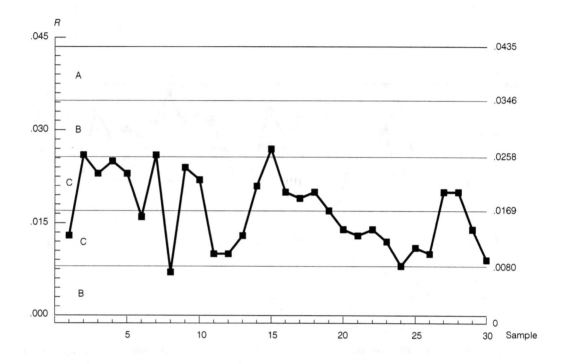

b) $\bar{x}$ chart:

Centerline = $\bar{\bar{x}}$ = .5056

Upper control limit = $\bar{\bar{x}} + A_2\bar{R}$ = .5056 + 1.023(.0169) = .5229

Lower control limit = $\bar{\bar{x}} - A_2\bar{R}$ = .5056 − 1.023(.0169) = .4883

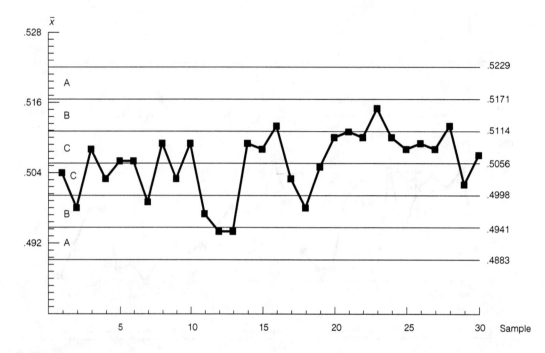

c)   The R chart indicates that the process dispersion is unchanged. However, the $\bar{x}$ chart shows that the process went out of control. [Nine points in a row in zone C or beyond (points 20–28) and two out of three points in a row in zone A or beyond (points 11–13).]

18.6   Centerline = $\bar{p}$ = .11

Upper control limit = $\bar{p} + 3\sqrt{\dfrac{\bar{p}(1-\bar{p})}{n}}$ = $.11 + 3\sqrt{\dfrac{(.11)(.89)}{100}}$ = .204

Lower control limit = $\bar{p} - 3\sqrt{\dfrac{\bar{p}(1-\bar{p})}{n}}$ = $.11 - 3\sqrt{\dfrac{(.11)(.89)}{100}}$ = .016

18.7 $\hat{p}$

A	$\bar{p} + 3\sqrt{\dfrac{\bar{p}(1-\bar{p})}{n}} = .204$
	$\bar{p} + 2\sqrt{\dfrac{\bar{p}(1-\bar{p})}{n}} = .173$
B	
	$\bar{p} + \sqrt{\dfrac{\bar{p}(1-\bar{p})}{n}} = .141$
C	
	$\bar{p} = .110$
C	
	$\bar{p} - \sqrt{\dfrac{\bar{p}(1-\bar{p})}{n}} = .079$
B	
	$\bar{p} - 2\sqrt{\dfrac{\bar{p}(1-\bar{p})}{n}} = .047$
A	
	$\bar{p} - 3\sqrt{\dfrac{\bar{p}(1-\bar{p})}{n}} = .016$

18.8   The sample proportions and the mean of the sample proportions are computed as follows.

Sample	Number of Defectives	Sample Proportions $\hat{p}_j$
1	9	.009
2	4	.004
3	8	.008
4	8	.008
5	8	.008
6	6	.006
7	4	.004
8	6	.006
9	7	.007
10	10	.010
11	3	.003
12	5	.005
13	8	.008
14	6	.006
15	4	.004

Sample	Number of Defectives	Sample Proportions $\hat{p}_j$
16	7	.007
17	5	.005
18	6	.006
19	5	.005
20	6	.006
21	12	.012
22	7	.007
23	4	.004
24	5	.005
25	7	.007
		$\bar{p} = .0064$

Centerline $= \bar{p} = .0064$

$$\text{Upper control limit} = \bar{p} + 3\sqrt{\frac{\bar{p}(1-\bar{p})}{n}} = .0064 + 3\sqrt{\frac{(.0064)(.9936)}{1,000}} = .01397$$

$$\text{Lower control limit} = \bar{p} - 3\sqrt{\frac{\bar{p}(1-\bar{p})}{n}} = .0064 - 3\sqrt{\frac{(.0064)(.9936)}{1,000}} = -.00117$$

Since the lower control limit is negative, we set it equal to zero.

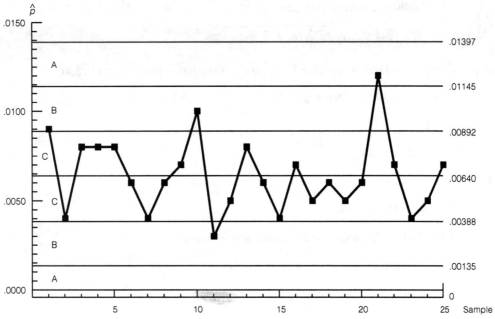

The process appears to be under control.

Chapter 19

19.1 a) Problem objective: Comparison of two populations

Data type: Qualitative

Other factors: Two categories

Statistical technique: z-test of $p_1 - p_2$

H_0: $(p_1 - p_2) = 0$
H_A: $(p_1 - p_2) > 0$

Test statistic: $z = \dfrac{(\hat{p}_1 - \hat{p}_2)}{\sqrt{\hat{p}\hat{q}(1/n_1 + 1/n_2)}}$

Rejection region: $z > z_\alpha = z_{.05} = 1.645$

Value of the test statistic: $z = 2.23$

Conclusion: Reject H_0.

There is enough evidence to conclude that North American car manufacturers improved the quality of their cars.

b) Confidence interval estimate:

$$(\hat{p}_1 - \hat{p}_2) \pm z_{\alpha/2}\sqrt{\hat{p}_1\hat{q}_1/n_1 + \hat{p}_2\hat{q}_2/n_2}$$

$$= (.096 - .0625) \pm 1.96\sqrt{(.096)(.904)/500 + (.0625)(.9375)/800}$$

$$= .0335 \pm .0308$$

LCL = .0027

UCL = .0643

19.2 Problem objective: Description of a single population

Data type: Quantitative

Other factors: Location is the measurement of interest

Statistical technique: t-interval estimate of μ

Confidence interval estimate:

$$\bar{x} \pm t_{\alpha/2}\frac{s}{\sqrt{n}} = 24.0 \pm 2.145\frac{9.67}{\sqrt{15}} = 24.0 \pm 5.36$$

LCL = 18.64

UCL = 29.36

19.3 Problem objective: Comparison of five populations

Data type: Quantitative

Other factors: Samples are independent; data are normal.

Statistical technique: Analysis of variance (single-factor, independent samples)

$H_0: \mu_1 = \mu_2 = \mu_3 = \mu_4 = \mu_5$
H_A: At least two means differ.

Test statistic: $F = MST/MSE$

Rejection region: $F > F_{\alpha, k-1, n-k} = F_{.10, 4, 20} = 2.25$

Value of the test statistic: $F = 2.40$

Conclusion: Reject H_0.

There is sufficient evidence to conclude that there are differences in house prices among the five areas.

19.4   Problem objective: Comparison of five populations

Data type: Qualitative

Other factors: None

Statistical technique: Chi-squared test of a contingency table

H_0: The two variables are independent.
H_A: The two variables are dependent.

Test statistic: $\chi^2 = \sum_{i=1}^{25} (o_i - e_i)^2 / e_i$

Rejection region: $\chi^2 > \chi^2_{\alpha,(r-1)(c-1)} = \chi^2_{.10,16} = 23.5418$

Value of the test statistic: $\chi^2 = 4.518$

Conclusion: Do not reject H_0.

There is not enough evidence to indicate that there are differences among the five areas in terms of types of homes.

19.5   a)   Problem objective: Comparison of two populations

Data type: Quantitative

Other factors: Location is the measurement of interest; independent samples; data are normal; we can assume $\sigma_1^2 = \sigma_2^2$ $\left(s_1^2 = .0147 \text{ and } s_2^2 = .0110 \right)$.

Statistical technique: Equal-variances t-test of $\mu_1 - \mu_2$

H_0: $(\mu_1 - \mu_2) = 0$
H_A: $(\mu_1 - \mu_2) < 0$

Test statistic: $t = \dfrac{(\bar{x}_1 - \bar{x}_2) - (\mu_1 - \mu_2)}{\sqrt{s_p^2 \left(1/n_1 + 1/n_2 \right)}}$

Rejection region: $t < -t_{\alpha, n_1 + n_2 - 2} = -t_{.05,10} = -1.812$

Value of the test statistic: $t = -2.80$

Conclusion: Reject H_0.

There is enough evidence to infer that the new technology prolongs battery lives.

b) Confidence interval estimate:

$$(\bar{x}_1 - \bar{x}_2) \pm t_{\alpha/2}\sqrt{s_p^2\left(1/n_1 + 1/n_2\right)} = (1.467 - 1.65) \pm 3.169\sqrt{.0128(1/6 + 1/6)}$$

$$= -.183 \pm .207$$

LCL = −.39

UCL = .024

19.6   Problem objective: Analysis of the relationship between two variables

Data type: Qualitative

Other factors: None

Statistical technique: Chi-squared test of a contingency table

H_0: The two variables are independent.
H_A: The two variables are dependent.

Test statistic: $\chi^2 = \sum\limits_{i=1}^{9} (o_i - e_i)^2/e_i$

Rejection region: $\chi^2 > \chi^2_{\alpha,(r-1)(c-1)} = \chi^2_{.01,4} = 13.2767$

Value of the test statistic: $\chi^2 = 5.04$

Conclusion: Do not reject H_0.

There is not enough evidence to support the repairman's belief.

19.7   Problem objective: Description of a single population

Data type: Qualitative

Other factors: Two categories

Statistical technique: z-test of p

H_0: $p = .10$
H_A: $p > .10$

Test statistic: $z = \dfrac{\hat{p} - p}{\sqrt{pq/n}}$

Rejection region: $z > z_\alpha = z_{.05} = 1.645$

Value of the test statistic: $z = 1.89$

Conclusion: Reject H_0.

There is sufficient evidence to support the official's belief.

19.8   Problem objective: Comparison of five populations

Data type: Quantitative

Other factors: Independent samples; data are normal.

Statistical technique: Analysis of variance (single-factor, independent samples)

H_0: $\mu_1 = \mu_2 = \mu_3 = \mu_4 = \mu_5$
H_A: At least two means differ.

Test statistic: $F = MST/MSE$

Rejection region: $F > F_{\alpha, k-1, n-k} = F_{.01, 4, 17} = 4.67$

Value of the test statistic: $F = 4.35$

Conclusion: Do not reject H_0.

There is not enough evidence to conclude that there are differences in gross sales among the days of the week.

19.9   Problem objective: Analysis of the relationship between two variables

Data type: Quantitative

Other factors: None

Statistical technique: Simple linear regression and correlation

H_0: $\beta_1 = 0$ H_0: $\rho = 0$

                   or

H_A: $\beta_1 < 0$ H_A: $\rho = 0$

Test statistic: $t = \dfrac{\hat{\beta}_1 - \beta_1}{s_{\hat{\beta}_1}}$ or $t = r\sqrt{\dfrac{(n-2)}{1-r^2}}$

Rejection region: $t < -t_{\alpha, n-2} = -t_{.01, 18} = -2.552$

Value of the test statistic: $t = -4.57$

Conclusion: Reject H_0.

There is enough evidence to conclude that the professor is correct.

19.10   Problem objective: Comparison of three populations

Data type: Quantitative

Other factors: Independent samples; data are normal.

Statistical technique: Analysis of variance (single-factor, independent samples)

H_0: $\mu_1 = \mu_2 = \mu_3$
H_A: At least two means differ.

Test statistic: $F = \text{MST/MSE}$

Rejection region: $F > F_{\alpha, k-1, n-k} = F_{.05, 2, 57} = 3.15$ (approximately)

Value of the test statistic: $F = 13.54$

Conclusion: Reject H_0.

There is sufficient evidence to conclude that there are differences in frequency of visits among the age categories.

19.11 Problem objective: Comparison of two populations

Data type: Quantitative

Other factors: Location is the measurement of interest; independent samples; data are normal; we can assume that $\sigma_1^2 = \sigma_2^2$ ($s_1^2 = 2.49$ and $s_2^2 = 1.98$).

Statistical technique: Equal-variances t-test of $\mu_1 - \mu_2$

H_0: $(\mu_1 - \mu_2) = 0$
H_A: $(\mu_1 - \mu_2) > 0$

Test statistic: $t = \dfrac{(\bar{x}_1 - \bar{x}_2) - (\mu_1 - \mu_2)}{\sqrt{s_p^2 (1/n_1 + 1/n_2)}}$

Rejection region: $t > t_{\alpha, n_1 + n_2 - 2} = t_{.05, 58} = 1.671$ (approximately)

Value of the test statistic: $t = 1.99$

Conclusion: Reject H_0.

There is sufficient evidence to conclude that females visit their doctors more frequently than males.

19.12 Problem objective: Comparison of two populations

Data type: Qualitative

Other factors: Two categories

Statistical technique: z-test of $p_1 - p_2$

H_0: $(p_1 - p_2) = 0$

H_A: $(p_1 - p_2) < 0$

Test statistic: $z = \dfrac{(\hat{p}_1 - \hat{p}_2)}{\sqrt{\hat{p}\hat{q}(1/n_1 + 1/n_2)}}$

Rejection region: $z < -z_\alpha = -z_{.05} = -1.645$

Value of the test statistic: $z = -1.13$

Conclusion: Do not reject H_0.

There is not enough evidence to conclude that males are more likely to visit their doctors for a routine checkup than are females.

19.13   Problem objective: Comparison of three populations

Data type: Qualitative

Other factors: None

Statistical technique: Chi-squared test of a contingency table

H_0: The two variables are independent.
H_A: The two variables are dependent.

Test statistic: $\chi^2 = \displaystyle\sum_{i=1}^{9} (o_i - e_i)^2 / e_i$

Rejection region: $\chi^2 > \chi^2_{\alpha,(r-1)(c-1)} = \chi^2_{.05,4} = 9.48773$

Value of the test statistic: $\chi^2 = 8.73$

Conclusion: Do not reject H_0.

There is not enough evidence to conclude that there are differences in the reasons for doctor visits among the age categories.

19.14   Problem objective: Description of a single population

Data type: Qualitative

Other factors: Two categories

Statistical technique: z-test of p

H_0: $p = .5$
H_A: $p < .5$

Test statistic: $z = \dfrac{\hat{p} - p}{\sqrt{pq/n}}$

Rejection region: $z < -z_\alpha = -z_{.05} = -1.645$

Value of the test statistic: $z = -3.10$

Conclusion: Reject H_0.

There is sufficient evidence to conclude that less than half of all visits are for routine checkups.

19.15   Problem objective: Description of a single population

Data type: Quantitative

Other factors: Location is the measurement of interest

Statistical technique: t-test of μ

H_0: $\mu = 1.5$
H_A: $\mu > 1.5$

Test statistic: $t = \dfrac{\bar{x} - \mu}{s/\sqrt{n}}$

Rejection region: $t > t_{\alpha, n-1} = t_{.05, 59} = 1.671$ (approximately)

Value of the test statistic: $t = 2.11$

Conclusion: Reject H_0.

There is enough evidence to conclude that the average patient visits his or her physician at least one and a half times per year.

19.16   Problem objective: Description of a single population

Data type: Qualitative

Other factors: Three categories

Statistical technique: Chi-squared test of a multinomial experiment

H_0: $p_1 = 1/3$, $p_2 = 1/3$, $p_3 = 1/3$
H_A: At least one p_i is not equal to its specified value.

Test statistic: $\chi^2 = \displaystyle\sum_{i=1}^{3} (o_i - e_i)^2 / e_i$

Rejection region: $\chi^2 > \chi^2_{\alpha, k-1} = \chi^2_{.05, 2} = 5.99147$

Value of the test statistic: $\chi^2 = .7$

Conclusion: Do not reject H_0.

There is not enough evidence to conclude that the purpose of the visit is equally divided among the three responses.

19.17   Problem objective: Comparison of two populations

Data type: Quantitative

Other factors: Location is the measurement of interest; matched pairs; data are normal.

Statistical technique: t-test of μ_D

H_0: $\mu_D = 0$
H_A: $\mu_D > 0$

Test statistic: $t = \dfrac{\bar{x}_D - \mu_D}{s_D/\sqrt{n_D}}$

Rejection region: $t > t_{\alpha,\, n_D - 1} = t_{.05,9} = 1.833$

Value of the test statistic: $t = 3.67$

Conclusion: Reject H_0.

There is enough evidence to conclude that the 1987 ball is livelier.

19.18   Problem objective: Comparison of three populations

Data type: Quantitative

Other factors: Blocked experiment; data are normal

Statistical technique: Analysis of variance (randomized blocks)

H_0: $\mu_1 = \mu_2 = \mu_3$
H_A: At least two means differ.

Test statistic: $F = \text{MST/MSE}$

Rejection region: $F > F_{\alpha,\, k-1,\, n-k-b+1} = F_{.05,2,8} = 4.46$

Value of the test statistic: $F = 1.49$

Conclusion: Do not reject H_0.

There is not enough evidence to show that productivity is affected by the shift starting time.